S0-BDN-271

Layered Learning in Multiagent Systems

Intelligent Robotics and Autonomous Agents Series
Ronald C. Arkin, editor

Behavior-Based Robotics, Ronald C. Arkin, 1998

Robot Shaping: an Experiment in Behavior Engineering, Marco Dorigo and Marco Colombetti, 1998

Layered Learning in Multiagent Systems: A Winning Approach to Robotic Soccer, Peter Stone, 2000

Layered Learning in Multiagent Systems
A Winning Approach to Robotic Soccer

Peter Stone

The MIT Press
Cambridge, Massachusetts
London, England

This book was set in Times Roman by the author using the LaTeX document preparation system.
Printed on recycled paper and bound in the United States of America.

Library of Congress Cataloging-in-Publication Data

Stone, Peter (Peter H.), 1971-
Layered learning in multiagent systems: A Winning Approach to Robotic Soccer/Peter Stone.
p. cm. —(Intelligent robotics and autonomous agents)
"A Bradford book." Includes bibliographical references.
ISBN 0-262-19438-4 (hc. : alk. paper)
1. Intelligent agents (Computer software). 2. Robotics. I. Title.
II.series.
QA76.76.I58 S76 2000
006.3—dc21 99-049153
CIP

To Tammy and Jasmine

Contents

Preface

This book represents the culmination of six enjoyable and productive years as a Ph.D. candidate and Postdoctoral Fellow in the Computer Science Department at Carnegie Mellon University (CMU) in Pittsburgh, Pennsylvania. It is not about robotic soccer per se. Rather, it is about building artificially intelligent agents for complex multiagent control tasks. Nonetheless, robotic soccer plays a central role in the text as the primary application domain and inspiration for all of the research contributions.

When I first arrived at CMU in the autumn of 1993, soccer was among my favorite pastimes. From when I first joined a team at the age of 7 through my years on the varsity team at the University of Chicago, soccer was a great form of exercise and camaraderie: a perfect distraction from my intellectual pursuits. It had never occurred to me that soccer could also become a major focus of my intellectual life.

Indeed, my first research topic as a Ph.D. student had nothing to do with soccer. I began by examining generative AI planning—particularly from the perspectives of integrating planning and learning, and of integrating planning and execution—within the CMU PRODIGY project. It was at the 1994 American Association of Artificial Intelligence (AAAI) conference in Seattle, Washington that I first considered the possibility of bringing soccer into my research.

What first attracted me to the demonstration of the Dynamite system at AAAI-94 (referred to in Section 1.1) was the fact that it was billed as a *soccer*-playing system: I had no intention of getting into robotics myself. However, I cannot deny that the thought immediately occurred to me that working on such a system would be a lot of fun. When I saw my advisor, Manuela Veloso, shortly after seeing the demo, I half-jokingly informed her that I was going to start working on robotic soccer. Her seemingly flippant answer surprised me: "Okay."

I then started thinking more seriously about robotic soccer as an artificial intelligence domain, and it didn't take me long to see the serious research possibilities. Because of my focus on planning and execution, I had already been considering real-time planning as an area of interest. And although the Dynamite system had only one robot on each team, I began thinking about the collaborative and adversarial possibilities involved in having multiple agents per team. By the beginning of my second year as a graduate student, Manuela and I were pursuing robotic soccer as a research domain full-force: both in simulation *and*—with the help of a string of undergraduates and eventually an electrical engineer Sorin Achim—with real robots.

About a year later, it came to my attention that there were two groups in Asia thinking about organizing international robotic soccer competitions: the beginnings of MiroSot and RoboCup. As one of the only groups already involved in robotic soccer at the time, we quickly became deeply involved.

Detailed histories of the competitions (Sections 8.1–8.5) and of prior and contemporary research within the robotic soccer domain (Section 9.2) are given in the main text. These histories, as well as the general references throughout the book, the description of the RoboCup soccer simulator (Section 2.2), and the details of the CMUnited simulator team (Sections 3.5 and B.1), cover up until December of 1998, at which time my Ph.D. dissertation was completed (Stone, 1998). This book is based closely upon my dissertation.

Since that time, we have entered CMUnited in one additional competition, RoboCup-99. Because the entry was based closely on the research reported in this book, its successful results are mentioned briefly in Chapter 8. Differences between the 1999 and 1998 versions of the team are noted in the text, along with differences between the 1999 (version 5) and 1998 (version 4) versions of the underlying simulator.

Meanwhile, the robotic soccer community as a whole continues to grow. RoboCup-99 in Stockholm was attended by more than 400 people comprising about 90 teams. RoboCup-99 saw the introduction of a legged robot competition using dog-like robots with 4 legs, and there is talk of introducing a humanoid league in the near future (Kitano and Asada, 1998).

As Hiroaki Kitano—president of the RoboCup Federation—is fond of saying, RoboCup's long-term goal is to enable the creation of a humanoid robotic soccer team that is capable of playing on a full-size field and beating the best human soccer team by the year 2050. Realistic? We'll see!

Acknowledgments

First and foremost, this book represents a great deal of time and effort not only on my part, but on the part of my Ph.D. advisor, Manuela Veloso. She helped me shape my research from day one as a graduate student, pushed me to get through the inevitable research setbacks, and encouraged me to achieve to the best of my ability. Without Manuela, this book would not have happened.

I also thank my other three members of my Ph.D. thesis committee, Andrew Moore, Herb Simon, and Victor Lesser for valuable discussions and comments regarding my research.

Almost all research involving robots is a group effort. The members of the CMU robosoccer lab have all contributed to making my research possible. Sorin Achim, who has been with our project almost from the beginning has tirelessly experimented with different robot architectures, always managing to pull things together and create working hardware in time for competitions. Kwun Han was a partner in the software development of the CMUnited-97 team, as well as an instrumental hardware developer for CMUnited-98. Mike Bowling successfully created a new software approach for the CMUnited-98 robots. He also collaborated on an early simulator agent implementation. Patrick Riley put up with many demands and requests in a short period of time as he helped me create the CMUnited-98 simulator software. He was also a partner in the development of the CMUnited-99 simulator team. And Manuela has heroically managed all of these projects while also staying involved in the low-level details. I have been proud to share CMUnited's success with all of these people.

Many other people at CMU have helped shape my research. Members of the PRODIGY group, including Jim Blythe, Jaime Carbonell, Eugene Fink, and Xuemei Wang, encouraged me in the early states of my research. Members of Reinforcement Learning group, especially Justin Boyan, Rich Caruana, Astro Teller, Belinda Thom, and Will Uther, have also provided me with comments and suggestions along the way. Mike Bowling and Tucker Balch helped me specifically with the writing of my thesis.

Outside of CMU, I owe thanks to other members of the robotic soccer community. First, Alan Mackworth deserves special credit for originally recognizing the challenges of this domain. He and his student, Michael Sahota, were very helpful in our initial forays into this domain. Among many others, I thank Hiroaki Kitano and Minoru Asada for their endless efforts in promoting robotic soccer and making the international RoboCup competitions possible. Special thanks go to Itsuki Noda, who created the soccer server, and who has been very receptive to suggestions for its continued development. Without Noda's soccer server, my research surely would have followed a different course. I also thank Steve Chien for inviting me to work with him at JPL during the summer of 1995.

On a more personal note, I have been lucky to have many close friends who have helped to make my time in Pittsburgh enjoyable. Astro Teller has been a friend and confidant throughout the entire process here. Belinda Thom and Justin Boyan also stand out as people with whom I spent many enjoyable hours away from the office.

My parents, Russell and Rala Stone, and my sister Mira have always been, and continue to be, there for me at all times. My daughter Jasmine has provided me with continual excuses for "study breaks." And most of all, my wife Tammy has been incredibly supportive, understanding, and encouraging as she has gone through the entire book-writing process with me.

This work has been supported through the generosity of the NASA Graduate Student Research Program (GSRP). This research is also sponsored in part by the Defense Advanced Research Projects Agency (DARPA), and Rome Laboratory, Air Force Materiel Command, USAF, under agreement numbers F30602-95-1-0018, F30602-97-2-0250 and F30602-98-2-0135 and in part by the Department of the Navy, Office of Naval Research under contract number N00014-95-1-0591. Views and conclusions contained in this document are those of the author and should not be interpreted as necessarily representing the official policies or endorsements, either expressed or implied, of NASA, the Defense Advanced Research Projects Agency (DARPA), the Air Force Research Laboratory (AFRL), the Department of the Navy, Office of Naval Research, or the U.S. Government.

I thank Bob Prior, Dave Kortenkamp, and Ron Arkin for inviting me to publish this book with MIT Press.

1 Introduction

Multiagent Systems (MAS) is the subfield of Artificial Intelligence (AI) that aims to provide both principles for construction of complex systems involving multiple *agents* and mechanisms for coordination of independent agents' *behaviors*. While there is no generally accepted definition of "agent" in AI, for the purposes of this book, an agent is an entity with perceptions, goals, cognition, actions, and domain knowledge, situated in an environment. The ways it acts, or its mappings from perceptions over time to actions, are called its "behaviors."

When a group of agents in a multiagent system share a common long-term goal, they can be said to form a *team*. Team members (or *teammates*) coordinate their behaviors by adopting compatible cognitive processes and by directly affecting each others' perceptory inputs including via communicative actions. Other agents in the environment that have goals opposed to the team's long-term goal are the team's *adversaries*.

This book contributes several techniques for generating successful team behaviors in real-time, noisy, collaborative and adversarial multiagent environments. As of yet, there has been little work within this type of multiagent system.

Because of the inherent complexity of this type of multiagent system, Machine Learning (ML) is an interesting and promising area to merge with MAS. ML has the potential to provide robust mechanisms that leverage upon experience to equip agents with a spectrum of behaviors, ranging from effective individual performance in a team, to collaborative achievement of independently and jointly set high-level goals. Using a hierarchical task decomposition, multiple ML modules can be combined to produce more effective behaviors than a monolithic ML module that learns straight from sensors to actuators.

By learning portions of their cognitive processes, selectively communicating with each other, and coordinating their behaviors via common knowledge, a group of independent agents can work together towards a common goal in a complex, real-time, noisy, adversarial environment.

1.1 Motivation

The line of research addressed in this book was originally inspired by the Dynamite test bed (Barman et al., 1993). Their successful implementation of two non-holonomic robots pushing a ping-pong ball towards opposite goals on a walled field was the first real robotic soccer system. While limited to a single robot on each team in 1994, Dynamite demonstrated the feasibility of creating robotic soccer agents for studying real-time, collaborative and adversarial multiagent systems. Inspired by their success, we set out to create a robotic soccer system with several robots on each team. In so doing, it was immediately clear that the research issues introduced by the extension from single to multiple robot teams would be numerous and challenging.

Dynamite operates in a real-time, noisy, adversarial domain. This book focuses on a domains with those same three characteristics plus an additional one:

Real-time domains are those in which success depends on acting in response to a dynamically changing environment.

Noisy domains are those in which agents cannot accurately perceive the world, nor can they accurately affect it.

Collaborative domains are those in which a group of agents share a common goal.

Adversarial domains are those in which there are agents with competing goals.

While no previous system has addressed a domain with all of these characteristics, there have been previous systems examining each of these characteristics individually. Pengi (Agre and Chapman, 1987) is a real-time system in which an agent in a video game environment must act quickly in response to a dynamically changing environment. All robotic domains (e.g. (Brooks, 1986; Arkin, 1987)) are noisy as real-world sensors perceive the world imperfectly and robotic actuators are typically unreliable. Collaborative environments have been examined in the field of MAS (Grosz, 1996; Sycara et al., 1996; Cohen et al., 1999), and adversarial domains have been considered in AI game playing systems such as for checkers (Samuel, 1959) and chess (Newell and Simon, 1972). However these adversarial domains are turn-taking as opposed to real-time, they are not noisy, and there are no collaborative agents.

Some of these four domain characteristics have also been considered in combination. Several multiagent robotic systems (Arkin, 1992; Mataric, 1994a; Parker, 1994) consider collaborative, noisy environments. Dynamite, mentioned above, operates in a real-time, noisy, adversarial environment. In this book, I consider real-time, noisy, collaborative and adversarial multiagent domains, using simulated robotic soccer with multiple agents on each team as a representative test bed. The challenges that arise in this domain have motivated my research.

One of the first observations made was that creating all of the behaviors and agent interactions directly would be an impossible task in such a complex multiagent domain. Thus, a primary research goal of this book is the investigation of whether and how ML techniques can be used to create a team of cooperating agents.

1.2 Objectives and Approach

Objectives

The principal question addressed in this book is:

Can agents learn to become individually skilled and to work together in the presence of both teammates and adversaries in a real-time, noisy environment with limited communication?

More specifically, the book contributes an agent structure enabling the use of ML techniques to improve an agent's behavior in domains with the following characteristics:

- A need for real-time decision-making;
- Sensor and actuator noise with hidden state.
- Independent agents with the same well-defined high-level goal: *teammates*
- Agents with a conflicting well-defined high-level goal: *adversaries*

Note that the intermediate or low-level goals of teammates and adversaries can differ indeterminately.

The agents are assumed to have at their disposal the following resources:

- Sensors of the environment that give partial, noisy information;
- The ability to process sensory information in order to update a world model;
- Noisy actuators that affect the environment;
- Low-bandwidth, unreliable communication capabilities.

This book contributes a successful method—using machine learning—of equipping such agents with effective behaviors in such a domain.

Approach

The general approach to answering the above question has been to create an existence proof: a full-fledged functioning multiagent system that incorporates learning in a real-time, noisy environment with both teammates and adversaries.

Robotic soccer is a domain which fits the above characteristics while being both accessible and suitably complex. Insofar as the main goal of any test bed is to facilitate the trial and evaluation of ideas that have promise in the real world, robotic soccer proved to be an excellent test bed for this book. All of the contributions of this book were originally developed in *simulated* robotic soccer. However, some were then applied in either real robotic soccer or in network routing.

An initial assumption was that, due to the complexity of the environment, agents in domains with the above characteristics would not be able to learn effective direct mappings from their sensors to their actuators, even when saving past states of the world. Thus, the approach taken was to break the problem down into several behavioral layers and to use ML techniques when appropriate. Starting with low-level behaviors, the process of creating new behavior levels and new ML subtasks continues towards high level strategic behaviors that take into account both teammate and opponent strategies.

In the process, a key advantage of such an approach surfaced: learning low-level behaviors can facilitate the learning of higher-level behaviors. Either by creating the behavioral components that make up the new learned behavior or by manipulating the input space of the new learned behavior, previously learned behaviors can enable the learning of increasingly complex behaviors. This new approach to multiagent machine learning is called *layered learning*.

Layered learning assumes that the appropriate behavior granularity and the aspects of the behaviors to be learned are determined as a function of the specific domain. Layered learning does not include an automated hierarchical decomposition of the task. Each layer is learned by applying or developing appropriate ML algorithms. Our research methodology consisted of investigating several levels of learning to demonstrate the effectiveness of combining multiple machine learning modules hierarchically.

1.3 Contributions

This book makes four distinct contributions to the fields of MAS and ML.

Team Member Agent Architecture. The team member agent architecture is suitable for domains with periodic opportunities for safe, full communication among team members, interleaved with periods of limited communication and a need for real-time action. This architecture includes mechanisms for task decomposition and dynamic role assignment as well as for communication in single-channel, low-bandwidth communication environments. It is implemented in both simulated and real robotic soccer.

Layered Learning. Layered learning is a hierarchical ML paradigm that combines multiple machine learning modules, each module directly affecting the next. Layered learning is described in general and then illustrated as a set of three interconnecting learned behaviors within a complex, real-time, collaborative and adversarial domain.

Team-Partitioned, Opaque-Transition Reinforcement Learning. Team-Partitioned, Opaque-Transition Reinforcement Learning (TPOT-RL) is a new multiagent reinforcement learning method applicable in domains in which agents have limited information about environmental state transitions. TPOT-RL partitions the learning task among team members, allowing the agents to learn simultaneously by directly observing the long-term effects of their actions in the environment. TPOT-RL is demonstrated to be effective both in robotic soccer and in another multiagent domain, network routing.

The CMUnited Simulated Robotic Soccer System. The CMUnited simulated robotic soccer team (CMUnited) is a fully implemented and operational team of simulated agents. Coupled with the detailed descriptions and source code in the appendices, CMUnited's algorithmic details presented throughout the book should enable future researchers to build upon CMUnited's successful implementation.

While the last of these contributions is inherently domain-specific, for each of the first three contributions, this book provides a general specification as well as an implementation within a complex domain: simulated robotic soccer. In addition, opportunities for generalization to other domains are discussed, illustrated, and implemented.

1.4 Reader's Guide to the Book

Following is a general description of the contents of each chapter as well as guidelines as to which chapters are relevant to which contribution. Since

CMUnited is described throughout the entire book, all chapters are relevant and it is not mentioned in the guidelines.

Chapter 2 introduces the domains used as test beds within the book: simulated and real robotic soccer as well as network routing. The simulated robotic soccer domain is used as an example throughout the book and all contributions are implemented in this domain. The team member agent architecture is also implemented in the real robotic soccer domain, while TPOT-RL is also implemented in network routing.

Chapter 3 describes the team member agent architecture. It is defined generally and then implemented in both simulated and real robotic soccer. This architecture is used in the implementations of layered learning and TPOT-RL.

Chapter 4 introduces the general layered learning method. The implementation of layered learning described in Chapters 5–7 also contribute to the complete description of layered learning.

Chapter 5 describes a learned, individual robotic soccer behavior. It is presented as the first learned layer in our layered learning implementation.

Chapter 6 presents a learned multiagent behavior built upon the individual behavior from Chapter 5. This second learned layer in our layered learning implementation also serves as the basis for the team learning algorithm described in Chapter 7, namely TPOT-RL.

Chapter 7 introduces the novel multiagent reinforcement learning algorithm, TPOT-RL. TPOT-RL builds upon the multiagent behavior described in Chapter 6 to create a team-level collaborative and adversarial behavior. This team-level behavior is the highest implemented learned layer in the simulated robotic soccer implementation of the layered learning paradigm. The chapter also includes a description and implementation of TPOT-RL in network routing, demonstrating its generalization to other multiagent domains.

Chapter 8 provides general results of the implemented robotic soccer systems in international competitions. While focussed evaluations are provided in several of the previous chapters, anecdotal evidence of the success of the overall approach is provided in this chapter.

Chapter 9 provides an extensive survey of work related to the research in this book. While several chapters contain their own related work sections describing the research most relevant to their contents, this chapter surveys the field of MAS from a machine learning perspective, and presents a broad overview of robotic soccer research around the world.

Chapter 10 summarizes the contributions of this book and outlines the most promising directions for future work.

Table 1.1 summarizes the relevance of each chapter to the book's contributions.

Table 1.1
Correspondence between the book's contributions and the book's chapters.

	Chapter								
Contribution	2	3	4	5	6	7	8	9	10
Team Member Agent Architecture	*	*	−	−	−	−	+	+	+
Layered Learning	*	+	*	*	*	*	+	+	+
TPOT-RL	*	+	−	−	+	*	+	+	+
CMUnited	*	*	*	*	*	*	*	*	+

* : essential; + : relevant; − : irrelevant

2 Substrate Systems

The innovations reported in this book are designed primarily for real-time, noisy, collaborative and adversarial domains. As such, simulated robotic soccer—the RoboCup soccer server (Noda et al., 1998) in particular—has served as an ideal research test bed. However, the positive results achieved are not limited to this domain. Throughout the book, the extent to which each result generalizes is discussed. In addition, some of the techniques developed in simulated robotic soccer have been applied in two other domains with some similar characteristics: real robotic soccer and network routing. This chapter compares and contrasts these three domains while specifying their details as they are used for empirical testing.

2.1 Overview

As the main test bed, all the contributions of this book are originally developed and implemented in simulated robotic soccer. It is a fully *distributed*, multiagent domain with both *teammates* and *adversaries*. There is *hidden state*, meaning that each agent has only a partial world view at any given moment. The agents also have *noisy sensors and actuators*, meaning that they do not perceive the world exactly as it is, nor can they affect the world exactly as intended. In addition, the perception and action cycles are *asynchronous*, prohibiting the traditional AI paradigm of using perceptual input to trigger actions. *Communication* opportunities are limited; the agents must make their decisions in *real-time*; and the actions taken by other agents, both teammates and adversaries, and their resulting state transitions are unknown. We refer to this last quality of unknown state transitions as *opaque transitions*. These italicized domain characteristics are appropriate for the development of all four of this book's contributions as presented in Section 1.3.

In order to test the generality of our simulator results, we transfer some of our techniques to our real robot system. In particular, portions of the team member agent architecture are implemented in the real robot system as well as in simulation. The real robot system is a completely different domain from the simulator. First, at the most basic level, the I/O is entirely different. While the simulator deals with abstract, asynchronous perceptions and actions, the robotic system processes real-time video images via an overhead camera and outputs motor control commands synchronously (i.e. triggered by perception) via radio. Second, the agents all share the same perception of the world, which makes the robotic system not completely distributed. However, functionally the robots are controlled independently: each is controlled by an independent function call using a turn-taking methodology. They can also be controlled by separate processes with a common sensory input stream. Three other differences of the robots from the simulator are the absence of communication among teammates (which is possible, but not used in our system), the absence of hidden state (agents have a full world view via an overhead camera), and a resulting full knowledge about the state transitions in the world. These domain differences prevent the use of identical agent programs in the two domains, but they do not limit the applicability of the flexible teamwork structure.

While developed within the context of robotic soccer, the multiagent algorithms presented in this book generalize beyond robotic soccer as well. To support this claim, we implement one of our algorithms in a different domain, namely network routing. We believe several other multiagent domains are also similar to robotic soccer. It is part of our future work to continue to identify other such multiagent domains (see Chapter 10).

Although network routing differs from robotic soccer in a lot of ways, in an abstract sense it is very similar. Even though our network routing simulator does not involve communication, noisy sensors and actuators, or adversaries, it retains the essential characteristics motivating the development of TPOT-RL: a distributed team of agents operating in real-time with opaque transitions. As reported in Chapter 7, TPOT-RL is successfully implemented in network routing as well as in robotic soccer.

Table 2.1 summarizes the domain comparison. The remainder of this chapter provides the domain specifications of simulated robotic soccer, real robotic soccer, and network routing as used experimentally in this book. I use this chapter to describe in detail the aspects of the domains that are not part of the book's contributions: the substrates upon which the contributions are built.

2.2 The RoboCup Soccer Server

The RoboCup soccer server (Noda et al., 1998) has been used as the basis for successful international competitions (RoboCup, 1997) and research challenges (Kitano et al., 1997). As one of the first users, I helped to test and tune it over the course of its development, and participated in its first test as the basis for a competition (Pre-RoboCup-96 at IROS-96). Experiments reported in this

Table 2.1
A comparison of the experimental domains used in this book.

	Simulator	Robots	Network routing
Distributed perception	yes	no	yes
Distributed action	yes	yes	yes
Asynchronous perception/action	yes	no	no
Teammates	yes	yes	yes
Adversaries	yes	yes	no
Hidden state	yes	no	yes
Noisy sensors	yes	yes	no
Noisy actuators	yes	yes	no
Communication	yes	no	no
Real-time	yes	yes	yes
Opaque transitions	yes	no	yes

book are conducted in several different versions of the simulator ranging from version 1 to version 4[1]. This section describes the version 4 of the simulator.

The soccer server is a complex and realistic domain. Unlike many AI domains, the soccer server embraces as many real-world complexities as possible. It models a hypothetical robotic system, merging characteristics from different existing and planned systems as well as from human soccer players. The server's sensor and actuator noise models are motivated by typical robotic systems, while many other characteristics, such as limited stamina and vision, are motivated by human parameters.

In this section I describe version 4 of the soccer server in detail. While not as detailed as the soccer server user manual (Andre et al., 1998a), this section defines all of the concepts and parameters that are important for the book.

I begin by giving a high-level overview of the simulator. Next I define define the simulated world including the field and all of the objects recognized by the simulator. I then specify the perceptions and actions available to agents in the simulator. Next I give a detailed illustrative sample trace of the interactions between the server and a client over a period of time. Finally, I summarize the challenging characteristics of this simulated robotic soccer domain.

1 Version 5, which was used at the 1999 RoboCup event, post-dates all of the experiments reported in this book. The main difference from version 4 is that players are given a neck so that they are able to look in a different direction from which they are moving.

Overview of the Simulator

The simulator, acting as a server, provides a domain and supports users who wish to build their own *agents* (also referred to as *clients* or *players*). Client programs connect to the server via UDP sockets, each controlling a single player. The soccer server simulates the movements of all of the objects in the world, while each client acts as the brain of one player, sending *movement commands* to the server. The server causes the player being controlled by the client to execute the movement commands and sends sensory information from that player's perspective back to the client.

When a game is to be played, two teams of 11 independently controlled clients connect to the server. The object of each team is to direct the ball into one of the goals at the ends of the field, while preventing the ball from entering the other goal.

The server's parameters that are relevant to this book are listed, along with their default values[2] and descriptions, in Table 2.4. Refer to this table as the parameters are alluded to in the text of this section.

The simulator includes a visualization tool, pictured in Figure 2.1. Each player is represented as a two-halved circle. The light side is the side towards which the player is facing. In Figure 2.1, all of the 22 players are facing the ball, which is in the middle of the field. The black bars on the left and right sides of the field are the goals.

The simulator also includes a *referee*, which enforces the rules of the game. It indicates changes in play mode, such as when the ball goes out of bounds, when a goal is scored, or when the game ends. It also enforces the *offsides* rule. Like in real soccer, a player is offsides if it is in the opponent's half of the field and closer to the opponent's goal line (the line along which the goal is located) than all or all but one of the opponent players when the ball is passed to it. The crucial moment for an offsides call is when the ball is kicked, not when it is received: a player can be behind all of the opponent defenders when it receives a pass, but not when a teammate kicks the ball towards it[3].

One of the real-world complexities embraced by the soccer server is asynchronous sensing and acting. Most AI domains use synchronous sensing and acting: an agent senses the world, acts, senses the result, acts again, and so on.

2 Several default values have changed from version to version of the simulator. Unless otherwise noted, this book uses the default values associated with version 4.

3 In real soccer, an offsides call is actually subjective based on the referee's opinion of whether the player in an offsides position is gaining an advantage by being there. The soccer server artificially operationalizes the offsides rule, making it an objective call.

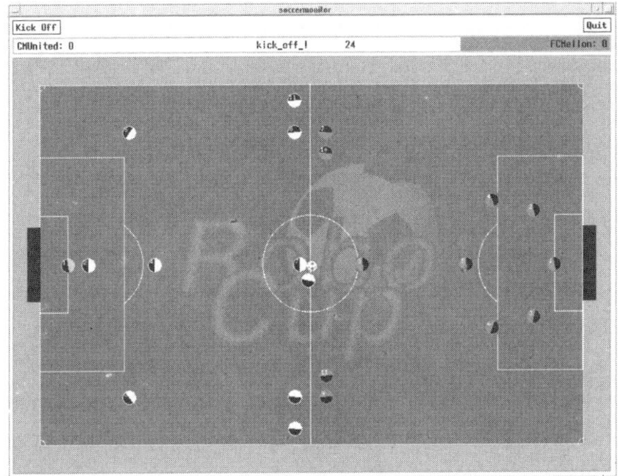

Figure 2.1
The soccer server display. Each player is represented as a two-halved circle. The light side is the side towards which the player is facing. All players are facing the ball, which is in the middle of the field. The black bars on the left and right sides of the field are the goals.

In this paradigm, sensations trigger actions. On the other hand, both people and complex robotic systems have independent sensing and acting rates. Sensory information arrives via different sensors at different rates, often unpredictably (e.g. sound). Meanwhile, multiple actions may be possible in between sensations or multiple sensations may arrive between action opportunities.

The soccer server uses a discrete action model: it collects player actions over the course of a fixed *simulator cycle* of length `simulator_step`, but only executes them and updates the world at the end of the cycle. If a client sends more than one movement command in a simulator cycle, the server chooses one randomly for execution. Thus, it is in each client's interest to try to send at most one movement command each simulator cycle. On the other hand, if a client sends no movement commands during a simulator cycle, it loses the opportunity to act during that cycle, which can be a significant disadvantage in a real-time adversarial domain: while the agent remains idle, opponents may gain an advantage. Each cycle, the simulator increments the simulated time counter by one.

Figure 2.2 illustrates the interactions between the server and two clients over the course of 3 simulator cycles at times t-1, t, and t+1. The thick central horizontal line represents the real time as kept by the server. The top and bottom horizontal lines represent the time-lines of two separate clients. Since they are separate processes, they do not know precisely when the simulator changes from one cycle to the next. The dashed arrows from the server towards a client represent perceptions for that client. The solid arrows from a client towards the server represent movement commands sent by that client. These arrows end at the point in time at which the server executes the movement commands, namely the end of the simulator cycle during which they are sent.

Client 1 sends movement commands after every perception it receives. This strategy works out fine in cycle t-1; but in cycle t it misses the opportunity to act because it receives no perceptions; and in cycle t+1 it sends two movement commands, only one of which will be executed.

Client 2, on the other hand, successfully sends one movement command every cycle. Note that in cycle t it must act with no new perceptual information, while in cycle t+1, it receives two perceptions prior to acting and one afterwards. Ideally, it would act after receiving and taking into account all three perceptions. However, it does not know precisely when the simulator cycle will change internally in the soccer server and it cannot know ahead of time when it will receive perceptions. Thus, in exchange for the ability to act every simulator cycle, it sometimes acts with less than the maximal amount of information about the world. However, as each simulator cycle represents only a short amount of real time (`simulator_step` msec), the world does not change very much from cycle to cycle, and the client can act accurately even if it takes some of its perceptions into account only before its *subsequent* action.

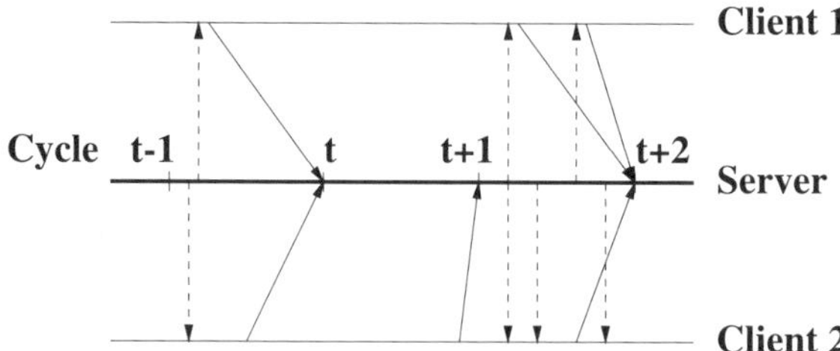

Figure 2.2
A sample period of the server-client interface over the course of 3 simulator cycles at times t-1, t, and t+1. The thick central horizontal line represents the real time as kept by the server. The top and bottom horizontal lines represent the time-lines of two separate clients. The dashed arrows from the server towards a client represent perceptions for that client. The solid arrows from a client towards the server represent movement commands sent by that client. These arrows end at the point in time at which the server executes the movement commands, namely the end of the simulator cycle during which they are sent.

Asynchronous sensing and acting, especially when the sensing can happen at unpredictable intervals, is a very challenging paradigm for agents to handle. Agents must balance the need to act regularly and as quickly as possible with the need to gather information about the environment. Along with asynchronous sensing and action, the soccer server captures several other real-world complexities, as will become evident throughout the remainder of this section.

The Simulated World

This subsection paraphrases a similar section in the soccer server user manual (Andre et al., 1998a).

FIELD AND OBJECTS

The soccer server is a two-dimensional simulation. There is no notion of height for any object on the field. The field has dimensions `field_length` × `field_width` with the goals of width `goal_width`, all of which are parameters defined in Table 2.4. There are up to 22 players on the field at a time along with 1 ball, all of which are modeled as circles. There are also several visible markers, including flags and side lines, distributed around the field as illustrated in Figure 2.3.

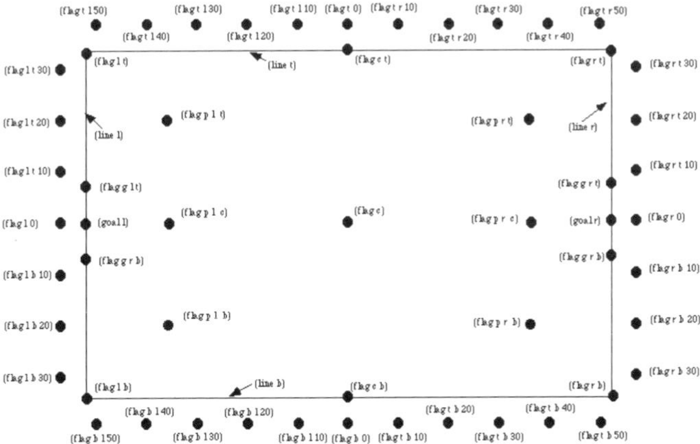

Figure 2.3
The locations and names of the visible markers in the soccer server. This figure originally appeared in the soccer server user manual(Andre et al., 1998a).

The players and the ball are all mobile objects. At the simulator cycle for time t, each object is in a specific position (p_x^t, p_y^t) and has a specific velocity (v_x^t, v_y^t). Each player is also facing in a specific direction θ^t. These positions are maintained internally as floating point numbers, but player sensations are only given to one decimal place. Thus, the perceived state space with the server parameters we use has more than $10^{9^{22}} = 10^{198}$ states: each of the 22 players can be in any of $680 \times 1050 \times 3600$ positions. Taking into account the ball, velocities, and past states, the actual state space is much larger than that.

Object Movement

As described in the user manual:

In each simulation step, the movement of each object is calculated in the following manner:

$$
\begin{aligned}
(u_x^{t+1}, u_y^{t+1}) &= (v_x^t, v_y^t) + (a_x^t, a_y^t) : accelerate \qquad (2.1)\\
(p_x^{t+1}, p_y^{t+1}) &= (p_x^t, p_y^t) + (u_x^{t+1}, u_y^{t+1}) : move\\
(v_x^{t+1}, v_y^{t+1}) &= \text{decay} \times (u_x^{t+1}, u_y^{t+1}) : decay\ speed\\
(a_x^{t+1}, a_y^{t+1}) &= (0, 0) : reset\ acceleration
\end{aligned}
$$

where, decay is a decay parameter specified by `ball_decay` or `player_decay`. (a_x^t, a_y^t) is the object's acceleration, which is derived from the *Power* parameter in `dash` (if the object is a player) or `kick` (if a ball) commands as follows:

$$(a_x^t, a_y^t) = Power \times (\cos(\theta^t), \sin(\theta^t))$$

In the case of a player, its direction is calculated in the following manner:

$$\theta^t = \theta^t + Angle$$

where *Angle* is the parameter of `turn` commands. In the case of a ball, its direction is given in the following manner:

$$\theta^t_{\text{ball}} = \theta^t_{\text{kicker}} + Direction$$

where θ^t_{ball} and θ^t_{kicker} are the directions of the ball and kicking player respectively, and *Direction* is the second parameter of a `kick` command (Andre et al., 1998a).

The commands and their parameters referred to above are specified precisely later in this section.

Collisions

As described in the user manual:

If at the end of the simulation cycle, two objects overlap, then the objects are moved back until they do not overlap. Then the velocities are multiplied by -0.1. Note that it is possible for the ball to go through a player as long as the ball and the player never overlap at the end of the cycle (Andre et al., 1998a).

NOISE

The soccer server adds evenly distributed probabilistic noise to all objects' movements. In particular, as described in the manual:

noise is added into Equation 2.1 as follows:

$$(u_x^{t+1}, u_y^{t+1}) = (v_x^t, v_y^t) + (a_x^t, a_y^t) + (\tilde{r}_{\mathrm{rmax}}, \tilde{r}_{\mathrm{rmax}})$$

where $\tilde{r}_{\mathrm{max}}$ is a random variable with uniform distribution in the range $[-\mathrm{max}, \mathrm{max}]$. rmax is a parameter that depends on the velocity of the object as follows:

$$\mathrm{rmax} = \mathrm{rand} \cdot |(v_x^t, v_y^t)|$$

where rand is a parameter specified by `player_rand` or `ball_rand`.
Noise is added also into a *Power* parameter in a `turn` command as follows:

$$Angle = (1 + \tilde{r}_{\mathrm{rand}}) \cdot Angle$$

(Andre et al., 1998a)

STAMINA

The soccer server prevents players from constantly running at maximum velocity (`player_sp_max`) by assigning each player a limited stamina. The stamina is modeled in three parts.

- `stamina` ∈ [0, `stamina_max`] is the actual limit of the *Power* parameter of a `dash` command.
- `effort` ∈ [`effort_min`, 1.0] represents the efficiency with which the player can move.
- `recovery` ∈ [`recovery_min`, 1.0] represents the rate at which stamina is replenished.

A player's stamina has both replenishable and non-replenishable components. The replenishable components are `stamina` and `effort`; `recovery` is non-replenishable.

The stamina parameters listed in Table 2.4 are used as follows:

- If a player tries to dash with power *Power*, the effective power of its dash is affected by `stamina` and `effort` while `stamina` is subsequently decremented:

–`effective_dash_power` = Min(`stamina`,*Power*) × `effort`.

–`stamina` = `stamina` − `effective_dash_power`.

• On every cycle, `effort` is decremented if `stamina` is below a threshold, and incremented if it is above a threshold:

–if `stamina` ≤ `effort_dec_thr` × `stamina_max` and `effort` > `effort_min`, then `effort` = `effort` − `effort_dec`.

–if `stamina` ≥ `effort_inc_thr` × `stamina_max` and `effort` < `1.0`, then `effort` = `effort` + `effort_inc`.

• On every cycle, `recovery` is decremented if `stamina` is below a threshold:

–if `stamina` ≤ `recover_dec_thr` × `stamina_max` and `recovery` > `recover_min`, then `recovery` = `recovery` − `recover_dec`.

• On every cycle, `stamina` is incremented based on the current value of `recovery`:

–`stamina` = `stamina` + `recovery` × `stamina_inc`.

–if `stamina` > `stamina_max`, then `stamina` = `stamina_max`.

Agent Perception

Agents receive three different types of sensory perceptions from the server: aural, visual, and physical. This subsection describes the characteristics of the sensory information, which are summarized in Table 2.2.

AURAL INFORMATION

The soccer server communication paradigm models a crowded, low-bandwidth environment. All 22 agents (11 on each team) use a single, unreliable communication channel. When an agent or the referee speaks, nearby agents on both teams can hear the message immediately. There is no perceptual delay. They hear a message in the format (`hear` *Time Direction Message*) where:

- *Time* is the current simulator cycle;
- *Direction* is the relative direction from whence the sound came;
- *Message* is the message content;

Note that there is no information about which player sent the message or that player's distance.

Agents have a limited communication range, hearing only messages spoken from within a distance specified by the parameter audio_cut_off_dist. They also have a limited communication capacity, hearing a maximum of hear_inc messages in hear_decay simulation cycles. Thus communication is extremely unreliable. Using the parameters in Table 2.4, if more than 1 agent speaks over the course of 2 simulation cycles, a player will miss hearing all but 1 of the messages. Messages from the referee are treated as privileged and are always transmitted to all agents.

In short, the characteristics of the low-bandwidth communication environment include:

- All 22 agents (including adversaries) on the same channel;
- Limited communication range and capacity;
- No guarantee of sounds getting through;
- Immediate communication: no perceptual delay.

VISUAL INFORMATION

As described in the user manual:

Visual information arrives from the server in the following basic format:

(see *Time ObjInfo ObjInfo* ...)
Time indicates the current time.
ObjInfo is information about a visible object in the following format:
(*ObjName Distance Direction DistChng DirChng FaceDir*)

```
ObjName = (player Teamname UNum)
        | (goal Side)
        | (ball)
        | (flag c)
        | (flag [l|c|r] [t|b])
        | (flag p [l|r] [t|c|b])
        | (flag [t|b] [l|r] [10|20|30|40|50])
        | (flag [l|r] [t|b] [10|20|30])
        | (flag [l|r|t|b] 0)
        | (line [l|r|t|b])
```

Distance, *Direction*, *DistChng* and *DirChng* are calculated by the following way:

$$
\begin{aligned}
p_{rx} &= p_{xt} - p_{xo} \\
p_{ry} &= p_{yt} - p_{yo} \\
v_{rx} &= v_{xt} - p_{xo} \\
v_{ry} &= v_{yt} - p_{yo}
\end{aligned}
$$

$$\begin{aligned}
Distance &= \sqrt{p_{rx}^2 + p_{ry}^2} \\
Direction &= \arctan\left(p_{ry}/p_{rx}\right) - a_o \\
e_{rx} &= p_{rx}/Distance \\
e_{ry} &= p_{ry}/Distance \\
DistChng &= (v_{rx} * e_{rx}) + (v_{ry} * e_{ry}) \\
DirChng &= [(-(v_{rx} * e_{ry}) + (v_{ry} * e_{rx}))/Distance] * (180/\pi)
\end{aligned}$$

where (p_{xt}, p_{yt}) is the absolute position of a target object, (p_{xo}, p_{yo}) is the absolute position of the sensing player, (v_{xt}, v_{yt}) is the absolute velocity of the target object, (v_{xo}, v_{yo}) is the absolute velocity of the sensing player, and a_o is the absolute direction the sensing player is facing. In addition, (p_{rx}, p_{ry}) and (v_{rx}, v_{ry}) are respectively the relative position and the velocity of the target, and (e_{rx}, e_{ry}) is the unit vector that is parallel to the vector of the relative position. *Facedir* is only included if the observed object is another player, and is the direction of the observed player relative to the direction of the observing player. Thus, if both players are facing the same direction, then *FaceDir* would be 0.
The (goal r) object is interpreted as the center of the goal. (flag c) is a virtual flag at the center of the field. (flag l b) is the flag at the lower left of the field. (flag p l b) is a virtual flag at the lower inside corner of the penalty box on the left side of the field. The remaining types of flags are all located 5 meters outside the playing field. For example, (flag t l 20) is 5 meters from the top sideline and 20 meters left from the center line. In the same way, (flag r b 10) is 5 meters right of the right sideline and 10 meters below the center of the right goal. Also, (flag b 0) is 5 meters below the midpoint of the bottom sideline.
In the case of (line ...), *Distance* is the distance to the point there the center line of the player's view crosses the line, and *Direction* is the direction of line.
All of the flags and lines are shown in Figure 2.3 (Andre et al., 1998a).

The frequency, range, and quality of visual information sent to a particular agent are governed by the integer server parameters `send_step` and `visible_angle`; and the player parameters `view_quality` ∈ {*high*,*low*}, `view_width` ∈ {*narrow*, *normal*,*wide*}, and `view_angle`, a floating point number. A player can directly control its `view_quality` and `view_width` via its actuators. By default, `view_quality` = *high*, `view_width` = *normal* and `view_angle` = `visible_angle`. In that case the agent receives visual information every `send_step` msec.

However, the agent can trade off the frequency of the visual information against its quality and width via its `view_mode` = {`view_quality`,`view_width`}. By using *low* `view_quality`—in which case it receives angle information, but no distances to object—the agent can get sights twice as frequently: every

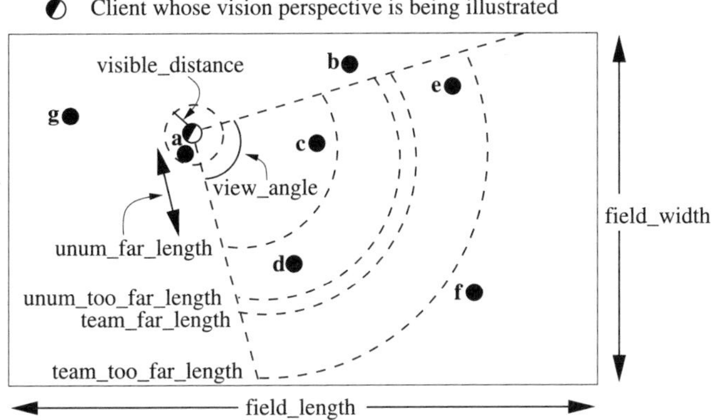

Figure 2.4
The visible range of an individual agent in the soccer server. The viewing agent is the one shown as two semi-circles. The light semi-circle is its front. The black circles represent objects in the world. Only objects within `view_angle`^{o}/2, and those within `visible_distance` of the viewing agent can be seen. `unum_far_length`, `unum_too_far_length`, `team_far_length`, and `team_too_far_length` affect the amount of precision with which a players' identity is given.

`send_step`/2. Similarly, the agent can get sights twice as frequently by switching to a *narrow* `view_width`, in which case `view_angle` = `visible_angle`/2. On the other hand, the player can use a *wide* `view_width` (`view_angle` = `visible_angle` × 2) at the expense of less frequent visual information (every `send_step` × 2 msec). With both `view_width` = *narrow* and `view_quality` = *low*, visual information arrives every `send_step`/4 msec.

The meaning of the `view_angle` parameter is illustrated in Figure 2.4. In this figure, the viewing agent is the one shown as two semi-circles. The light semi-circle is its front. The black circles represent objects in the world. Only objects within `view_angle`^{o}/2, and those within `visible_distance` of the viewing agent can be seen. Thus, objects *b* an *g* are not visible; all of the rest are.

As object *f* is directly in front of the viewing agent, its angle would be reported as 0 degrees. Object *e* would be reported as being at roughly -40°, while object *d* is at roughly 20°.

Also illustrated in Figure 2.4, the amount of information describing a player varies with how far away the player is. For nearby players, both the team and the uniform number of the player are reported. However, as distance increases, first the likelihood that the uniform number is visible decreases, and then even the team name may not be visible. It is assumed in the server that `unum_far_length` $\leq$ `unum_too_far_length` $\leq$ `team_far_length` $\leq$ `team_too_far_length`. Let the player's distance be *dist*. Then

- If *dist* $\leq$ `unum_far_length`, then both uniform number and team name are visible.
- If `unum_far_length` $<$ *dist* $<$ `unum_too_far_length`, then the team name is always visible, but the probability that the uniform number is visible decreases linearly from 1 to 0 as *dist* increases.
- If *dist* $\geq$ `unum_too_far_length`, then the uniform number is not visible.
- If *dist* $\leq$ `team_far_length`, then the team name is visible.
- If `team_far_length` $<$ *dist* $<$ `team_too_far_length`, then the probability that the team name is visible decreases linearly from 1 to 0 as *dist* increases.
- If *dist* $\geq$ `team_too_far_length`, then neither the team name nor the uniform number is visible.

For example, in Figure 2.4, assume that all of the labeled black circles are players. Then player c would be identified by both team name and uniform number; player d by team name, and with about a 50% chance, uniform number; player e with about a 25% chance, just by team name, otherwise with neither; and player f would be identified simply as an anonymous player.

Finally, the precision of information regarding an object's distance decreases with its distance. As written in the user manual:

> In the case that an object in sight is a ball or a player, the value of distance to the object is quantized in the following manner:
>
> $$d' = \text{Quantize}(\exp(\text{Quantize}(\log(d), 0.1)), 0.1)$$
>
> where d and d' are the exact distance and quantized distance respectively, and
>
> $$\text{Quantize}(V, Q) = \text{rint}(V/Q) \cdot Q$$
>
> This means that players can not know the exact positions of very far objects. For example, when the distance is about 100.0, the maximum noise is about 10.0, while when the distance is less than 10.0, the noise is less than 1.0.
> In the case of flags and lines, the distance value is quantized in the following manner.
>
> $$d' = \text{Quantize}(\exp(\text{Quantize}(\log(d), 0.01)), 0.1)$$
>
> (Andre et al., 1998a)

This visual paradigm creates a huge amount of hidden state for each individual agent. In addition, with the parameters identified in Table 2.4, by default, the agents receive visual information less frequently (every 150 msec) than they can act (every 100 msec). Thus, unless they are to miss many action opportunities, the agents must sometimes choose more than one sequential action from a given state.

With these parameters, play occurs in *real time*: the agents must react to their sensory inputs at roughly the same speed as human or robotic soccer players. Our own robots have been able to act between 3 and 30 times per second. Human reaction times have been measured in the 200-500 msec range (Woodworth, 1938).

PHYSICAL INFORMATION

Upon request from an agent, the server also sends physical information about the agent. Such `sense_body` information includes:

- the agent's current `stamina`, `effort`, and `recovery` values;
- the agent's current speed;
- the agent's current `view_quality` and `view_width` values.

The agent's speed is given as a magnitude only: it must infer the direction of its movement from visual cues.

Table 2.2 summarizes types of sensory information available to soccer server agents.

Table 2.2
The soccer server agents' sensors.

Name	When received	Information type	Limitations
see	every `send_step` msec (default)	visual	limited angle, precision decreases with distance
hear	instantaneously when a nearby agent (or the referee) speaks	aural	limited distance and frequency
sense_body	upon request	physical	none

Agent Action

Agents can send several different types of commands to the simulator as their actuators: they change the world in some way. This subsection describes the characteristics of the different commands which are summarized in Table 2.3.

Communication

Agents can “say” any text string up to 512 ASCII characters in length. Both teammates and opponents will hear the complete message subject to the range and frequency constraints described in the previous subsection.

An agent can speak as often as it wants. But since teammates can only hear one message every 2 cycles, it is useless to speak more frequently than that.

Movement

The agent has just four actuators for physically manipulating the world: `turn`, `dash`, `kick`, and `catch`. The server only executes one of these commands for each player at the end of each simulator cycle. If an agent sends more than one such command during the same cycle, only one is executed non-deterministically. Since the simulator runs asynchronously from the agents, there is no way to keep perfect time with the server's cycle. Therefore any given command could be missed by the server. It is up to the agent to determine whether a given command has been executed by observing the future state of the world.

The movement commands are all parameterized with real number arguments indicating the *Angle* and/or *Power* associated with the action. As always, angles are relative to the direction the agent is currently facing (θ^t).

The details of the movement commands are as follows:

Turn(*Angle*): -180 $\leq$ *Angle* $\leq$ 180 indicates the angle of the turn. Rotation efficiency is reduced for moving players. That is, the higher a player's speed, the smaller a fraction of *Angle* the agent will actually turn according to the equation:

$$\text{actual\_angle} = Angle/(1.0 + \texttt{inertia\_moment} * \texttt{player\_speed})$$

Dash(*Power*): -30 $\leq$ *Power* $\leq$ 100 indicates the power of the dash. Agents only move in the direction they are facing, either forwards or backwards. To move in another direction, they must first turn. Dashing efficiency is reduced for players with low stamina as indicated in the specification of the simulated world above. A dash sets the acceleration in Equation 2.1 for one simulation cycle. It does not cause a sustained run over time. In order to keep running, the agent must keep issuing dash commands. *Power* is multiplied by the server parameter `dash_power_rate` before being applied in Equation 2.1.

Kick(*Power*, *Angle*): 0 $\leq$ *Power* $\leq$ 100 indicates the power of the kick, -180

$\leq$ *Angle* $\leq$ 180, the angle at which the ball is accelerated. Like the dash, the kick sets the ball's acceleration in Equation 2.1. There are four points about the kick model of the server that should be understood.

- A kick changes the ball's velocity by vector addition. That is, a kick accelerates the ball in a given direction, as opposed to setting the velocity. Thus multiple kicks on successive cycles can move the ball faster than a single kick.

- An agent can kick the ball when it is within `kickable_area` which is defined as `ball_size` + `player_size` + `kickable_margin`). The ball being within `kickable_area` is a precondition for successfully executing a kick.

- The ball and the player can collide as indicated in the specification of the simulated world above. Thus in order to smoothly kick the ball, a player must take care to avoid kicking the ball into itself.

- The actual power with which the ball is kicked depends on its relative location to the player. As presented in the user manual:

  Let `dir_diff` be the absolute value of the angle of the ball relative to the direction the player is facing (if the ball is directly ahead, this would be 0). Let `dist_ball` be the distance from the center of the player to the ball. Then the kick power rate is figured as follows:

  `kick_power_rate` * (1 - .25 * `dir_diff` / 180 -
  .25 * (`dist_ball` - `player_size` - `ball_size`) / `kickable_area`)

  This number is then multiplied by the *Power* parameter passed to the kick command before applying Equation 2.1.
  According to this paradigm, the strongest kick occurs when the ball is as close as possible to the player and directly in front of it. The power decreases as distance and/or angle increases (Andre et al., 1998a).

Catch(*Angle*): -180 $\leq$ *Angle* $\leq$ 180 indicates the angle of the catch. Only the goaltender can catch, and only within its own penalty box. These conditions are preconditions of the catch command. A catch is only effective if the ball is within a rectangle of size `catchable_area_w` × `catchable_area_l` with one edge on the player and extending in the direction indicated by *Angle*. The ball being in such a position is another precondition for successfully executing a catch.

PERCEPTION CONTROL

The two remaining commands available to agents control the types of sensations they receive. The `sense_body` command requests physical information from the server[4]. The `change_view` command specifies a `view_quality` (low/high) and a `view_width` (narrow/normal/wide). As described in the previous subsection, higher quality and greater width lead to less frequent visual The `sense_body` command can be executed up to 3 times per simulator cycle (by convention), while `change_view` can be executed once per cycle.

Table 2.3 summarizes all of the actuators available to agents in the soccer server. The types and ranges of the arguments are shown along with when the commands are executed by the server. In the table, "cycle" refers to a simulation cycle of length `simulator_step`. As described in the text, only `kick` and `catch` have preconditions.

Table 2.3
The soccer server agents' commands. In the table, "cycle" refers to a simulation cycle of length `simulator_step`.

Syntax	Argument meaning	Type	Range	When executed	Frequency limit
say(x)	message to be broadcast	ascii text	$\leq$ 512 characters	instantly	1 heard every 2 cycles
turn(x)	angle to turn	float	$-180 \leq x \leq 180$	end of cycle	
dash(x)	power to dash	float	$-30 \leq x \leq 100$	end of cycle	1 of these per cycle
kick(x, y)	power to kick, angle to kick	float float	$0 \leq x \leq 100$, $-180 \leq y \leq 180$	end of cycle	
catch(x)	angle to catch	float	$-180 \leq x \leq 180$	end of cycle	
sense_body()				instantly	3 per cycle
change_view(x, y)	view quality view width	discrete discrete	high/low narrow/normal/wide	instantly	1 per cycle

Sample Trace

Figure 2.5 illustrates the format of the interface between the server and a specific client. In the pictures, the white arrow and text are added for reference purposes: they are not part of the actual display. The input/output trace below the pictures is given from the perspective of the client labeled "CLIENT."

4 The sense_body command becomes obsolete in version 5 of the simulator as the server automatically sends sense_body perceptual information to each client every simulator cycle.

In Figure 2.5(a) the client is about to run to the ball and kick it towards the goal. Figure 2.5(b) shows the resulting scene after the kick. In the input/output trace below the pictures, as specified earlier in this section, dashes are followed by a power (they are always in the direction that the player is facing), turns are followed by an angle, and kicks are followed by a power and an angle. Sensory information from the server comes in the form of "hear," "see," and "sense_body" strings representing aural, visual, and physical information respectively. In all cases, the number after the type indicator ("hear," "see", or "sense_body") indicates the elapsed time in the match. Aural information then indicates whether it is the referee speaking or else from what angle the sound came. Visual information includes the distances followed by angles of the visible objects. If an object is close enough, two additional numbers indicate the object's relative velocity. In the case of other players, a fifth number indicates the relative direction that the player is facing. Sense_body information indicates the client's physical parameters.

Since the client's vision is limited to 45° on either side of the direction it is facing (the black semi-circle is the back of the player, the light semi-circle is the front), not all objects are visible at each sensory step. For example, at the beginning of the trace in Figure 2.5 (time 94), the client sees two teammates and two opponents (one of which is indicated by "`player opponent 1`"). However by the end of the trace (time 112), it is no longer able to see the teammates. Similarly, by the end of the trace, it is no longer able to see the center of the penalty area: (flag p r c).

The method of communication is illustrated by the message from teammate 2 that is heard at time 103 ("shoot the ball"), and by the spoken response "shooting now." Two messages from the referee at time 113, indicating the successful goal and the subsequent restart, are also present at the end of the trace. The capacity limits on hearing do not apply to messages from the referee.

Both the sensors and the actions in the simulator are noisy. Notice that even though the player begins by facing directly at the stationary ball (the ball's angle is 0) and dashes straight toward it, the ball does not remain directly in front of the player: in the subsequent visual string, the ball's angle is -2. Also notice that the nearby players (CMUnited 2 and Opponent 1) are identified by team and number. The players that are farther away are only identified by team name. Although not apparent from this trace, when players are far enough away, even their team may not be visible.

The trace in Figure 2.5 begins at elapsed time 94 and continues through 113. Each time increment occurs in 100 msec of real time and visual sensor in-

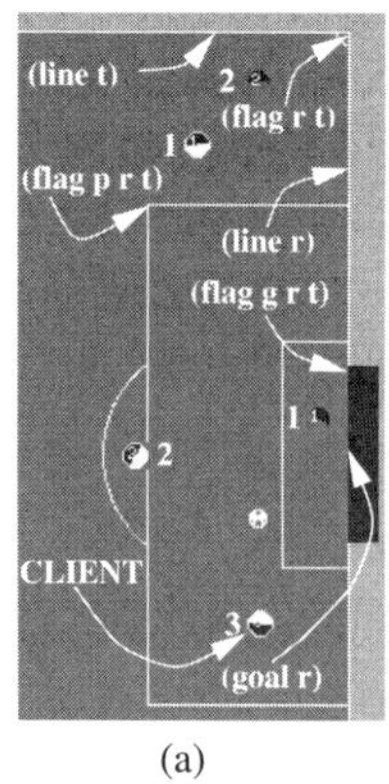

(a)

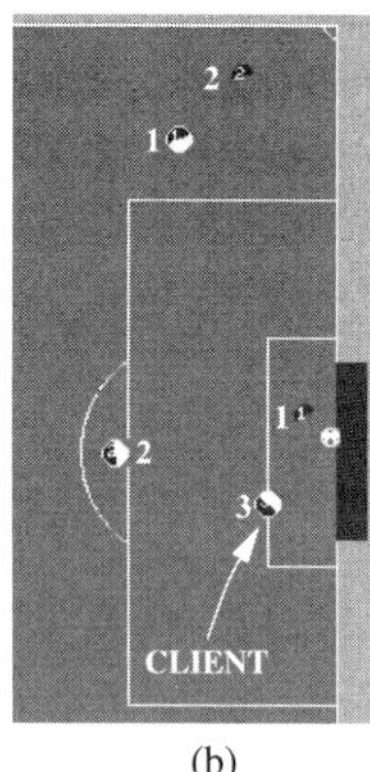

(b)

```
(see 94 ((goal r) 15.3 27) ((flag r t) 47.9 8) ((flag p r t) 34.8 -15) ((flag p r c) 16.4 -34 0 0)
   ((flag g r t) 21.8 19) ((ball) 8.2 0 0 0) ((player CMUnited) 40.4 -8)
   ((player CMUnited 2) 16.4 -37 0 0 117) ((player Opponent 1) 16.4 15 0 0 -148)
   ((player Opponent) 44.7 0) ((line t) 47.5 89))
—> (sense_body)
(sense_body 95 (view_mode high normal) (stamina 1280 1) (effort 1) (recovery 1) (speed 0.39))
—> (dash 100.00)
(see 96 ((goal r) 13.6 31) ((flag r t) 46.1 8) ((flag p r t) 33.1 -16) ((flag p r c) 14.9 -39 -0.298 -0.9)
   ((flag g r t) 19.9 20 -0.398 0.5) ((ball) 6.7 -2 -0.402 0) ((player CMUnited) 36.6 -8)
   ((player CMUnited 2) 14.9 -41 -0.298 -0.9 117) ((player Opponent 1) 14.9 17 -0.298 0.5 -148)
   ((player Opponent) 40.4 0) ((line t) 45.6 89))
—> (dash 100.00)
—> (sense_body)
(sense_body 97 (view_mode high normal) (stamina 1120 1) (effort 1) (recovery 1) (speed 0.44))
—> (dash 100.00)
   .
   .
   .
(hear 103 -70 shoot the ball) (see 104 ... ((ball) 1.8 6 0.108 5.4) ... )
—> (say shooting now)
—> (kick 100.00 65.40)
(hear 104 self shooting now)
—> (sense_body)
(sense_body 105 (view_mode high normal) (stamina 980 1) (effort 1) (recovery 1) (speed 0))
—> (turn 31.76)
(see 106 ... ((ball) 4.1 14 1.23 7) ... )
—> (turn 14.00)
   .
   .
   .
—> (dash 100.00)
(see 112 ((goal r) 6.8 12) ((flag r t) 38.5 -32) ((flag g r t) 12.3 -14 -0.246 0) ((ball) 7.4 2 0.74 1.5)
   ((player Opponent 1) 7.4 -18 -0.148 -0.2 107) ((player Opponent) 33.1 -44) ((line r) 8.2 -40))
(hear 113 referee goal_l_1)
(hear 113 referee kick_off_r)
```

Figure 2.5
A trace of the soccer server's input and output to the client controlling player 3 (indicated "CLIENT"). It in the position shown in (a), moves to the ball and shoots it towards the goal, ending in the position shown in (b). Commands from the player are preceded by "—>."

Table 2.4
Soccer server version 4 parameters along with their default values used in this book. This table is adapted from the parameter table in the soccer server user manual (Andre et al., 1998a).

Parameter Name	Default	Explanation
field_width	68	Width of the field.
field_length	105	Length of the field.
goal_width	14.02	Width of the goal.
simulator_step	100	Milliseconds in each simulation cycle.
unum_far_length	20	Distance below which object velocities and players' uniform numbers are always visible.
unum_too_far_length	40	Distance above which object velocities and players' uniform numbers are never visible.
team_far_length	40	Distance below which uniform colors always visible.
team_too_far_length	60	Distance above which uniform colors never visible.
player_size	0.8	Radius of a player.
player_decay	0.4	Decay rate of player speed. If 1.0, a player keeps its speed; if 0.0, a player loses all its speed in 1 cycle.
player_rand	0.1	Amount of noise added in players' movements and turns.
player_speed_max	1.0	Maximum player speed in 1 cycle (i.e. players can achieve maximum speed of 10 m/sec when `simulator_step`=100).
ball_size	0.085	Radius of the ball.
ball_decay	0.96	Decay rate of the ball speed.
ball_rand	0.05	Amount of noise added in the movement of the ball.
ball_speed_max	2.7	Maximum ball speed in 1 cycle (i.e. the ball can achieve maximum speed of 27 m/sec when `simulator_step`=100).
stamina_max	2000.0	Maximum stamina of a player.
stamina_inc_max	20.0	Amount of stamina that a player gains in a simulation cycle.
recover_dec_thr	0.3	Decrement threshold for player's recovery.
recover_dec	0.0002	Decrement step for player's recovery.
recover_min	0.5	Minimum player recovery.
effort_dec_thr	0.3	Decrement threshold for player's effort capacity.
effort_dec	0.005	Decrement step for player's effort capacity.
effort_inc_thr	0.6	Increment threshold for player's effort capacity.
effort_inc	0.01	Increment step for player's effort capacity.
effort_min	0.6	Minimum value for player's effort capacity.
audio_cut_dist	50.0	Maximum distance a spoken message can reach.
hear_inc	1	Maximum hearing capacity of a player. A player can hear `hear_inc` messages in `hear_decay` cycles.
hear_decay	2	Decay of hearing capacity of a player.
inertia_moment	5.0	Inertia moment of a player. It affects its turns.
kickable_margin	1.0	The area within which the ball is kickable is: kickable_area = kickable_margin + ball_size + player_size.
catchable_area_l	2.0	Goaltender catchable area length.
catchable_area_w	1.0	Goaltender catchable area width.
catch_probability	1.0	The probability for a goaltender to catch the ball.
dash_power_rate	0.01	Rate by which the *Power* argument in the `dash` command is multiplied.
kick_power_rate	0.016	Rate by which the *Power* argument in the `kick` command is multiplied.
visible_angle	90	Angle of a player's view cone in standard view mode.
send_step	150	Length of the interval for sending visual information to a player in the standard view mode (milliseconds).

formation arrives every 150 msec. The entire trace, from the moment pictured in Figure 2.5(a) until the ball enters the goal in Figure 2.5(b), occurs in about 2 seconds.

Summary

The parameters governing the operation of the soccer server as referred to in this section are summarized in Table 2.4. Their default values are also given.

All of the simulator features described in this section combine to make it a very challenging and realistic environment in which to conduct research. Table 2.5 summarizes the challenges that agents must face.

Table 2.5
Challenges for the soccer server agents.

- Sensing and acting is asynchronous.
- The players' vision is limited, giving them a partial view of the world with lots of hidden state.
- The players can communicate by speaking a message that is audible to all nearby players.
- All players are controlled by separate processes, enforcing a distributed approach.
- Each player has limited stamina;
- There are many sources of noise:
  - –Noise in actuator parameters;
  - –Noise in object motion;
  - –Noise in visual perceptions.
- Percepts sent to the agent or commands from the agent may be lost:
  - –There is no guarantee that any sent commands are ever executed;
  - –The agent must verify whether commands are executed from the sensory information it receives.
- Everything happens in real time:
  - –Visual information arrives at 150 msec intervals (with *high* `view_quality` and *normal* `view_width`);
  - –Aural information arrives asynchronously whenever it is issued;
  - –Agents can act (physically) at most once every 100 msec.

2.3 The CMUnited-97 Real Robots

While originating from similar motivations, robotic soccer with real robots is quite a different domain than the soccer server. Robotic soccer with real robots is the subject of an entirely separate research challenge from the simulator challenge (Asada et al., 1998). Whereas the soccer server provides an abstract sensor and actuator interface, the real robots must perceive the world via real NTSC video images, and they move by controlling the speeds of real motors. Therefore the sources and types of noise differ from the evenly distributed, probabilistic models incorporated into most simulations (including the soccer server). Although it is quicker and easier to get to the point of creating basic behaviors in simulation[5], it is also easy to ignore real-world complexities that may be abstracted away by the simulator. As presented in Chapter 3, the robots are used in this book to validate the team member agent architecture which was first implemented in the soccer server.

Building a fully functioning robot system can be a frustrating process full of false starts and dead ends. The CMUnited-97 real robots (Veloso et al., 1998b, 1999c) are the culmination of more than two years of development. After building one preliminary version (Achim et al., 1996), we were able to build CMUnited-97, an autonomous team of robots that won the RoboCup-97 small-robot competition at IJCAI-97 in Nagoya, Japan (Veloso et al., 1998a). The CMUnited real robot team is an on-going effort. In 1998, the team entered and won the RoboCup-98 small-robot competion with CMUnited-98, a different team of robots and mostly different software (Veloso et al., 1999a). This section describes the CMUnited-97 robots since they are the ones used for the research reported in this book.

The robots are no bigger than 180 cm^2 in area (footprint) and operate on a field with the same size and surface as a ping-pong table. Their object is to push an orange golf ball into one of the goals at the ends of the field. A team consists of up to 5 robots playing at one time. Figure 2.6 shows a picture of the CMUnited-97 robotic agents on the field. One of the 6 robots was used as a reserve in case any of the others temporarily malfunctioned.

Overall Architecture

The architecture of our system addresses the autonomous robotic control task by viewing the overall system as the combination of the robots, the camera, an image processor, and several clients as the minds of the small-size robot players. Figure 2.7 sketches the building blocks of the architecture.

The complete system is fully autonomous consisting of a well-defined and challenging processing cycle:

5 After downloading the soccer server, it took about 3 days to create a simple go-to-the-ball-and-shoot behavior. It took at least 6 months of development before we were able to create such a behavior using the real robots.

- The overhead camera with framegrabber grabs still images of the field.
- The image processor finds the ball's and the robots' locations and orientations in the still images.
- The client control modules use the objects' position information to produce control information. Each control module controls one robot. Actions are abstract commands indicating how the robots should move.

Figure 2.6
The CMUnited-97 robot team that competed in RoboCup-97. One of the 6 robots was used as a reserve in case any of the others temporarily malfunctioned.

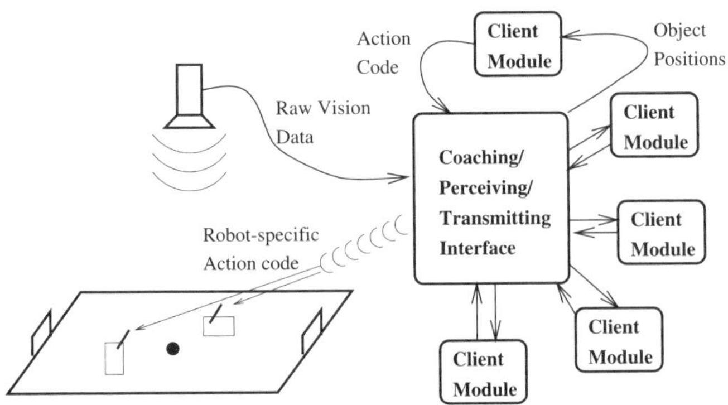

Figure 2.7
The CMUnited-97 robot architecture with global perception and distributed action.

• The wireless communication link transmits the control information from the host computer to the robots. Each robot has an identification binary code that is used on-board to detect commands intended for that robot. The abstract commands from the control modules are converted to a sequence of motor control bytes.
• The robot hardware receives the motor commands and moves the robots.

Table 2.6 summarizes the inputs and outputs of the five components of the complete robot architecture.

Table 2.6
The functional layers of the robot architecture with their inputs and outputs.

Functionality	Entity	Input	Output
vision	camera/framegrabber	continuous visual data	still frames
perception	image processor	still frames	robots' and ball's coordinates
skills and strategy	client control modules	robots' and ball's coordinates	abstract commands
communication	radio link	abstract commands	motor commands
movement	robots	motor commands	robot movement

The remainder of Section 2.3 is organized as follows. First, I describe our development of a preliminary image processor as well as the portions of the current image processor developed principally by Han (Han and Veloso, 1997) that are relevant to understanding the sensing capabilities of the robot agents. Second, I precisely specify the perception and abstract actions that are the inputs and outputs of the client control modules. Details of the other hardware components (the camera, framegrabber, radio link and the physical robots) can be found in (Achim et al., 1996). The client control modules are part of the research reported in this book and are therefore described in detail in a later chapter (Section 3.7).

The Image Processor

In this subsection I describe the preliminary image processor that we developed as part of our initial CMUnited-96 robot implementation (Achim et al., 1996). Then I describe the portions of the CMUnited-97 vision system developed principally by Han (Han and Veloso, 1997) that are relevant to understanding the sensing capabilities of the robot agents.

The robots need sensory information describing the positions of the robots and the ball on the field. The vision system provides this sensory information by way of an overhead camera, framegrabber, and image processor. The fact that perception is achieved by a video camera that overlooks the entire field offers an opportunity to get a complete, global view of the world state. Although this setup may simplify the sharing of information among multiple agents, it presents a challenge for reliable and real-time processing of the movement of multiple moving objects—in our case, the ball, five agents on our team, and five agents on the opposing team.

The CMUnited-96 Vision System

In our initial robot implementation (Achim et al., 1996) which we entered in the MiroSot-96 competition (Kim, 1996), I was the principal developer of the image processor. In that system, we use a standard camcorder mounted above the field. It produces NTSC video output that is then processed by the framegrabber.

The framegrabber takes raw, continuous image data and converts it into digital frames at a maximum rate of 30 frames per second. The framegrabber produces still images such as the one shown in Figure 2.8. The format is a

Figure 2.8
An example of a still image of our initial CMUnited-96 robot implementation captured by the framegrabber. Each robot has two different color patches so that we can detect both position and orientation. Each shade in this greyscale image is a different color in reality

320×240 array of pixels, each having a red, green, and blue value ranging from 0–255.

Fast image processing to discover the positions and orientations of the objects on the field is a significant challenge. Our method is color-based. By knowing the color of the ball and coding each robot with two different colors, one per half as shown in Figure 2.8 (each shade in the greyscale image is a different color in reality), it is possible to scan the image for pixels that are within a certain threshold distance from these colors.

Once one such pixel is found, the center of a color region is found by computing the center of gravity of all the pixels in a local region that match that color within a threshold. For example, the ball is orange. Thus, to find the ball, the entire image can be scanned for a pixel that is close to orange. Then, in a small region around that pixel, the coordinates of all of the orange pixels are averaged to indicate the center of the ball. For the robots, the centers of the two halves are found in the same way, making it trivial to compute the centers and orientations of the robots.

One important technique for speeding up the image processing is to rely on the assumption that objects will not move very far from frame to frame. Thus we can search for objects in a small region around their previous locations. Our image processing algorithm is summarized in Table 2.7.

Table 2.7
A high-level view of our algorithm for locating a given robot in a still frame used by the CMUnited-96 vision-processing software.

To find robot R, consisting of colors $C1$ and $C2$, at time T:

- Find a pixel of color $C1$ near the location of robot R at time $T - 1$. (At time 0, the entire image must be scanned.)
- Find the center of gravity of all $C1$-colored pixels near that pixel.
- Find the center of gravity of all $C2$-colored pixels near that pixel.
- Use the two centers of gravity to compute the center and the orientation of the robot.

While we use several techniques to speed up the CMUnited-96 vision processing, it still does not operate at frame rate: while the images are grabbed 30 times/sec, we can only process them roughly 7 times/sec. The ability to operate reliably at frame rate is a significant improvement in the CMUnited-97 vision system.

The CMUnited-97 Vision System

In contrast to the robots detected by the algorithm laid out in Table 2.7, the CMUnited-97 robots are all marked with the same two colors. Thus there is the added challenge of keeping track of which robot is which. Our image processor, developed principally by Han, successfully keeps track of five individual identical-looking teammates as well as five opponents. The ball's position and velocity are calculated at frame rate using a Kalman-Bucy filter (Han and Veloso, 1997).

Agent Perception and Action

This subsection specifies the perception and action capabilities of the robot team CMUnited-97 which is used as a substrate system in this book. The cognition component comprising the client control modules is described in Section 3.7 since it is an implementation of the team member agent architecture.

Perception

While the agents all get the same sensory information from a centralized image processor, the control decisions are made in a distributed manner. The agents are controlled either one at a time by the same process, or by completely separate processes all receiving the same visual information.

Visual information arrives at the framegrabber's image processing rate: 30 frames/sec. The vision system sends sensory information to each of the agents in the following form:

- 5 teammates: absolute (x, y, θ) position and orientation coordinates.
- 5 opponents: absolute (x, y) position coordinates. Orientation markers are team-dependent and thus cannot be reliably detected.
- Ball: absolute (x, y) coordinates as well as (dx, dy) velocity information.

Position information is accurate to within about 1cm and orientation information is accurate to within about 10 degrees, but the noise does not follow any regular distribution. Since the camera always sees the entire field, there is no hidden state.

The field is 274cm in length and 153cm in width. Therefore, each of the 10 robots can be in any of 274*153 possible positions, with the 5 teammates having any of 36 possible orientations. In addition, the ball can be in the same number of positions. Not considering the continuous ball velocity and the past states of the world, the perceived state space has $(274 * 153)^{11} > 10^{49}$

different states. Of course, the actual state space is infinitely large since the robot positions and orientations can vary continuously.

ACTION

The output of the client modules is abstract commands indicating how the robots should move. Note that the two motors on the robots can be controlled separately. The motors have encoders which enable precise control (Achim et al., 1996). Two types of commands are available:

Distance mode: Each motor moves a specified distance in a specified direction. Used for precise on-the-spot-turns.

Velocity mode: Each motor accelerates to a specified velocity. Used for continuous straight or curved movement.

The communication link converts the abstract commands to a stream of motor control bytes which can then be executed by the motor controllers on the robots. The commands are executed reliably and can be sent at the vision system's frame rate: 30 times/sec. Thus perception and action are synchronous with sensations triggering actions.

2.4 Network Routing

Network routing is a domain with enough similar characteristics to robotic soccer that the new TPOT-RL algorithm is effective, but enough differences to validate its generalizability. As a domain for the experiments reported in Chapter 7, we use a modified version of a publicly available packet routing simulator (Boyan and Littman, 1994).

In this simulator, a network at time t consists of:

• A set of *nodes* $N = \{n_0, \ldots, n_{m-1}\}$, $|N| = m$. Each node n_i consists of a queue of packets $K_{n_i} \subseteq K$, $|K_{n_i}| = k_{t,n_i}$ at time t. As packets are introduced into and removed from the queue, K_{n_i}, and consequently k_{t,n_i}, changes over time.

• A set of *links* $L \subseteq \{\{n_i, n_j\} | n_i, n_j \in N\}$ connecting pairs of nodes. From any node n_i, $L_{n_i} \subseteq N$ is the set of links from n_i: $L_{n_i} = \{n \in N | \{n, n_i\} \in L\}$. $|L_{n_i}| = l_{n_i}$.

• A set of *packets* $K = \{k_0, \ldots, k_{z_t-1}\}$, $|K| = z_t$ at time t. Each packet k_i is introduced at a source node $k_{i_{source}} \in N$ and travels towards its destination node

$k_{i_{dest}} \in N$. The packet also stores the time at which it left its source, $k_{i_{stime}}$, and when it arrives, the time at which it reaches its destination $k_{i_{dtime}}$. $k_{i_{path}} \subseteq L$ is an ordered list of links along which k_i has traveled from $k_{i_{source}}$ to its current position along with the times at which it has traversed each link. As packets are introduced into and removed from the network, K, and consequently z_t, changes over time.

• A *node capacity* C_{node} indicating the maximum number of packets allowed in a node's packet queue: $\forall i, k_{t,n_i} \leq C_{node}$.

• A *network capacity* C_{net} indicating the number of packets that can be active at one time in the network: $z_t \leq C_{net}$.

Two other parameters affecting the simulation are t_l which is the time it takes a packet to traverse a link and t_n which is the time it takes for a node to process one packet. If at time t, packet k enters the queue K_{n_i} at node n_i, it will stay there for $k_{t,n_i} t_n$ seconds.

As described by its authors, the network routing simulator is ...

> ... a discrete event simulator to model the motion of packets through a local area network. Packets are periodically introduced into the network at a random node with a random destination. Multiple packets at a node are stored in an unbounded FIFO queue; however, we set a limit on the total number of packets active in the network at a time.... In unit time, a node takes the top packet in its queue, examines its destination, and chooses a neighboring node to which to send the packet. A packet sent directly to its destination node is removed from the network immediately (Littman and Boyan, 1993).

At any give time, the state space can have up to C_{net} packets with a source, destination, and current location all in N ($|N| = m$). Thus the instantaneous size of the state space is:

$$|S| = (m^3)^{C_{net}} \tag{2.2}$$

In addition, each packet has traversed some subset of the $|L|$ links in the network, and the agents internal states' keep track of network statistics over time, thus increasing the effective size of the state space indefinitely.

The packet routing problem can be viewed as a multiagent collaborative problem by modeling each node as having an independent agent which makes the routing decisions at that node. When a node gets a packet, its agent must decide to which neighboring node it should forward the packet. This decision certainly depends on the packet's destination and might also depend upon the node's perception of the current state of the network. The team's goal is to route packets efficiently so that nodes do not reach their queue capacities and so that packets arrive at their destinations as quickly as possible.

This formulation of network routing is a team problem: all the agents are trying to work together to achieve optimal network performance. While neither the sensors nor the actuators are noisy, there is no explicit inter-agent communication, and there are no adversaries, the overall task is similar to robotic soccer in that unpredictable changes in network traffic, like unpredictable changes in opponent behaviors, can dynamically change the task characteristics. In addition, teammates' actions and their resulting state transitions are unknown. This last quality is that of opaque transitions and is a key characteristic enabling the effective use of the TPOT-RL algorithm.

Agent Perception and Action

PERCEPTION

When faced with the decision of where to send a particular packet k_i at time t, the sensory information available to an agent at a given node n_j is:

- $k_{i_{source}}$, the packet's source;
- $k_{i_{dest}}$, the packet's destination;
- $k_{i_{stime}}$, the time the packet left its source;
- $k_{i_{path}}$, the links traversed (with times) by the packet;
- K_{t,n_j}, the queue of packets waiting to be processed.

In addition, the agent can keep track of the traffic along its links. Since it either sends or receives every packet that travels along one of these links, it can keep local traffic statistics over time. Finally, the agent gets periodic overall network performance statistics as the feedback of the team's performance.

ACTION

The actions the agent can take are straightforward: the agent at node n_j can send packet k_i to a neighboring node along any of the links in L_{n_j}. Sensing and acting are synchronous in this domain: actions are triggered by a perception that the world has changed.

Example Network

Figure 2.9 illustrates our simulation of the packet routing problem. Nodes are represented as circles and links are lines. Suppose that node A receives a packet destined for node B along link 1. It must then decide whether to forward it along link 2, link 3, or possibly back along link 1.

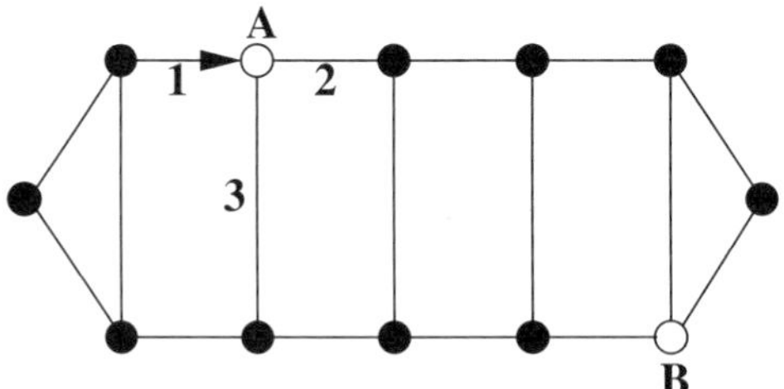

Figure 2.9
An example of the packet routing problem. Nodes are represented as circles and links are lines. In this case, node A is receiving a packet destined for node B along link 1 and must decide along which link to route it.

This simulator is meant to be a test bed for learning experiments rather than a realistic simulation of network routing. Nonetheless, it has been used by researchers other than the simulator's creators to test reinforcement learning approaches (Subramanian et al., 1997).

3 Team Member Agent Architecture

In order to create a coherent *team of agents*, the entire agent architecture must be designed with the team in mind. "Collaboration must be designed into systems from the start; it cannot be patched on. (Grosz, 1996)"

A multiagent system which involves several agents that collaborate towards the achievement of a joint objective is viewed as a *team* of agents. Most proposed teamwork structures (e.g. joint intentions (Cohen et al., 1999), shared plans (Grosz, 1996)) rely on agents in a multiagent system to negotiate and/or contract with each other in order to initiate team plans. However, in dynamic, real-time domains with unreliable communication, complex negotiation protocols may take too much time and/or be infeasible due to communication restrictions.

Simulated robotic soccer provides a time-critical environment in which agents in a team alternate between periods of limited and unlimited communication. Before games and at half-times, the team can effectively communicate with no limitations: each agent can be given the entire internal decision-making mechanisms of all of its teammates. However, as described in Section 2.2, during the course of a game, the agents must act independently in a dynamic, real-time, low-bandwidth communication environment: if the agents take the time to fully synchronize while playing, they may miss critical action opportunities and concede an advantage to the opponents.

These domain characteristics motivate the introduction of the concept of *periodic team synchronization* (PTS) domains. In PTS domains, during the limited communication periods, agents need to act autonomously, while still working towards a common team goal. Time-critical environments require real-time response and therefore eliminate the possibility of heavy communication among team agents. However, in PTS domains, agents can periodically synchronize in a safe, full-communication setting.

In this chapter, I describe our general team member agent architecture suitable for creating teams of agents in PTS domains (Stone and Veloso, 1999c). This architecture includes a mechanism for defining pre-determined multiagent protocols accessible to the entire team, called *locker-room agreements*. Within this team member agent architecture and using the locker-room agreement, we define our flexible teamwork structure that allows for task decomposition and dynamic role assignment in PTS domains (Stone and Veloso, 1999b). In addition, we define a communication protocol in service of the locker-room agreement that is suitable for use during low-communication periods in a class of PTS domains: domains such as the soccer server with single-channel, low-bandwidth communication environments (Stone and Veloso, 1998b).

The team member agent architecture described in this chapter defines a complete agent, including perception, cognition, and action. It is fully implemented as a simulated robotic soccer team.

This chapter is organized as follows. Section 3.1 expands upon the introduction of PTS domains and the two main contributions of this chapter: a flexible teamwork structure and a low-bandwidth communication paradigm. Section 3.2 presents the general agent architecture within which both the flexible teamwork structure and the low-bandwidth communication paradigm are situated. Sections 3.3 and 3.4 formally present the teamwork structure and the communication paradigm respectively. Section 3.5 gives details of our full implementations of both main contributions of this chapter within the simulated robotic soccer domain. Section 3.6 presents extensive empirical results testing the effectiveness of these implementations. Section 3.7 describes the implementation of the team member agent architecture and flexible formations within a second domain, namely real robotic soccer, and Section 3.8 is devoted to discussion and related work.

3.1 PTS Domains

We define periodic team synchronization domains as domains with the following characteristics:

• There is a team of autonomous agents A that collaborate towards the achievement of a joint long-term goal G.

• Periodically, the team can synchronize with no restrictions on communication: the agents can in effect inform each other of their entire internal states and decision-making mechanisms with no adverse effects upon the achievement of G. These periods of full communication can be thought of as times at which the team is "off-line."

• In general (i.e. when the agents are "on-line"):

–The domain is *dynamic* and *real-time* meaning that team performance is adversely affected if an agent ceases to act for a period of time: G is either less likely to be achieved, or likely to be achieved farther in the future. That is, consider agent a_i. Assume that all other agent behaviors are fixed and that were a_i to act optimally, G would be achieved with probability p at time t. If a_i stops acting for a random period of time and then resumes acting optimally, either:

$*G$ will be achieved with probability p' at time t with $p' < p$; or

$*G$ will be achieved with probability p at time t' with $t' > t$.

–The domain has *unreliable communication*, either in terms of transmission reliability or bandwidth limits. In particular:

$*$If an agent $a_i \in A$ sends a message m intended for agent $a_j \in A$, then m arrives with some probability $q < 1$; or

$*$Agent a_i can only receive x messages every y time units.

In the extreme, if $q = 0$ or if $x = 0$, then the periods of full communication are interleaved with periods of *no* communication, requiring the agents to act completely autonomously. In all cases, there is a cost to *relying* on communication. If agent a_i cannot carry on with its action until receiving a message from a_j, then the team's performance could suffer. Because of the unreliable communication, the message might not get through on the first try. And because of the dynamic, real-time nature of the domain, the team's likelihood of or efficiency at achieving G is reduced.

The soccer server provides a PTS domain since teams can plan strategies before the game, at halftime, or at other breakpoints; but during the course of the game, communication is limited. Its communication protocol involves a single, low-bandwidth, unreliable communication channel for all 22 agents (see Chapter 2).

In PTS domains, teams are long-term entities so that it makes sense for them to have periodic, reliable, private synchronization opportunities in which they can form off-line agreements for future use in unreliable, time-critical environments. This view of teams is complementary to teams that form on the fly for a specific action and keep communicating throughout the execution of that action as in (Cohen et al., 1999). Instead, in PTS domains, teams define coordination protocols during the synchronization opportunity and then disperse into the environment, acting autonomously with limited or no communication.

It has been claimed that pre-determined team actions are not flexible or robust to failure (Tambe, 1997). In the context of PTS domains, a key contribution of our work is the demonstration that certain pre-determined multiagent protocols can facilitate effective teamwork while still retaining flexibility. We call these pre-determined protocols *locker-room agreements*. Formed during the periodic synchronization opportunities, locker-room agreements are remembered identically by all agents and allow them to coordinate efficiently.

In this chapter, I present the *team member agent architecture*, an agent architecture suited for team agents in PTS domains. The architecture allows for an agent to act collaboratively based on locker-room agreements.

A first approach to PTS domains is to break the task at hand into multiple rigid roles, assigning one agent to each role. Thus each component of the task is accomplished and there are no conflicts among agents in terms of how they should accomplish the team goal. However such an approach is subject to several problems: inflexibility to short-term changes (e.g. one robot is non-operational), inflexibility to long-term changes (e.g. a route is blocked), and a lack of facility for reassigning roles.

We introduce instead *formations* as a teamwork structure within the team member agent architecture. A formation decomposes the task space defining a set of roles with associated behaviors. In a general scenario with heterogeneous agents, subsets of homogeneous agents can flexibly switch roles within formations, and agents can change formations dynamically.

Within these PTS domains and our flexible teamwork structure, several challenges arise. Such challenges include:

- how to represent and follow locker-room agreements;
- how to determine the appropriate times for agents to change roles and/or formations;
- how to ensure that all agents are using the same formation; and
- how to ensure that all roles in a formation are filled: since the agents are autonomous and do not share memory, they could easily become uncoordinated.

Also within the team member agent architecture, we introduce a communication paradigm appropriate for agents in PTS domains with single-channel, low-bandwidth, unreliable communication during the dynamic, real-time (online) phases. Not all PTS domains have such communication environments, but agents operating in those that do can implement this communication paradigm within their locker-room agreements.

In a nutshell, the contributions of this chapter are: the introduction of the concepts of PTS domains and locker-room agreements; the definition of a general team member agent architecture for defining a flexible teamwork structure; the facilitation of smooth transitions among roles and entire formations; a method for using roles to define pre-compiled multi-step, multiagent plans; and techniques for dealing with the obstacles to inter-agent communication during the low-communication periods of PTS domains with single-channel, low-bandwidth, unreliable communication during the "on-line" periods.

In addition to simulated robotic soccer, there are several other examples of PTS domains, such as hospital/factory maintenance (Decker, 1996b), search and rescue (Kitano et al., 1999), multi-spacecraft missions (Stone, 1997), and battlefield combat (Tambe, 1997). There are also several other domains with similar communication requirements to the ones considered here. For example, aural communication in crowded settings is one. Both people and robots using aural sensors (e.g. (Fujita and Kageyama, 1997)) must contend with multiple simultaneous audible streams. They also have a limit to the amount of sound they can process in a given amount of time, as well as to the range within which communication is possible. Another example of such a communication environment is arbitrarily expandable systems. If agents are not aware of what other agents exist in the environment, then all agents must use a single universally-known communication channel, at least in order to initiate communication.

3.2 Architecture Overview

The team member agent architecture is suitable for PTS domains. Individual agents can capture locker-room agreements and respond to the environment while acting autonomously. Based on a standard agent paradigm, our team member agent architecture allows agents to sense the environment, to reason about and select their actions, and to act in the real world. At team synchronization opportunities, the team also makes a locker-room agreement for use by all agents during periods of limited communication. Figure 3.1 shows the functional input/output model of the architecture.

The agent keeps track of three different types of state: the *world state*, the *locker-room agreement*, and the *internal state*. The agent also has two different types of behaviors: *internal behaviors* and *external behaviors*.

The world state reflects the agent's conception of the current state of the real world, both via its sensors and via the predicted effects of its actions. This conception can be represented as a belief state in terms of probability distributions or confidence values. The world state is updated as a result of interpreted sensory information. It may also be updated according to the predicted effects of the external behavior module's chosen actions. The world state is directly accessible to both internal and external behaviors.

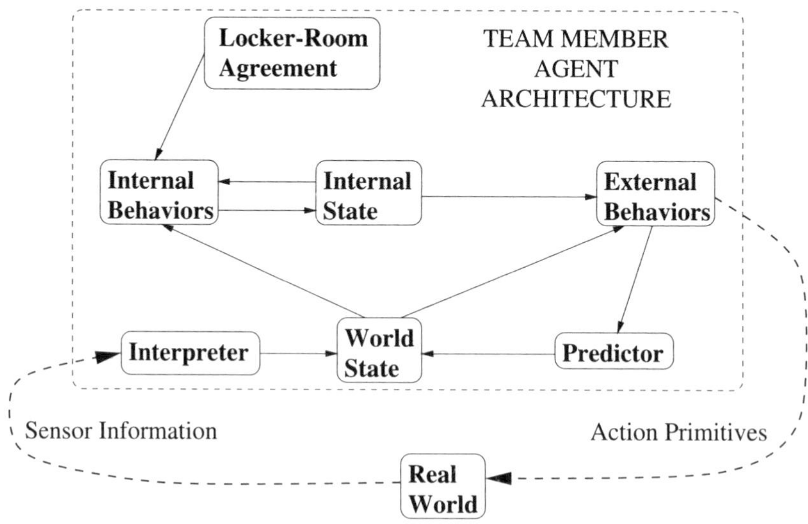

Figure 3.1
A functional input/output model of the team member agent architecture for PTS domains.

The locker-room agreement is set by the team when it is able to privately synchronize. It defines the flexible teamwork structure and the inter-agent communication protocols, if any. It is identical for all team members. The locker-room agreement is accessible only to internal behaviors.

The internal state stores the agent's internal variables. It may reflect previous and current world states, possibly as specified by the locker-room agreement. For example, the agent's role within a team behavior could be stored as part of the internal state. A window or distribution of past world states could also be stored as a part of the internal state. The agent updates its internal state via its internal behaviors.

The internal behaviors update the agent's internal state based on its current internal state, the world state, and the team's locker-room agreement.

The external behaviors reference the world and internal states, and select the actions to send to the actuators. The actions affect the real world, thus altering the agent's future percepts and predicted world states. External behaviors consider only the world and internal states, without direct access to the locker-room agreement.

Internal and external behaviors are similar in structure. They are both sets of condition/action pairs where conditions are logical expressions over the inputs and actions are themselves behaviors as illustrated in Figure 3.2. In both cases, a behavior is a directed acyclic graph (DAG) of arbitrary depth. The leaves of the DAGs are the behavior types' respective outputs: internal state changes for internal behaviors and action primitives for external behaviors. One leaf is illustrated in Figure 3.2.

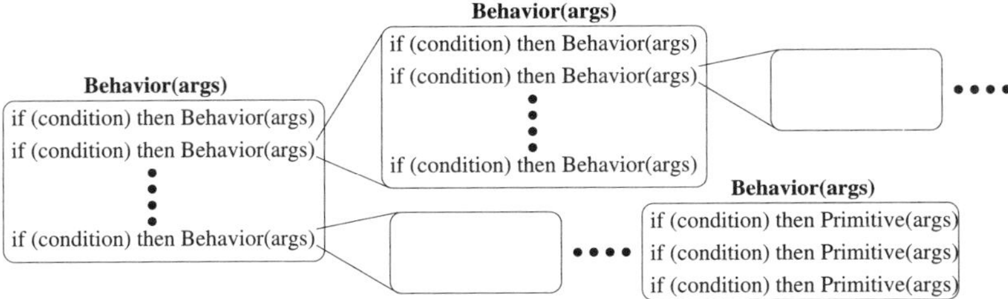

Figure 3.2
Behaviors in the team member agent architecture. Both internal and external behaviors are organized as directed acyclic graphs.

This notion of behavior is consistent with that laid out in (Mataric, 1994a). In particular, behaviors can be nested at different levels: selection among lower-level behaviors can be considered a higher-level behavior, with the overall agent behavior considered a single "do-the-task" behavior. There is one such *top-level* internal behavior and one top-level external behavior; they are called when it is time to update the internal state or act in the world, respectively.

The following section introduces the teamwork structure that builds upon this team member agent architecture. The teamwork structure is designed for use in PTS domains. It exploits the locker-room agreement and the behavior definitions of the team member agent architecture.

3.3 Teamwork Structure

Common to all players, the locker-room agreement includes the team structure used by team members while they are acting in a time-critical environment with limited or no communication. In this section, I present our teamwork structure. It defines:

1. Flexible agent *roles* with protocols for switching among them;
2. Collections of roles built into team *formations*; and
3. Multi-step, multiagent plans for execution in specific situations: *set-plays*.

The teamwork structure indirectly affects the agents' external behaviors by changing the agents' internal states via internal behaviors.

Roles

A *role*, r, consists of a specification of an agent's internal and external behaviors. The conditions and arguments of any behavior can depend on the agent's current role, which is a function of its internal state. At the extreme, a top-level external behavior could be a switch, calling an entirely different behavior subgraph for each possible role. However, the role can affect the agent's overall behavior at any level of its behavior graph: it could affect just the arguments of a behavior deeply embedded in the behavior graph.

Roles may be *rigid*, completely specifying an agent's behavior. Or they may be *flexible*, leaving a certain degree of autonomy to the agent filling the role. For example, consider an agent that has access to a clock and that can blow a whistle. Role r could rigidly specify that the agent filling it must blow a whistle on the hour every hour. On the other hand, role r could leave some flexibility to the agent that fills it, specifying that no fewer than 25% but no more than 75% of the times that the hour changes, the agent must blow a whistle. In this case, the agent must stay within a parametric range in order to successfully fill the role, but on every given hour change, it can choose for itself what to do. By specifying ranges of parameters or behavior options, the agent filling role r can be given an arbitrary amount of flexibility. In this sense, a role can be thought of as a "soft constraint" on an agent's behavior.

A role in the robotic soccer domain, can be a position such as a midfielder. In the hospital maintenance domain, a role could specify the wing of the hospital whose floors the appropriate agent should keep clean, while in the web search domain, it could specify a server to search.

Formations

We achieve collaboration between agents through the introduction of *formations*. A formation decomposes the task space defining a set of roles. Formations include as many (possibly redundant) roles as there are agents in the team, so that each role is filled by one agent. In addition, formations can specify subformations, or *units*, that do not involve the whole team. A unit consists of a subset of roles from the formation, a *captain*, and intra-unit interactions among the roles.

For a team of n agents $A = \{a_1, a_2, \ldots, a_n\}$, any formation is of the form

$$F = \{R, U_1, U_2, \ldots, U_k\}$$

where R is a set of roles $R = \{r_1, r_2, \ldots, r_n\}$ such that $i \neq j \Rightarrow r_i \neq r_j$. Note that there are the same number of roles as there are agents. However, it is possible to define redundant roles such that the behavior specification of r_i is equivalent to that of r_j $(i \neq j)$. Each unit U_i is a subset of R: $U_i = \{r_{i1}, r_{i2}, \ldots, r_{ik}\}$ such that $r_{ia} \in R$, $a \neq b \Rightarrow r_{ia} \neq r_{ib}$ and r_{i1} is the *captain*, or unit leader. The map $A \mapsto R$ is not fixed: roles can be filled by different homogeneous agents. A single role may be a part of any number of units and formations.

Units are used to deal with local problem solving issues. Rather than involving the entire team in a sub-problem, the roles that address it are organized into a unit. Captains are unit-members with special privileges in terms of directing the other unit members.

Roles and formations are introduced independently from the agents that are to fill them. The locker-room agreement specifies an initial formation; an initial map from agents to roles; and run-time triggers for dynamic changing of formations. At any given time, each agent has an opinion as to what formation the team is currently using. Agents keep mappings $A \mapsto R$ from teammates to roles in the current formation. All this team structuring information is stored in the agent's internal state. It can be altered via the agent's internal behaviors.

Since agents are autonomous and operating in a PTS domain, during the periods of limited communication there is no guarantee that they will all think that the team is using the same formation, nor that they have accurate maps $A \mapsto R$. In fact, the only guarantee is that each agent knows its own current role. Thus, in our implementation of the teamwork structure, we create robust behaviors for team agents which do not depend upon having correct, up-to-date knowledge of teammates' internal states: they degrade gracefully. When limited communication is available, efficient low-bandwidth communication protocols can allow agents to inform each other of their roles periodically. Figure 3.3 illustrates a team of agents smoothly switching roles and formations over time.

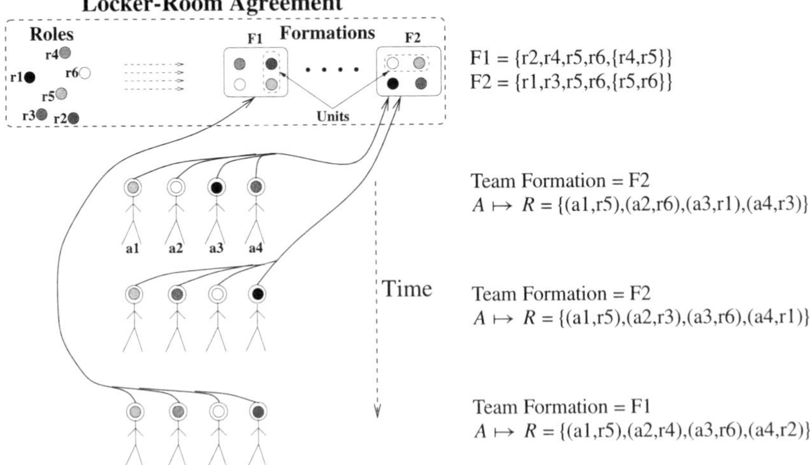

Figure 3.3
A team of agents smoothly switching roles and formations over time. Different roles are represented as differently shaded circles. Formations are possibly overlapping collections of roles. Units within the formations are indicated within a dotted enclosure. The definitions of all roles, formations, and units are part of the locker-room agreement and are known to all agents. An agent's current role is indicated by the shaded circle in its head and its current formation is indicated by an arrow to the formation. The agents first switch roles while staying in the same formation; then they switch to an entirely new formation.

Set-Plays

As a part of the locker-room agreement, the team can define multi-step, multi-agent plans to be executed at appropriate times. Particularly if there are certain situations that occur repeatedly, it makes sense for the team to devise plans for those situations ahead of time. We define a set-play as the combination of:

- A *trigger* condition indicating the set of states in which the set-play is activated; and
- A set of *set-play roles* $R_{sp} = \{spr_1, \ldots, spr_m\}, m \leq n$ defining the actions to be taken by the participants in the set-play. Each set-play role spr_i includes:

  –A *set-play behavior* to be executed; and

  –A *termination* condition indicating the set of states in which an agent should cease filling the set-play role and resume its normal behavior.

The set-plays are defined in the locker-room agreement so that they are known to all agents on the team. Note that a set-play need not involve the entire team: $m \leq n$. The locker-room agreement also includes a general function to map roles in a formation to roles in a set-play: $R \mapsto R_{sp}$. Thus set-play roles are not assigned to pre-determined agents; instead they are filled by whichever agent is filling the appropriate role in the team's current formation.

3.4 Communication Paradigm

The teamwork structure defined in Section 3.3 is designed to be appropriate for all PTS domains. In the subclass of PTS domains with single-channel, low-bandwidth, unreliable communication during the periods of limited communication, such as the soccer server, the communication paradigm defined in this section is also appropriate. The communication paradigm further illustrates the use of the locker-room agreement within the team member agent architecture. Recall that PTS domains may have no communication possible during the "on-line" periods. In those cases, our communication paradigm does not apply.

Domains with single-channel, low-bandwidth, unreliable communication raise several challenges for inter-agent communication. The locker-room agreement can be used to make inter-agent communication more efficient and reliable. The five challenges addressed by our communication approach are:

1. Team members need some method of identifying which messages on the single channel are intended for which agent.

2. Since there is a single communication channel, agents must be prepared for active interference by hostile agents. A hostile agent could mimic messages it has previously heard at random times.

3. Since the communication channel has low bandwidth, the team must prevent itself from "talking all at once." Many communication utterances call for responses from all team members. However, if all team members respond simultaneously, few of the responses will get through.

4. Since communication is unreliable, agents must be robust to lost messages: their behaviors cannot depend upon receiving communications from a teammate.

5. Teams must determine how to maximize the chances that they are using the same team strategy (formation) despite the facts that each is acting autonomously and that communication is unreliable.

The characteristics and challenges of this communication environment are summarized in Table 3.1.

Table 3.1
The characteristics and challenges of the type of communication environment considered in this book.

Communication Environment	Challenges
• Many agents, teams	• Message targeting and distinguishing
• Single-channel	• Robustness to active interference
• Low-bandwidth	• Multiple simultaneous responses
• Unreliable	• Robustness to lost messages
	• Team coordination

In order to meet these challenges, we specify that a team uses messages with the following fields, all of whose syntax and semantics are defined within the locker-room agreement:

- The <team-identifier> identifies messages from within the team as opposed to another team in an adversarial environment.
- The <unique-team-member-ID> is a different sequential integer assigned to each team member.
- The <encoded-time-stamp> is a security code that can be used to verify a message's authenticity.
- The <time-stamped-team-strategy> indicates the current formation that the sender believes the team is using.
- The <selected-internal-state> contains portions of the sender's internal state.
- The <message-type> and <message-data> contain the semantic content of the individual message. The messages can use any syntactic and semantic codes (KQML (Finin et al., 1994) and KIF (Genesereth and Fikes, 1992) for example). The locker-room agreement also includes a mapping from message type to response requirements.
- The <target> indicates the intended recipient(s) of the message. It could be intended for a single team member identified either by <unique-team-member-ID> or by role within the team's current formation; for a unit of the current formation; or for all team members.

In addition to this protocol which is defined within the locker-room agreement, some internal state variables need to be devoted to communication. When an agent hears a message, it interprets it and updates the world state to reflect any information transmitted by the message. It also stores the content of the message as a special variable `last-message`. Furthermore, based on the locker-room agreement, an internal behavior then updates the internal state. If the message requires a response, three variables in the internal state are manipulated by an internal behavior: `response`, `response-flag`, and `communicate-delay`. `response` is the actual response that should be given by the agent as determined in part by the locker-room agreement. All three of these variables are then referenced by an external behavior to determine when a response should be given. For example one condition-action pair of the top-level external behavior might be: `if (response-flag set and communicate-delay=0) then say(response)`.

These message fields and internal state variables are components of our novel communication paradigm and represent contributions of our team member agent architecture. The remainder of this section details how these particular message fields and internal state variables can be used to meet the challenges summarized in Table 3.1.

Message Targeting and Distinguishing

Since there is a single communication channel, agent a_i hears messages sent by all agents whether or not they are intended for it. Messages sent by agents from another team are completely ignored. Messages sent by a teammate are identified by the <team-identifier> field. Since all team members know the locker-room agreement, agents monitor all messages from teammates to determine their teammates' internal states, even if the content of the message is intended for another teammate.

Agents can distinguish messages that are intended for them by checking the <team-identifier> and <target> fields. An agent a_i pays attention to a message from a member of the same team that is targeted to a_i, to the entire team, or to some subset of the team that includes a_i. The <target> field could identify an individual agent either by its unique ID number or by the role that it is currently playing. Thus, a message could be sent to the agent playing a particular role without knowing which agent that is. Similarly, a message could be targeted towards all agents in a unit of the team's current formation.

Robustness to Active Interference

The only further difficulty related to an agent distinguishing which messages are intended for it arises in the presence of active interference. Consider a hostile agent h which hears a message that is directed to a_i at time t. h has full access to the message since all agents use the same communication channel. Thus if h remembers the message and sends an identical message at time u, agent a_i will mistakenly believe that the message is from a teammate. Although the message was appropriate at time t, it may be obsolete at time u and it could potentially confuse a_i as h might intend.

This potential difficulty is avoided with the <encoded-time-stamp> field. Even a simple time stamp is likely to safeguard against interference since h is not privy to the locker-room agreement: it does not necessarily know which field is the time stamp. However, if h discovers which field is the time stamp by noticing that it always matches the time of the message, it could alter the field based on the time elapsed between times t and u. Indeed, if there is a globally accessible clock, h would simply have to replace t with u in the message. However, the team can safeguard against such interference techniques by encoding the time-stamp using an injective function chosen as a part of the locker-room agreement. This function can use any of the other message fields as arguments in order to make decryption as difficult as possible. The only requirement is that a teammate receiving the message can invert the function to determine the time at which the message was sent. If the time at which it was sent is either too far in the past or in the future (according to the locker-room agreement), then the message can be safely ignored. In particular, the locker-room agreement has a variable `message-lag-tolerance` encoding this time. If a message sent at time t arrives at time u with $u - t >$ `message-lag-tolerance`, then the message is ignored.

By observing enough messages and comparing them with the actual time, it is theoretically possible for hostile agents to crack simple codes and alter the <encoded-time-stamp> field appropriately before sending a false message. However, the function can be made arbitrarily complex so that such a feat is intractable within the context of the domain. If secrecy is critical and computation unconstrained, a theoretically safe encryption scheme can be used. The degree of complexity necessary depends upon the number of messages that will be sent after the locker-room agreement. With few enough messages, even a simple linear combination of the numerical message fields suffices.

Multiple Simultaneous Responses

The next challenge to meet is that of messages that require responses from several teammates. However, not all messages are of this type. For example, a message meaning "where are you?" requires a response, while "look out behind you" does not. Therefore it is first necessary for agents to classify messages in terms of whether or not they require responses as a function of the <message-type> field. Since the low-bandwidth channel prevents multiple simultaneous responses, the agents must also reason about the number of intended recipients as indicated by the <target> field. Taking these two factors into account, there are six types of messages, indicated here as a1,a2,a3,b1,b2, and b3:

	Response requested	
Message Target	no	yes
Single agent	a1	b1
Whole team	a2	b2
Part of team	a3	b3

When hearing any message, the agent updates its internal belief of the other agent's status as indicated by the <time-stamped-team-strategy> and <selected-internal-state> fields. However, only when the message is intended for it does it consider the content of the message. Then it uses the following algorithm in response to the message:

1. If the message requires no response (types a1,a2,a3), the agent simply updates its internal state.
2. If the message requires a response, then set `response` to the appropriate response message, `response-flag` = 1 and
   - If the agent was the only target (type b1), respond immediately: `communicate-delay` = 0;
   - If the message is sent to more than one target (types b2 and b3), set `communicate-delay` based on the difference between the <unique-team-member-ID> of the message sender and that of the receiver. Thus each teammate responds at a different time, leaving time for teammate messages to go through.

An internal behavior decrements `communicate-delay` as time passes. An external behavior uses the communication condition-action pair presented above:

```
if (response-flag set and communicate-delay=0)
then say(response)
```

where say is an actuator primitive. Players also set the `communicate-delay` variable in the event that they need to send multiple messages to the same agent in a short time. This communication paradigm allows agents to continue acting in real-time while reasoning about the appropriate time to communicate.

Robustness to Lost Messages

In order to meet the challenge raised by unreliable communication leading to lost messages, agents must not depend on communication to act. Communication is structured so that it helps agents update their world and internal states. But agents do not stop acting while waiting for communications from teammates. As brought up in (Tambe, 1996a), such a case could cause infinite looping if a critical teammate fails to respond for any reason. As well as continuing to act while waiting for `communicate-delay` to expire, agents ensure that they do not rely on inter-agent communication by continuing to act while waiting for responses from teammates. They also maintain world and internal states without help from teammates. Communication can improve the reliability of an agent's world state by elucidating some of an agent's hidden state; but communication is not necessary for an agent to maintain a reasonable approximation of the world state.

Team Coordination

Finally, team coordination is difficult to achieve in the face of the possibility that autonomous team members may not agree on the <time-stamped-team-strategy> or the mapping from teammates to roles within the team strategy. Again, there are no disastrous results should team members temporarily adopt different strategies; however they are more likely to achieve their goal G if they can stay coordinated.

One method of coordination is via the locker-room agreement. Agents agree on globally accessible environmental cues as triggers for switches in team strategy. Another method of coordination which complements this first approach is via the time stamp. When hearing a message from a teammate indicating that the team strategy is different from the agent's current idea of the team strategy, the agent adopts the more recent team strategy: if the received message's team strategy has a time-stamp that is more recent than that on the agent's current team strategy, it switches; otherwise it keeps the same team strategy and informs its teammate of the change. Thus changes in team strategy can quickly propagate through the team.

In particular, suppose that agent a_i hears at time t that the team formation is F_1. It then hears a message from agent a_j indicating that the team formation was set to F_2 at time u. If $t < u$, then F_2 is a more recent team decision and it updates its notion of the team's formation to F_2. However, if $u < t$, it is agent a_j that has an obsolete view of the formation. a_i then sends a message to a_j indicating in the <time-stamped-team-strategy> field that the formation was set to F_1 at time t, thus causing a_j to update its notion of the team's formation. In the event that $t = u$, the locker-room agreement must specify an order of precedence among roles in order for the agents to determine which agent's idea of the current formation to regard as correct.

Depending on the available bandwidth in the particular application, the <selected-internal-state> can also be used to facilitate team coordination by helping to keep the team members up-to-date regarding the mapping $A \mapsto R$, and perhaps regarding object locations that might be hidden to individual agents.

3.5 Implementation in Robotic Soccer

Robotic soccer is a very good example of a PTS domain: teams can coordinate before the game, at half-time, and at other break points, but communication is limited during play. In addition, as described in Chapter 2, the soccer server models a single-channel, low-bandwidth, unreliable communication environment.

This section provides a detailed description of a specific implementation of the team member agent architecture, the teamwork structure, and the communication approach presented in Sections 3.2–3.4. The implementation is that of the CMUnited-98 simulated robotic soccer team[1].

The implementation is described in great detail. In particular, the first subsection presents the low-level action cycle, skills, and world model of CMUnited-98 agents. Further details, particularly implementation details of the skills, are available in Appendix B. The low-level details presented in this first subsection are important for gaining an understanding of the basic agent perception and action capabilities. In the context of the team member agent

1 The subsequent CMUnited-99 team uses the same team member agent architecture, teamwork structure, and communication approach.

architecture, they represent the interpreter, the world state, the predictor, and the external behaviors. These portions of the agent architecture are concerned principally with issues relating to an individual agent. On the other hand, the teamwork structure and communication paradigm implementations, presented in the subsequent two subsections, deal with collaborative, team issues. They are defined within the locker-room agreement, internal behaviors, and internal state.

Action Cycle and World Model

This subsection defines the portions of the CMUnited-98 simulated robotic soccer agent implementation that relate to an individual agent. In the context of the team member agent architecture presented in Section 3.2, this subsection covers the interpreter, the world state, the predictor, and the external behaviors.

TIMING ACTIONS

A CMUnited-98 agent is capable of perception, cognition, and action. By perceiving the world, it builds a model of the current world state. Then, based on a set of behaviors, it chooses an action appropriate for this world state.

A driving factor in the design of the agent architecture is the fact that the simulator operates in fixed cycles of length `simulator_step` (100 msec). As presented in Section 2.2, the simulator accepts commands from clients throughout a cycle and then updates the world state all at once at the end of the cycle. Only one action command (dash, kick, turn, or catch) is executed for a given client during a given cycle.

Therefore, agents (simulator clients) should send exactly one action command to the simulator in every simulator cycle. If more than one command is sent in the same cycle, a random one is executed, possibly leading to undesired behavior. If no command is sent during a simulator cycle, an action opportunity has been lost: opponent agents who have acted during that cycle may gain an advantage. In the team member agent architecture, sending an action corresponds to executing the top-level external behavior.

Since the simulator updates the world at the end of every cycle, it is advantageous to try to determine the state of the world at the end of the previous cycle when choosing an action for the current cycle. As such, the basic agent loop during a given cycle t is as follows:

- Assume the agent has consistent information about the state of the world at the end of cycle $t-2$ and has sent an action during cycle $t-1$.

• While the server is still in cycle $t - 1$, upon receipt of a sensation (see, hear, or sense_body), process the sensation in the interpreter and store the new information in temporary structures. Do not update the world state.

• When the server enters cycle t (determined either by a running clock or by the receipt of a sensation with time stamp t), use all of the information available (temporary information from sensations and predicted effects of past actions) to **update the world state** to match the server's world state (the "real world state") at the end of cycle $t - 1$. Then **choose and send an action** to the server for cycle t: execute the top-level external behavior.

• Repeat for cycle $t + 1$.

While the above algorithm defines the overall agent loop, much of the challenge is involved in updating the world state effectively and choosing an appropriate action. The remainder of this subsection goes into these processes in detail.

The World State

When acting based on a world model, it is important to have as accurate and precise a model of the world as possible at the time that an action is taken. In order to achieve this goal, CMUnited-98 agents gather sensory information over time, extracting its meaning via the interpreter, and process the information by incorporating it into the world state immediately prior to acting.

There are several objects in the world, such as the goals and the field markers which remain stationary and can be used for self-localization. Mobile objects are the agent itself, the ball, and 21 other players (10 teammates and 11 opponents). These objects are represented in a type hierarchy as illustrated in Figure 3.4.

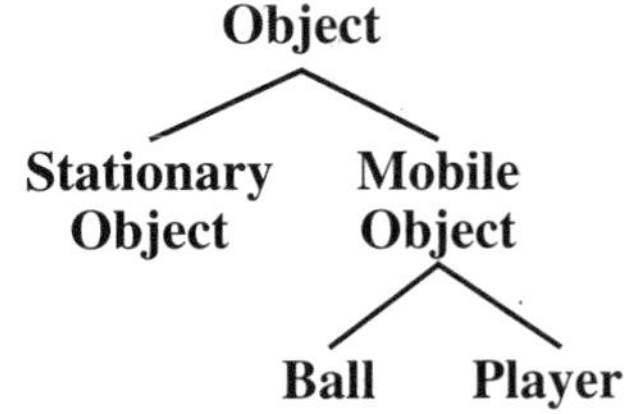

Figure 3.4
The agent's object type hierarchy.

Each agent's world state stores an instantiation of a stationary object for each goal, sideline, and field marker; a ball object for the ball; and 21 player objects. Since players can be seen without their associated team and/or uniform number, the player objects are not identified with particular individual players. Instead, the variables for team and uniform number can be filled in as they become known.

Mobile objects are stored with confidence values within [0,1] indicating the confidence with which their locations are known. The confidence values are needed because of the large amount of hidden state in the world: no object is seen consistently. While it would be a mistake to only remember objects that are currently in view, it is also wrong to assume that a mobile object will stay still (or continue moving with the same velocity) indefinitely. By decaying the confidence in unseen objects over time, agents can determine whether or not to rely on the position and velocity values (Bowling et al., 1996).

All information is stored as global coordinates even though both sensor and actuator commands are specified in relative coordinates (angles and distances relative to the agent's position on the field). Global coordinates are easier to store and maintain as the agent moves around the field because the global coordinates of stationary objects do not change as the agent moves, while the relative coordinates do. It is a simple geometric calculation to convert the global coordinates to relative coordinates on demand as long as the agent knows its own position on the field.

The variables associated with each object type are as follows:

Object :

- Global (x, y) position coordinates
- Confidence within [0,1] of the coordinates' accuracy

Stationary Object : nothing additional

Mobile Object :

- Global (dx, dy) velocity coordinates
- Confidence within [0,1] of the coordinates' accuracy

Ball : nothing additional

Player :

- Team
- Uniform number
- Global θ facing angle
- Confidence within [0,1] of the angle's accuracy

Updating the World State

Information about the world can come from

- Visual information;
- Audial information;
- Sense_body information; and
- Predicted effects of previous actions.

Visual information arrives to the interpreter as relative distances and angles to objects in the player's view cone. Audial information could include information about global object locations from teammates. Sense_body information pertains to the agent's own status including stamina, view mode, and speed.

Whenever new information arrives at the interpreter, it is stored in temporary structures with time stamps and confidences (1 for visual information, possibly less for audial information). Visual information is stored as relative coordinates until the agent's exact location is determined.

When it is time to act during cycle t, all of the available information is used to best determine the server's world state at the end of cycle $t-1$. If no new information arrived pertaining to a given object, the velocity and actions taken are used by the predictor to predict the new position of the object and the confidence in that object's position and velocity are both decayed.

When the agent's world state is updated to match the end of simulator cycle $t-1$, first the agent's own position is updated to match the time of the last sight; then those of the ball and players are updated.

The Agent Itself: Since visual information is given in coordinates relative to the agent's position, it is important to determine the agent's exact position at the time of the sight. When updating the world state to match the end of simulator cycle $t-1$, there may have been visual information with time stamp $t-1$ and/or t (anything earlier would have been incorporated into the previous update of the world state at the end of cycle $t-1$).
If the latest visual information has time stamp $t-1$, then the agent's own position is not updated until after the other objects have been updated since their coordinates are given relative to the old agent position. If the latest visual information has time stamp t, or if there has been no new visual information since the last world-state update, the agent's status can be updated immediately. In either case, the following process is used to update the information about the agent:

- If new visual information has arrived:
  - –The agent's position can be determined accurately by using the relative coordinates of one seen line and the closest stationary object.
- If no visual information has arrived:
  - –Bring the velocity up to date, possibly incorporating the predicted effects of any actions (a dash) taken during the previous cycle.
  - –Using the previous position and velocity, predict the new position and velocity.
- If available, reset the agent's speed as per the sense_body information. Assume velocity is in the direction the agent is facing.
- Bring the player's stamina up to date either via the sense_body information or from the predicted action effects.

The Ball: As the key focus of action initiative in the domain, the ball's position and velocity drives a large portion of the agents' decisions. As such, it is important to have as accurate and up-to-date information about the ball as possible.
The ball information is updated as follows:

- If there was new visual information, use the agent's absolute position at the time (determined above), and the ball's temporarily stored relative position to determine the ball's absolute position at the time of the sight.
- If velocity information is given as well, update the velocity. Otherwise, check if the old velocity is correct by comparing the new ball position with the expected ball position.
- If no new visual information arrived or the visual information was from cycle $t-1$, estimate its position and velocity for cycle t using the values from cycle $t-1$. If the agent kicked the ball on the previous cycle, the predicted resulting ball motion is also taken into account.
- If the ball should be in sight (i.e. its predicted position is in the player's view cone), but isn't (i.e. visual information arrived, but no ball information was included), set the confidence to 0.
- Information about the ball may have also arrived via communication from teammates. If any heard information would increase the confidence in the ball's position or velocity at this time, then it is used as the correct information. Confidence in teammate information can be determined by the time of the information (did the teammate see the ball more recently?)

and the teammate's distance to the ball (since players closer to the ball see it more precisely).

Ball velocity is particularly important for agents when determining whether or not (or how) to try to intercept the ball, and when kicking the ball. However, velocity information is often not given as part of the visual information string, especially when the ball is near the agent and kickable. Therefore, when necessary, the agents attempt to infer the ball's velocity indirectly from the current and previous ball positions.

Teammates and Opponents: The biggest challenge related to keeping track of player positions is that the visual information often does not identify the player that is seen (see Figure 2.4). One might be tempted to ignore all ambiguously-specified players. However, for strategic planning it is very useful to have a complete picture of the player positions around the field.

In general, player positions and velocities are determined and maintained in the same way as in the case of the ball. A minor addition is that the direction a player is facing is sometimes available from the visual information.

When a player is seen without full information about its identity, previous player positions can be used to help disambiguate the identity. Knowing the maximum distance a player can move in any given cycle, it is possible for the agent to determine whether a seen player could be the same as a previously identified player. If it is physically possible, the agent assumes that they are indeed the same player.

Since different players can see different regions of the field in detail, communication can play an important role in maintaining accurate information about player locations.

From the complete set of player locations, an agent can determine both the defensive and offensive offsides lines. It is particularly important for forwards to stay in front of the last opponent defender in order to avoid being called offsides. Forwards periodically look towards the opponent defenders in order to increase the reliability of their location information.

AGENT SKILLS: LOW-LEVEL EXTERNAL BEHAVIORS

Once the agent has determined the server's world state for cycle t as accurately as possible, it can choose and send an action to be executed at the end of the cycle. That is, it must execute its external behavior. At the top level, it first chooses its *behavior mode* or its local goal within the team's overall strategy. The behavior mode determines the subgraph of the external behavior to be executed. The subgraphs contain several low-level *skills* which provide the agent with basic capabilities. The output of the skills are primitive movement commands.

The skills available to CMUnited-98 players include kicking, dribbling, ball interception, goaltending, defending, and clearing. The implementation details of these skills are described in Appendix B.

The common thread among these skills is that they are all *predictive, locally optimal skills* (PLOS). They take into account predicted world states as well as predicted effects of future actions in order to determine the optimal primitive action from a local perspective, both in time and in space.

One simple example of PLOS is each individual agent's stamina management. The server models stamina as having a replenishable and a non-replenishable component. Each is only decremented when the current stamina goes below a fixed threshold. Each player monitors its own stamina level to make sure that it never uses up any of the non-replenishable component of its stamina. No matter how fast it should move according to the behavior the player is executing, it slows down its movement to keep itself from getting too tired. While such behavior might not be optimal in the context of the team's goal, it is locally optimal considering the agent's current tired state.

Even though the skills are predictive, the agent *commits* to only one action during each cycle. When the time comes to act again, the situation is completely reevaluated. If the world is close to the anticipated configuration, then the agent will act similarly to the way it predicted on previous cycles. However, if the world is significantly different, the agent will arrive at a new sequence of actions rather than being committed to a previous plan. Again, it will only execute the first step in the new sequence.

Behavior Modes: The Top-Level External Behavior

Given all of the individual skills available to the CMUnited-98 agents, it becomes a significant challenge to coordinate the team so that the players are not all trying to do the same thing at the same time. Of course one and only one agent should execute the goaltending behavior. But it is not so clear how to determine when an agent should move towards the ball, when it should defend, when it should dribble, or clear, etc.

A player's top-level external behavior decision is its behavior mode. Implemented as a rule-based system, the behavior mode determines the abstract behavior that the player should execute. For example, there is a behavior mode for the set of states in which the agent can kick the ball. Then, the decision of what to do with the ball is made by way of a more involved decision mechanism represented as a subgraph of the external behavior. On each action cycle, the first thing a player does is re-evaluate its behavior mode.

The behavior modes include:

Goaltend: Only used by the goaltender.

Localize: Find own field location if it's unknown.

Face Ball: Find the ball and look at it.

Handle Ball: Used when the ball is kickable.

Active Offense: Go to the ball as quickly as possible. Used when no teammate could get there more quickly.

Auxiliary Offense: Get open for a pass. Used when a nearby teammate has the ball.

Passive Offense: Move to a position likely to be useful offensively in the future.

Active Defense: Go to the ball even though another teammate is already going. Used in the defensive end of the field.

Auxiliary Defense: Mark an opponent.

Passive Defense: Track an opponent or go to a position likely to be useful defensively in the future.

The detailed conditions and effects of each behavior mode are described in Appendix C. However, they will also become more clear as the role-based flexible team structure is described in this section.

The remainder of this section details the implementations of both main contributions of this chapter: the flexible teamwork structure and the communication paradigm. Both implementations are unified within the CMUnited simulated robotic soccer system, building upon the action cycle and world state model presented here.

Teamwork Structure Implementation

One approach to task decomposition in the soccer server is to assign fixed coordinate positions to agents.[2] Such an approach leads to several problems: i) short-term inflexibility in that the players cannot adapt their positions to the

---

2 One of the teams in Pre-RoboCup-96 used and depended upon these assignments: the agents passed to the fixed positions regardless of whether or not there was a teammate there.

ball's location on the field; ii) long-term inflexibility in that the team cannot adapt to opponent strategy; and iii) local inefficiency in that players often get tired running across the field back to their positions after chasing the ball. Our formations allow for flexible teamwork and combat these problems. (The term "position" is often used to denote the concept of "role" in the soccer domain. In this section I use the two terms interchangeably.)

This subsection describes the CMUnited simulator team implementation of the teamwork structure presented in Section 3.3. In the context of the team member agent architecture in Section 3.2, it covers the locker-room agreement, the internal behaviors, and the internal state.

Domain Instantiations of Roles and Formations

Figure 3.5 shows a simplified top-level external behavior used by a team agent. The agent's top priority is to locate the ball. If the ball's location is known, it moves towards the ball or goes to its position (i.e. to assume its role), depending on its internal state. It also responds to any requested communications from teammates. The sub-behaviors of the top-level behavior are all behavior modes.

External Behavior: Play Soccer()

If (Ball Lost)	Face Ball()
If (Ball known AND Chasing)	Handle Ball(args1)
If (Ball known AND Not Chasing)	Passive Offense(args2)
If (Commuincate Flag Set)	Communicate()

Figure 3.5
An example of a simplified top-level external behavior for a robotic soccer player.

The referenced "handle ball" and "passive offense" behaviors may be affected by the agent's current role and/or formation. Such effects are realized by references to the internal state either at the level of function arguments (args1, args2), or within sub-behaviors. None of the actions in the condition-action pairs here are action primitives; rather, they are calls to lower level behaviors.

The definition of a position includes *home coordinates*, a *home range*, and a *maximum range*, as illustrated in Figure 3.6. The position's home coordinates are the default location to which the agent should go. However, the agent has some flexibility, being able to set its actual home position anywhere within

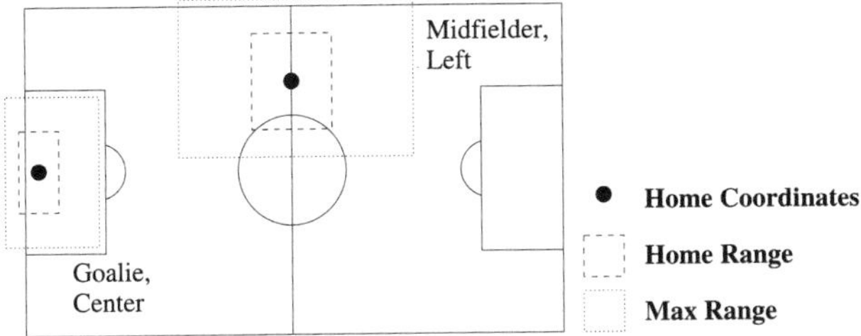

Figure 3.6
Different positions with home coordinates and home and max ranges.

the home range. When moving outside of the max range, the agent is no longer considered to be in the position. The home and max ranges of different positions can overlap, even if they are part of the same formations.

A formation consists of a set of positions and a set of units (as defined in Section 3.3). The formation and each of the units can also specify inter-position behavior specifications for the member positions, as illustrated in Figure 3.7(a). In this case, the formations specify inter-role interactions, namely the positions to which a player should consider passing the ball. We use decision tree learning to enable players to decide where to pass from among these options (see Chapter 6). Figure 3.7(b) illustrates the units, the roles involved, and their captains. Here, the units contain defenders, midfielders, forwards, left players, center players, and right players.

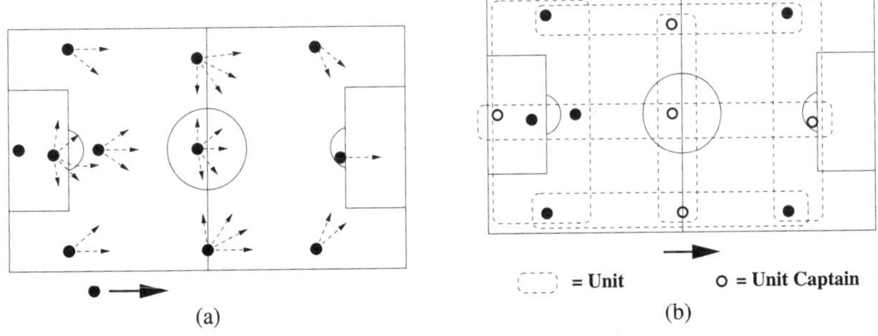

Figure 3.7
(a) A possible formation (4-3-3) for a team of 11 players. Arrows represent passing options. (b) Positions can belong to more than one unit.

Since the players are all autonomous, in addition to knowing its own role, each one has its own belief of the team's current formation along with the time at which that formation was adopted, and a map of teammates to positions. Ideally, the players have consistent beliefs as to the team's state, but this condition cannot be guaranteed between synchronization opportunities.

For example, consider the passive offense behavior in Figure 3.5. This external behavior references the agent's internal state via a series of function calls. Specifically, the agent is to move to some location within the home range of its current position in the team's current formation:

$$\texttt{TargetLocation} \in \texttt{HomeRange(MyPosition(CurrentFormation()))} \quad (3.1)$$

where `HomeRange(p)` returns the home range of position p; `MyPosition(f)` returns a player's own current position in formation f; and `CurrentFormation()` returns the player's own opinion of the team's current formation. Thus the internal behaviors that determine the player's current position and formation affect its external behavior. Notice that by specifying a range of possible locations, the role leaves some flexibility to the autonomous player: it can choose which specific `TargetLocation` to move to within the range.

Different roles can also have entirely different external behaviors. As presented in Section 3.3, each role could have an entirely different external behavior subgraph.

Our teamwork structure for PTS domains allows for several significant features in our simulated soccer team. These features are: (i) the definition of switching among multiple formations with units; (ii) flexible position adjustment and position switching; (iii) and pre-defined, special-purpose plays (set-plays).

Dynamic Switching of Formations

We implemented several different formations, ranging from very defensive (8-2-0) to very offensive (2-4-4).[3] The full definitions of all of the formations are a part of the locker-room agreement. Therefore, they are all known to all teammates. However during the periods of full autonomy and limited communication, it is not necessarily known what formation the rest of the teammates are using. Three approaches can be taken to address this problem:

3 Soccer formations are typically described as X-Y-Z where X, Y, and Z are the number of defenders, midfielders, and forwards respectively. It is assumed that the eleventh player is the goaltender (LaBlanc and Henshaw, 1994).

Static formation: the formation is set by the locker-room agreement and never changes;

Run-time formation switch: during team synchronization opportunities, the team defines globally accessible run-time evaluation metrics as formation-changing indicators.

Communication-triggered formation switch: one team member determines that the team should switch formations and communicates the decision to teammates.

Both run-time formation switches and communication-triggered formation switches are internal behaviors. The run-time triggers and communication protocols are defined in the locker-room agreement. When a run-time evaluation metric indicates that the formation should change, or when a heard communication triggers a formation change, an internal behavior changes the player's opinion of the team's formation in its internal state.

This change in internal state can then affect external behaviors. For example, a switch in formations changes the output of the `CurrentFormation()` function in Equation 3.1. The outputs of `MyPosition()` and `HomeRange()` are also altered: the new formation consists of a different collection of roles with different home ranges. Thus the passive offense external behavior changes as a result of the formation switch.

The CMUnited simulator team uses run-time formation switches. Based on the time left and score difference, the team switches to an offensive formation if it was losing near the end of the game and a defensive formation if it was winning. Specifically, the team starts out in a 4-4-2 formation. If $\Delta Minutes$ is the number of minutes left in the game, and $\Delta Score$ is the difference in score ($\Delta Score > 0$ if the team is winning; $\Delta Score < 0$ if the team is losing), then the team uses the following run-time formation-switching algorithm:

- If $\Delta Score < 0$ and $-\Delta Score \geq \Delta Minutes$, switch to a 3-3-4 formation;
- If $\Delta Score > 0$ and $\Delta Score \geq \Delta Minutes$, switch to a 8-2-0 formation;
- Otherwise switch to (or stay in) a 4-4-2 formation.

Since each agent is able to independently keep track of the score and time, the agents are always able to switch formations simultaneously.

Communication-triggered formation switches have also been implemented and tested. Details are presented later in this section in the context of the communication paradigm implementation.

Flexible Positions

As emphasized throughout, homogeneous agents can play different positions. But such a capability raises the challenging issue of when the players should change positions. In addition, with teammates switching positions, a player's internal player-position map $A \mapsto R$ could become incorrect and/or incomplete. The locker-room agreement provides procedures to the team that allow for coordinated role changing. In CMUnited's case, the locker-room agreement designates an order of precedence for the positions within each unit. Unless their pursuit of the ball leads them from their position, players only switch into a more important position than their current position.

By switching positions within a formation, the overall joint performance of the team can be improved. Position-switching has the potential to save player energy and to allow them to respond more quickly to the ball. However, switching positions can also cause increased player movement if a player has to move across the field to occupy its new position. Players must weigh the possible costs and benefits before deciding to switch positions.

Like switching formations, switching positions can change external behaviors via their references to the internal state. In Equation 3.1, switching positions changes the value returned by `MyPosition()`, thus also affecting the value of `HomeRange()`: the player executing the passive offense external behavior chooses its location from a different range of possible positions.

In addition to having the flexibility to switch to a different position, CMUnited-98 agents also have flexibility *within* their positions. That is, the external behavior references the internal state to determine a range of possible locations that are determined by the player's current position. However, within this range, the role does not specify the player's precise location. For example, in the passive offense external behavior (equation 3.1), the player must choose its `TargetLocation` from within the home range of its current position.

In the CMUnited multiagent approach, the player positions itself flexibly such that it *anticipates* that it will be useful to the team, either offensively or defensively. The agents can exercise this flexibility within its external behaviors in three ways:

- Opponent marking;
- Ball-dependent positioning;
- Strategic positioning using attraction and repulsion (SPAR).

When marking opponents, agents move next to a given opponent rather than staying at the default position home. The opponent to mark can be chosen by the player (e.g. the closest opponent), or by the unit captain which can ensure that all opponents are marked, following a preset algorithm as part of the locker-room agreement. The low-level agent behavior used when marking an opponent is specified in Appendix B (Section B.1).

When using ball-dependent positioning, the agent adjusts its location within its range based on the instantaneous position of the ball. For example, when the ball is on the same side of the field as the agent, the agent tries to move to a point on the line defined by its own goal and the ball. When the ball is on the other side of the field, the player adjusts its position back towards its own goal.

Ball-dependent positioning is an improvement over rigid roles in which agents stay in a fixed home position. However, by taking into account the positions of other agents as well as that of the ball, an even more informed positioning decision can be made. The idea of *strategic position by attraction and repulsion* (SPAR) is one of the novel contributions of the CMUnited-98 software. It was developed jointly in simulation and on the CMUnited-98 small-robot platform (Veloso et al., 1999b).

When positioning itself using SPAR, the agent uses a multi-objective function with attraction and repulsion points subject to several constraints. To formalize this concept, we introduce the following variables:

- P - the desired position for the passive agent in anticipation of a passing need of its active teammate;
- n - the number of agents on each team;
- O_i - the current position of each opponent, $i = 1, \ldots, n$;
- T_i - the current position of each teammate, $i = 1, \ldots, (n - 1)$;
- B - the current position of the active teammate and ball;
- G - the position of the opponent's goal.

SPAR extends potential fields approaches (Latombe, 1991) to highly dynamic, multiagent domains. The probability of collaboration in the robotic soccer domain is directly related to how "open" a position is to allow for a successful pass. Thus, SPAR maximizes the distance to other agents and minimizes the distance to the ball and to the goal according to several forces, namely:

- *Repulsion* from opponents, i.e. maximize the distance to each opponent: $\forall i, \max dist(P, O_i)$

- *Repulsion* from teammates, i.e. maximize the distance to other passive teammates: $\forall i, \max dist(P, T_i)$
- *Attraction* to the active teammate and ball: $\min dist(P, B)$
- *Attraction* to the opponent's goal: $\min dist(P, G)$

This formulation is a multiple-objective function. To solve this optimization problem, we restate the problem as a single-objective function. As each term may have a different relevance (e.g. staying close to the goal may be more important than staying away from opponents), we want to apply a different weighting function to each term, namely f_{O_i}, f_{T_i}, f_B, and f_G, for opponents, teammates, the ball, and the goal, respectively. Our anticipation algorithm then maximizes a weighted single-objective function with respect to P:

$$\max(\sum_{i=1}^{n} f_{O_i}(dist(P, O_i)) + \sum_{i=1}^{n-1} f_{T_i}(dist(P, T_i)) - f_B(dist(P, B)) - f_G(dist(P, G)))$$

In our case, we use $f_{O_i} = f_{T_i} = x$, $f_B = 0$, and $f_G = x^2$. For example, the last term of the objective function above expands to $(dist(P, G))^2$.

One constraint in the simulator team relates to the position, or role, that the passive agent is playing relative to the position of the ball. The agent only considers locations that are within one of the four rectangles illustrated in Figure 3.8: the one closest to the position home of the position that the agent is currently playing. This constraint helps ensure that the player with the ball will have several different passing options in different parts of the field. In addition, players do not need to consider moving too far from their positions to support the ball.

Since this position-based constraint already encourages players to stay near the ball, we set the ball-attraction weighting function f_B to the constant function $y = 0$. In addition to this first constraint, the agents observe three additional constraints. In total, the constraints in the simulator team are:

- Stay in an area near one's home position;
- Stay within the field boundaries;
- Avoid being in an offsides position;
- Stay in a position in which it would be possible to receive a pass.

This last constraint is evaluated by checking that there are no opponents in a cone with vertex at the ball and extending to the point in consideration.

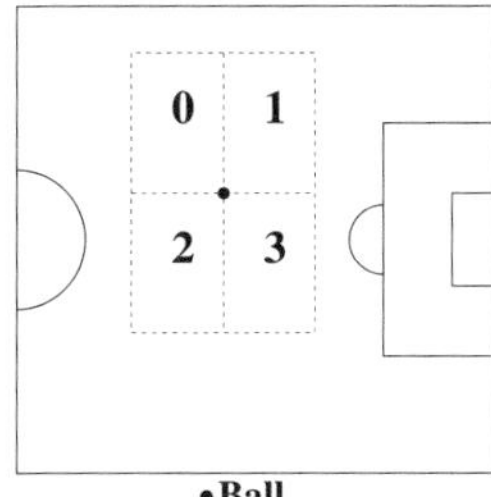

Figure 3.8
The four possible rectangles, each with one corner at the ball's location, considered for positioning by simulator agents when using SPAR.

In our implementation, the maximum of the objective function is estimated by sampling its values over a fine-grained mesh of points that satisfy the above constraints.

Using this SPAR algorithm, agents are able to *anticipate* the collaborative needs of their teammates by positioning themselves in such a way that the player with the ball has several useful passing options.

PRE-PLANNED SET-PLAYS

The final implemented improvement facilitated by our flexible teamwork structure is the introduction of set-plays, or pre-defined, special-purpose plays. As a part of the locker-room agreement, the team can define multi-step, multiagent plans to be executed at appropriate times. Particularly if there are certain situations that occur repeatedly, it makes sense for the team to devise plans for those situations.

In the robotic soccer domain, several situations occur repeatedly. For example, after every goal, there is a kickoff from the center spot; and when the ball goes out of bounds, there is a goal-kick, a corner-kick, or a kick-in. In each of these situations, the referee informs the team of the situation. Thus all the players know to execute the appropriate set-play. A particular referee's message is the trigger condition for each set-play. Associated with each set-play role is a set-play behavior indicating a location on the field as well as an action to execute when the ball arrives. The player in a given role might pass to the player filling another role, shoot at the goal, or kick the ball to some fixed location. The termination condition for each role is either the successful execution of the prescribed action or the passage of a specified amount of time from the beginning of the set-play.

The locker-room agreement specifies that the roles in the current team formation are mapped to the set-play roles in the way requiring the least movement of agents from their position homes. That is $F \mapsto R_{sp}$ is chosen to minimize

$$\sum_{spr \in R_{sp}} Dist(r, spr)$$

where $Dist(r, spr)$ is the distance from the home location of role r to the home location of its associated set-play role spr. This assignment of roles to set-play roles is part of each agent's internal behavior.

For example, Figure 3.9 illustrates a sample corner-kick set-play. The set-play designates five set-play roles, each with a specific location, which should be filled before the ball is put back into play. Based on the home positions of the current formation, each individual agent can determine the best mapping from positions to set-play locations, i.e. the mapping that requires the least total displacement of the 5 players. If there is no player filling one of the necessary formation roles, then there must be two players filling the same role, one of which must move to the vacant role. In the event that no agent chooses to do so, the set-play can proceed with any single set-play role unfilled. The only exception is that some player must fill the set-play role responsible for kicking the ball back into play. A special-purpose protocol is incorporated into the set-play behaviors to guarantee such a condition.

Once the set-play roles are filled, each player executes the action associated with its set-play role as an external behavior. As illustrated by the role starting the corner-kick in Figure 3.9, a player could choose among possible actions, perhaps based on the opponent positions at the time of execution. No individual player is guaranteed of participating in the play. For example, the uppermost set-play position is there just in case one of the other players misses a pass or shoots wide of the goal: no player will pass directly to it. Each player leaves its set-play role to resume its former role either after successfully kicking the ball, or after a pre-specified, role-specific amount of time.

The set-plays significantly improved CMUnited's performance. During the RoboCup-97 and RoboCup-98 simulator competitions, several goals were scored as a direct result of set-plays.

Communication Paradigm Implementation

In our teamwork structure, players are organized into team formations with each player filling a unique role. However players can switch among roles and

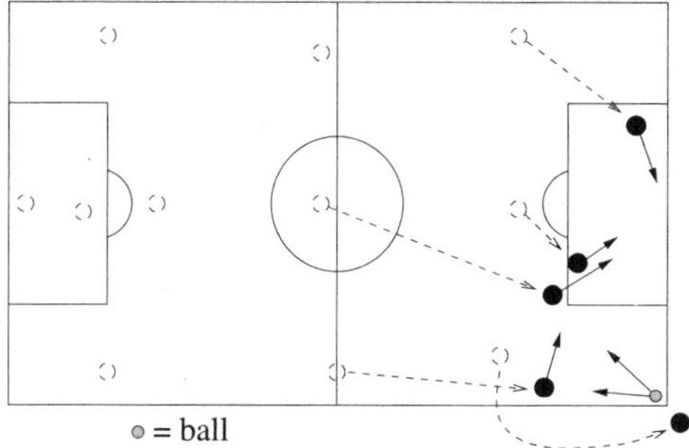

Figure 3.9
A sample corner-kick set-play. The dashed circles show the positions in the team's current formation and dashed arrows indicate the locations of the set-play roles—black circles—that they would fill. Solid arrows indicate the direction the ball is to be kicked as part of each set-play role.

the entire team can change formations. Both formations and roles are defined as part of the locker-room agreement, and each player is given a unique ID number. It is a significant challenge for players to remain coordinated, both by all believing that they are using the same formation and by filling all the roles in the formation. Since agents are all completely autonomous, such coordination is not guaranteed.

In PTS domains with limited communication (as opposed to no communication) possible during the dynamic, real-time periods, inter-agent communication can help the team stay coordinated. Communication protocols defined in the locker-room agreement combine with heard messages to trigger internal behaviors that alter the agent's internal state.

This subsection describes the CMUnited simulator team implementation of the communication paradigm presented in Section 3.4. All of the agent messages are of the format:

(CMUnited <Uniform-number> <Encoded-stamp> <Formation-number> <Formation-set-time> <Position-number> <target> <Message-type> [<Message-data>])

For example, player 8 might want to pass to player 6 but not know precisely where player 6 is at the moment. In this case, it could send the message `(CMUnited 8 312 1 0 7 6 Where-are-you?)`. "`CMUnited 8`" is the sender's team and number; "`312`" is the <Encoded-stamp>, in this case an agreed-upon linear combination of the current time, the formation number, and the sender's position number; "`1 0`" is the team formation player 8 is using followed by the time at which it started using it; "`7`" is player 8's current position;

"6" indicates that the message is for player 6; and "Where-are-you?" is a message type indicating that a particular response is requested: the recipient's coordinate location. In this case, there is no message data.

All teammates that hear such a message update their internal states to indicate that player 8 is playing position 7. However only player 6 sets its response and response-flag internal state variables. In this case, since the target is a single player, the communicate-delay flag remains at 0. Were the message targeted towards the whole team or to a subset of the team, then communicate-delay would equal:

- IF (my number > sender number) THEN
((my number − sender number − 1) × 2) × communicate-interval
- ELSE
(((sender number − my number − 1) × 2) + 1) × communicate-interval

where communicate-interval is the time between audible messages for a given agent (hear_decay = 2 simulator cycles in the case of the soccer server). Thus, assuming no further interference, player 8 would be able to hear responses from all targets.

Once player 6 is ready to respond, it might send back the message (CMUnited 6 342 1 0 5 all I'm-at 4.1 -24.5). Notice that player 6 is using the same team formation but playing a different position from player 8: position 5. Since this message doesn't require a response (as indicated by the "I'm-at" message type), the message is accessible to the whole team ("all"): all teammates who hear the message update their world states to reflect the message data. In this case, player 6 is at coordinate position (4.1, −24.5).

Were player 8 not to receive a response from player 6 before passing, it could still pass to its best estimate of player 6's location: should the message fail to get through, no disaster would result. Such is the nature of most communication in this domain. Should there be a situation which absolutely requires that a message get through, the sending agent could repeat the message periodically until hearing confirmation from the recipient that the message has arrived. However, such a technique consumes the single communication channel and should be used sparingly.

Notice that in the two example messages above, both players are using the same team-formation. However, such is not always the case. Even if they use common environmental cues to trigger formation changes, one player might miss the cue. In order to combat such a case, players update the team formation if a teammate is using a different formation that was set at a later time as detailed in Section 3.4. For example, if player 6's message had begun "`(CMUnited 6 342 3 50 ...`" indicating that it had been using team formation 3 since time 50, an internal behavior in player 8 would have changed its internal state to indicate the new team strategy.

Other examples of message types used in our implementation of simulated robotic soccer players include:

- Request/respond ball location
- Request/respond teammate location
- Inform pass destination
- Inform going to the ball
- Inform taking/leaving position

3.6 Results

Although the flexible teamwork structure and communication paradigm implementations are merged into a single robotic soccer system, we are able to isolate the effects of each contribution through controlled testing. This section presents empirical results demonstrating the effectiveness of both main contributions of this chapter: the flexible teamwork structure and the low-bandwidth communication paradigm.

Teamwork Structure Results

The flexible teamwork structure improves over a rigid structure by way of three characteristics: flexible positioning within roles, set-plays, and changeable formations. We tested the benefits of the first two characteristics by playing a team with flexible, changeable positions and set-plays against a "default team" with rigid positions and no set-plays. The behaviors of the players on the two teams are otherwise identical. The advantage of being able to change formations—the third characteristic—depends on the formation being used by the opponent. Therefore, we tested teams using each defined formation against each other.

Standard games in the soccer server system last 10 minutes. However, due to the large amount of noise, game results vary greatly. All reported results are cumulative over several games. Compiled statistics include the number of 10-minute games won, the total cumulative goals scored by each team, average goals per game, and the percentage of time that the ball was in each half of the field. The last statistic gives a rough estimate of the degree to which each team was able to control the ball.

Flexible Positions and Set-Plays

In order to test the flexible teamwork structure, we ran a team using ball-dependent flexible positions with set-plays against one using rigid positions and no set-plays. Both teams used a 4-4-2 formation. As shown in Table 3.2, the flexible team significantly outperformed the default team over the course of 38 games.

Table 3.2
Results when a flexible team plays against a rigid team. The flexible team won 34 out of 38 games with 3 ties.

(Game = 10 min.)	Flexible and Set-Plays	Default
Games won	34	1
Total goals	223	82
Avg. goals	5.87	2.16
Ball in own half	43.8%	56.2%

Further experimentation showed that both aspects of the flexible team contribute significantly to the team's success. Table 3.3 shows the results when a team using flexible positions but no set-plays plays against the default team and when a team using set-plays but rigid positions plays against the default team, again over the course of 38 games. Both characteristics provide a significant advantage over the default team, but they perform even better in combination.

Table 3.3
Results when only using flexible positions and only using set-plays. Each individually works better than using neither.

Only Flexible Positions

(Game = 10 min.)	Flexible	Default
Games won	26	6
Total goals	157	87
Avg. goals	4.13	2.29
Ball in own half	44.1%	55.9%

Only Set-Plays

(Game = 10 min.)	Flexible	Default
Games won	28	5
Total goals	187	108
Avg. goals	4.92	2.84
Ball in own half	47.6%	52.4%

Formations

In addition to the above tests, we tested the various formations against each other, as reported in Table 3.4. Each entry shows the goals scored for and against when a team using one formation played against a team using another formation over the course of 24 10-minute games. The right-most column collects the total goals scored for and against the team using that formation when playing against all the other teams. In all cases, the teams used flexible positions, but no set-plays.

Table 3.4
Comparison of the different formations. Entries in the table show the number of goals scored. Total (and percentage) cumulative goals scored against all formations appear in the right-most column.

formations	4-3-3	4-4-2	3-5-2	8-2-0	3-3-4	2-4-4	totals
4-3-3		68–60	68–54	24–28	59–64	70–65	289–271 (51.6%)
4-4-2	60–68		68–46	22–24	51–57	81–50	282–245 (53.5%)
3-5-2	54–68	46–68		13–32	61–72	75–73	249–313 (44.3%)
8-2-0	28–24	24–22	32–13		27–28	45–36	156–96 (61.9%)
3-3-4	64–59	57–51	72–61	28–27		87–69	308–267 (53.6%)
2-4-4	65–70	50–81	73–75	36–45	69–87		293–385 (43.2%)

The results show that the defensive formation (8-2-0) does the best in terms of the percentage of goals scored for versus those allowed against. However the total goals scored when using the defensive formation is quite low. On the other hand, the 3-3-4 formation performs well with a high goal total.

This study allowed us to devise an effective formation-switching strategy for the RoboCup competitions. For example, our RoboCup-97 team (Stone and Veloso, 1998a) used a 4-4-2 formation in general, switching to an 8-2-0 formation if winning near the end of the game, or a 3-3-4 formation if losing. This strategy, along with the flexible teamwork structure as a whole, and the communication paradigm, helped us to perform well in the RoboCup-97 and RoboCup-98 tournaments (see Chapter 8).

Communication Paradigm Results

While contributing to the overall success of the CMUnited simulator team, our communication paradigm is also demonstrably effective in controlled experimentation. In this subsection, I report results reflecting the agents' robustness to active interference, their ability to handle messages that require responses from multiple team members, and their ability to maintain a coordinated team strategy.

Robustness to Interference

Relying on communication protocols involves the danger that an opponent could actively interfere by mimicking an agent's obsolete messages: since there is a single communication channel, opponents can hear and mimic messages intended for teammates. However, the <Encoded-stamp> field guards against such an attempt. As a test, we played a communicating team (team C) against a team that periodically repeats past opponent messages (team D). Team C set: <Encoded-stamp> = <Uniform-number> × (`send` − `time` + 37). Thus teammates could determine `send-time` by inverting the same calculation (known to all through the locker-room agreement). Messages received more than a second after the `send-time` were disregarded (`message-lag-tolerance` = 1 sec). The one-second leeway accounts for the fact that teammates may have slightly different notions of the current global time.

In our experiment, agents from team D sent a total of 73 false messages over the course of a 5-minute game. Not knowing team C's locker-room agreement, they were unable to adjust the <Encoded-stamp> field appropriately. The number of team C agents hearing a false message ranged from 0 to 11, averaging 3.6. In all cases, each of the team C agents hearing the false message correctly ignored it. Only one message truly from a team C player was incorrectly ignored by team C players, due to the sending agent's internal clock temporarily diverging from the correct value by more than a second. Although it did not happen in the experiment, it is also theoretically possible that an agent from team D could mimic a message within a second of the time that it was originally sent, thus causing it to be indistinguishable from a valid message. However, in this case, the content of the message is presumably still appropriate and consequently unlikely to confuse team C.

Handling Multiple Responses

Next we tested our method of handling multiple simultaneous responses to a single message. Placing all 11 agents within hearing range, a single agent periodically sent a "`Where-are-you?`" message to the entire team and recorded the responses it received. In all cases, all 10 teammates heard the original message and responded. However, as shown in Table 3.5, the use of our method dramatically increased the number of responses that got through to the sending

Table 3.5
The number of responses that get through to agents when responses are delayed and when they are not. When the team uses `communicate-delay` as specified in Section 3.5, an average of 7.1 more responses get through than when not using it. Average response time remains under one second. Both experiments were performed 50 times.

	Number of Responses			Response Time (sec)		
	Min	Max	Avg	Min	Max	Avg
No Delay	1	1	1.0	0.0	0.0	0.0
Delay	6	9	8.1	0.0	2.6	0.9

agent. When the team used `communicate-delay` as specified in Section 3.5, message responses were staggered over the course of about 2.5 seconds, allowing most of the 10 responses to get through. When all agents responded at once (no delay), only one response (from a random teammate) was heard.

TEAM COORDINATION

Finally, we tested the team's ability to maintain coordinated team strategies when changing formations via communication. One player was given the power to toggle the team's formation between a defensive and an offensive formation. Announcing the change only once, the rest of team had to either react to the original message, or get the news from another teammate via other communications. As described in Section 3.5, the <Formation-number> and <Formation-set-time> fields are used for this purpose. We ran two different experiments, each consisting of 50 formation changes. In the first, a midfielder made the changes, thus making it possible for most teammates to hear the original message. In the second experiment, fewer players heard the original message since it was sent by the goaltender from the far end of the field. Even so, the team was able to change formations in an average time of 3.4 seconds. Results are summarized in Table 3.6.

3.7 Transfer to the Real Robots

As described in Chapter 2, the CMUnited-97 real robot platform differs from the soccer server platform in many ways, including agent perception and action capabilities. In addition, the robots do not have any inter-agent communication abilities. Nonetheless, the real robot soccer domain is a PTS domain and many components of the CMUnited simulator implementation described in

Table 3.6
The time it takes for the entire team to change team strategies when a single agent makes the decision. Even when the decision-making agent is at the edge of the field (goaltender) so that fewer than half of teammates can hear the single message indicating the switch, the team is completely coordinated after an average of 3.4 seconds.

Decision-Maker	Entire Team Change Time (sec) Min	Max	Avg	Var	Heard From Decision-Maker
Goaltender	0.0	23.8	3.4	17.8	46.6%
Midfielder	0.0	7.9	1.3	2.8	80.6%

Section 3.5 are directly transferable to the CMUnited-97 small-robot software. In particular, the teamwork structure transfers very easily and has been used successfully (Veloso and Stone, 1998). Since the robots do not use inter-agent communication, the communication paradigm is not appropriate for transfer.

The specific software components that transfered from the simulation to the real robot implementations include:

- The world model;
- Skill functionalities;
- Behavior modes;
- Team structure including the locker-room agreement

The objects in the world are defined according to the same type hierarchy depicted in Figure 3.4 and the same information is stored about each object. The one exception is that opponent orientation is not discernible by the small-robot vision system.

Since the movement capabilities and action command syntax of the robots differ greatly from those of the simulated agents, the low-level agent skill implementations are entirely different. However, the *functionalities* of the skills are similar. For example, like the simulated agents, the real robots also have ball-interception and goaltending skills. The implementation details of the robots' skills are provided in Appendix B.

With slightly less complex behaviors than the simulated agents, the robots need fewer behavior modes. However, they still choose one of several behavior modes as the top-level action decision. The default position-holding behavior occurs when the robot is in an *inactive* state. However, when the ball is nearby, the robot changes into an *active* state. In the active state, the robot moves towards the ball, attempting either to pass it to a teammate or to shoot it towards the goal based on an evaluation function that takes into account teammate and opponent positions. A robot that believes itself to be the intended receiver of a pass moves into the *auxiliary* state in which it tries to intercept a moving ball towards the goal. There is also a special *goaltend* mode for the goaltender. The CMUnited-97 decision function sets the robot that is closest to the ball into the active state; other robots filling a forward role (if any) into the auxiliary state; and all other robots (other than the goaltender) into the inactive state.

Most significantly within the context of this chapter, the team structure implementation described in Section 3.5 transfered directly to the real robot software. Changing nothing in the code except for the actual formation configurations (to accommodate teams of 5 rather than teams 11), the robots are instantly able to benefit from the advantages of the teamwork structure:

- Dynamic formations;
- Flexible positions; and
- Set-plays.

As in the simulator implementation, the formation defines a set of roles, or positions, with associated behaviors. It is specified within the locker-room agreement, a part of the team member agent architecture described in Section 3.2. The robots are dynamically mapped into the positions. Each robot is equipped with the knowledge required to play any position in each of several formations.

Positions are defined as flexible regions within which the player attempts to move towards the ball. For example, a robot playing the "right-wing" (or "right forward") position remains on the right side of the field near the opponents' goal until the ball comes towards it. Positions are classified as defender, midfielder, or forward based on the locations of these regions. They are also given behavior specifications in terms of which other positions should be considered as potential pass-receivers.

In the CMUnited-97 small-robot team, only the ball-dependent flexible positioning is implemented. However, the subsequent CMUnited-98 software was used in conjunction with the simulator to develop the SPAR flexible positioning algorithm (Veloso et al., 1999b).

At any given time each of the robots plays a particular position on the field. However, each robot has all of the knowledge necessary to play any position. Therefore the robots can—and do—switch positions on the fly. For example, robots A and B switch positions when robot A chases the ball into the region of robot B. Then robot A continues chasing the ball, and robot B moves to the position vacated by A.

The pre-defined positions known to all players are collected into formations, which are also commonly known. An example of a formation is the collection of positions consisting of the goaltender, one defender, one midfielder, and two attackers. Another possible formation consists of the goaltender, two defenders and two attackers. For illustration, see Figure 3.10.

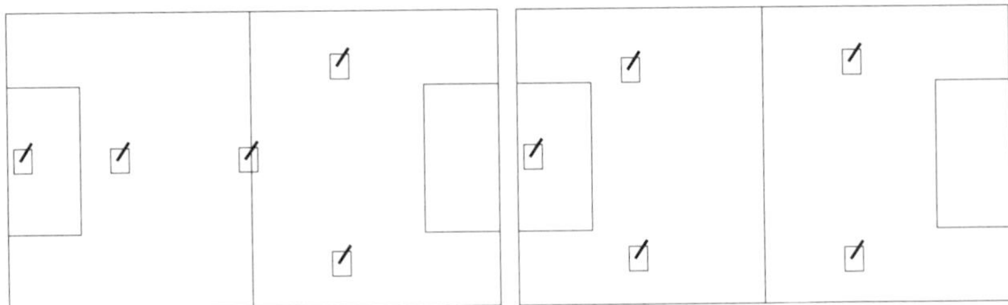

Figure 3.10
Two different defined formations. Notice that several of the positions are reused between the two formations.

The CMUnited-97 robots only used a single set-play: on a kickoff, one robot would pass the ball up the wing to another robot which would then shoot towards the goal. However, the concept of set-plays was originally developed in a previous real-robot soccer implementation (Achim et al., 1996). In that case, our 3-robot team was equipped with about 10 set-plays for several different restart situations.

3.8 Discussion and Related Work

This chapter has presented a team member agent architecture appropriate for PTS domains. While the implementation described here is in robotic soccer, it is easy to see how the architecture would apply to other sports, such as American football. In that case, the synchronization opportunities are more frequent, but formations can change during the course of a game, roles are defined with some flexibility so that agents can adjust to opponent behaviors on the fly, and agents must communicate efficiently both between plays on a drive and during plays.

There are several other examples of non-sports-related PTS domains. Having successfully developed and deployed an autonomous spacecraft (Pell et al., 1998), NASA is now interested in multi-spacecraft missions, or constellations (Stone, 1997). Since spacecraft pointing constraints limit the communication both between the spacecraft and ground control, and among the spacecraft, the spacecraft must be able to act autonomously while still working towards the constellation's overall goal. Using interferometry missions—in which several spacecraft coordinate parts of a powerful imaging instrument to view distant objects—as an example, the locker-room agreement could be used to define several formations to be used for viewing objects that are at various distances or in different parts of the sky. Depending on the relative locations of these objects, the various spacecraft might interchange roles as they image different objects.

Search and rescue scenarios could also be formulated as PTS domains. If several robotic agents are trying to locate victims in a remote disaster sight, they may have to act quickly and autonomously. Nonetheless, before beginning the search, they could define several formations corresponding to different geographical areas of focusing their search. Within these formations, agents would need to be assigned flexible roles given that the precise situation may not be known or may change unexpectedly. The agents might also agree, as part of their locker-room agreement to switch formations either after a certain time or as a result of some limited communication, perhaps from a unit captain.

Other PTS domains that could be applications for the team member agent architecture are hospital/factory maintenance (Decker, 1996b) and battlefield combat (Tambe, 1997). While in this book network routing is used to generalize the TPOT-RL algorithm (see Chapter 7), it could also be formulated as a PTS domain if the network nodes are permitted to freely use network bandwidth during periods of otherwise low usage. They could then exchange policies and feedback with regards to network performance.

The remainder of this section summarizes the previous work most closely related to the teamwork structure and communication paradigm as presented in this chapter.

Teamwork Structure

Two popular multiagent teamwork structures, joint intentions (Cohen et al., 1999) and shared plans (Grosz, 1996), consider a team to be a group of agents that negotiate and/or contract with each other in order to initiate a team plan. Both of these teamwork structures as well as STEAM (Tambe, 1997), another teamwork structure based on joint intentions and shared plans, include complex communication protocols for forming and disbanding a team in pursuit of a goal. The team forms dynamically and stays in close communication until the execution of the plan is completed. In contrast, the teamwork structure presented in this chapter supports a persistent team effort towards a common high-level goal in the face of limited communication.

The concept of the locker-room agreement facilitates coordination with little or no communication. Taking advantage of the property of PTS domains that the team and its long-term goal are persistent, our teamwork structure eliminates the need for the overhead inherent in previous paradigms.

Although it has been claimed that pre-determined team actions are not flexible or robust to failure (Tambe, 1997), the locker-room agreement provides a mechanism for pre-defining team actions with enough flexibility to succeed. In particular, set-plays are pre-determined team actions that can be executed without the need to negotiate or use extensive inter-agent communication: the locker-room agreement provides enough flexibility that the agents are able to seamlessly assume the appropriate roles.

While I use the term "formation" to refer to the largest unit of the teamwork structure, soccer formations are not to be confused with military-type formations in which agents must stay in precise relative positions. Despite this dual usage of the term, I use it because formation is a standard term within the soccer domain (LaBlanc and Henshaw, 1994). For an example of a multiagent system designed for military formations, see (Balch and Arkin, 1995).

Castelfranchi (1995) classifies different types of commitments in multiagent environments. In this context, locker-room agreements can be viewed as C-commitments, or commitments by team members to do the appropriate thing at the right time, as opposed to S-commitments with which agents adopt each other's goals. In the context of (Conte et al., 1999), the creation of a locker-room agreement is norm acceptance while its use is norm compliance. Within the framework presented in (Müller, 1999), the architecture is for interactive software and hardware multiagents.

As mentioned in Section 3.2, the concept of behavior in the context of our team member agent architecture is consistent with that laid out by Mataric (Mataric, 1994a). There, "behavior" is defined as "a control law with a particular goal, such as wall-following or collision avoidance." Behaviors can be nested at different levels with selection among lower-level behaviors consisting of a higher-level behavior. Similarly, internal and external behaviors in our system maintain team coordination goals, physical positioning goals, communication goals, and environmental information goals (such as knowledge of where the ball is). These behaviors are combined into top-level internal and external behaviors.

Communication Paradigm

Most inter-agent communication models assume reliable point-to-point message passing with negligible communication costs. In particular, KQML assumes point-to-point message passing, possibly with the aid of facilitator agents (Finin et al., 1994). Nonetheless, KQML performatives could be used for the content portions of our communication scheme. KQML does not address the problems raised by having a single, low-bandwidth communication channel.

When communication is reliable and the cost of communication relative to other actions is small, agents have the luxury of using reliable, multi-step negotiation protocols. For example, in Cohen's convoy example (Cohen et al., 1999), the communication time required to form and maintain a convoy of vehicles is insignificant compared to the time it takes the convoy to drive to its destination. Similarly, message passing among distributed information agents is typically very quick compared to the searches and services that they are performing. Thus, it makes sense for agents to initiate and confirm their coalition while guaranteeing that they will inform each other if they have trouble fulfilling their part of the joint action.

With only a single team present, a situation similar to the one considered here is examined in (Maio and Rizzi, 1995). In that case, like in the soccer server, messages sent are only heard by agents within a circular region of the sender. Communication is used for cooperation and for knowledge sharing. Like in the examples presented in the soccer domain, agents attempt to update each other regarding their own internal states when communicating. However, the exploration task considered there is much simpler than soccer, particularly in that there are no opponents using the same communication channel and in that the nature of the task allows for simpler, less urgent communication.

Although communication in the presence of hostile agents is well studied in military contexts from the standpoint of encryption, the problem considered here is not the same. While any encryption scheme could be used for the message content, the work presented here assumes that the adversaries cannot decode the message. Even so, they can disrupt communication by mimicking past messages textually: presumably past message have some meaning to the team that uttered them. Our method of message coding based on a globally accessible clock circumvents this latter problem.

Even when communication time is insignificant compared to action execution, such as in a helicopter fighting domain, it can be risky for agents to rely on communication. As pointed out in (Tambe, 1996a), if the teammate with whom an agent is communicating gets shot down, the agent could be incapacitated if it requires a response from the teammate. This work also considers the cost of communication in terms of risking opponent eavesdropping and the benefits of communication in terms of shifting roles among team members. However, the problems raised by a single communication channel and the possibility of active interference are not considered.

Another approach that recognizes the danger of basing behaviors upon multi-step communication protocols is ALLIANCE (Parker, 1994). Since a primary goal of this work is fault-tolerance, only broadcast communications are used. Agents inform each other of what they are currently doing, but never ask for responses. In ALLIANCE, the team uses time-slice communication so that each agent periodically gets exclusive use of the single communication channel.

A possible application of our communication method is to robots using audio communication. This type of communication is inherently single-channel and low-bandwidth. An example of such a system is the Robot Entertainment Systems which uses a tonal language (Fujita and Kageyama, 1997). Agents can communicate by emitting and recognizing a range of audible pitches. In such a system, the number of bits per message would have to be lowered, but the general techniques presented in this chapter still apply.

Another example of such a communication environment is arbitrarily expandable systems. If agents aren't aware of what other agents exist in the environment, then all agents must use a single universally-known communication channel, at least in order to initiate communication.

4 Layered Learning

As described in Section 3.2, our agents build up a world model and then use it as the basis for behaviors that respond effectively to the environment. Internal behaviors update the internal state while external behaviors produce executable actuator commands. Spanning both internal and external behaviors, *layered learning* (Stone and Veloso, 1998c, 1999a) is our bottom-up hierarchical approach to agent behaviors that allows for machine learning at the various levels.

The introduction and implementation of layered learning is one of the main contributions of this book. Layered learning is a machine learning paradigm defined as a set of principles for the construction of a hierarchical, learned solution to a complex task. This chapter lays out the principles of layered learning (Section 4.1), formalizes layered learning (Section 4.2), and gives an overview of the implementation which is detailed in Chapters 5–7 (Section 4.3). In Section 4.4, I discuss some of the general multiagent learning issues that arise within layered learning and within our implementation in particular. Section 4.5 presents related work.

4.1 Principles

Layered learning is defined by four principles as summarized in Table 4.1. In this section, I identify, motivate, and specify these four principles.

Table 4.1
The key principles of layered learning.

1. A mapping directly from inputs to outputs is not tractably learnable.
2. A bottom-up, hierarchical task decomposition is given.
3. Machine learning exploits data to train and/or adapt. Learning occurs separately at each level.
4. The output of learning in one layer feeds into the next layer.

Principle 1: Motivated by robotic soccer, layered learning is designed for domains that are too complex for learning a mapping directly from from the input to the output representation, or in the case of an agent, from an agent's sensory inputs to its actuator outputs. We assume that any domain that fits the description in Section 1.2—limited communication, real-time, noisy environments with both teammates and adversaries—is too complex for agents to learn direct mappings from their sensors to actuators.

Instead, the layered learning approach consists of breaking a problem down into several task layers. At each layer, a concept needs to be acquired. A machine learning (ML) algorithm abstracts and solves the local concept-learning task.

Principle 2: Layered learning uses a bottom-up incremental approach to hierarchical task decomposition. Starting with low-level subtasks, the process of creating new ML subtasks continues until reaching the high-level task that deal with the full domain complexity. The appropriate learning granularity and subtasks to be learned are determined as a function of the specific domain. The task decomposition in layered learning is not automated. Instead, the layers are defined by the ML opportunities in the domain.

Layered learning can, however, be combined with any algorithm for learning abstraction levels. In particular, let A be an algorithm for learning task decompositions within a domain. Suppose that A does not have an objective metric for comparing different decompositions. Applying layered learning on the task decomposition and quantifying the resulting performance can be used as a measure of the utility of A's output.

Figure 4.1 illustrates an abstract layered learning task decomposition within a collaborative and adversarial multiagent domain. Learning can begin with individual behaviors, which facilitate multiagent collaborative behaviors, and eventually lead to full-team collaborative and adversarial behaviors.

Figure 4.1
A sample task decomposition within the layered learning framework in a collaborative and adversarial multiagent domain. Layered learning is designed for use in domains that are too complex to learn a mapping straight from sensors to actuators. We use a hierarchical, bottom-up approach

Principle 3: Machine learning is used as a central part of layered learning to exploit data in order to *train* and/or *adapt* the overall system. ML is useful for training functions that are difficult to fine-tune manually. It is useful for adaptation when the task details are not completely known in advance or when they may change dynamically. In the former case, learning can be done off-line and frozen for future use. In the latter, on-line learning is necessary: since the learner needs to adapt to unexpected situations, it must be able to alter its behavior even while executing its task. Like the task decomposition itself, the choice of machine learning method depends on the subtask.

Principle 4: The key defining characteristic of layered learning is that each learned layer directly affects the learning at the next layer. A learned subtask can affect the subsequent layer by (i) constructing the set of training examples (ii) providing the features used for learning, or (iii) pruning the output set. In general, machine learning algorithms—e.g. neural networks, Q-learning (Watkins, 1989), and decision trees (Quinlan, 1993)—require an input and output representation, a target mapping from inputs to outputs, and training examples. The goal of learning is to generalize the target mapping from the training examples which provide the correct outputs for only a portion of the input space.

When using ML for behavior learning (as opposed to classification), training examples are generated by placing an agent in a situation corresponding to a specific instance of the input representation; allowing it to act; and then giving some reward, or indication of the merit of the action in the context of the target mapping. In this case, previous learned layers can (i) provide a portion of the behavior used during training by either determining the actions available or affecting the reinforcement received. Previous learned layers can also (ii) create the inputs to the learning algorithm by affecting or determining the agent's input representation. In addition, the previous learned layer can be used to (iii) limit the output behaviors considered by the agent. All three possibilities are illustrated in our simulated robotic soccer implementation outlined in Section 4.3 and detailed in subsequent chapters.

If each learned layer in a task decomposition directly affects the learning at the next layer, then the system is a layered learning system, even if the domain does not have identical properties to those considered in this book. Without this characteristic, the approach does not fall within the realm of layered learning.

In summary, layered learning is a hierarchical machine learning paradigm designed to allow for machine learning in complex domains. Layered learning allows for a bottom-up definition of subtasks at different hierarchical levels. Machine learning opportunities are identified when data is available or the task is unpredictable and hand-coded solutions are too complex to generate. Individual learned subtasks are organized, learned, and combined in a layered fashion, each facilitating the creation of the next.

4.2 Formalism

Consider the learning task of identifying a hypothesis h from among a class of hypotheses H which map a set of state feature variables S to a set of outputs O such that, based on a set of training examples, h is most likely (of the hypotheses in H) to represent unseen examples.

When using the layered learning paradigm, the complete learning task is decomposed into hierarchical subtask layers $\{L_1, L_2, \ldots, L_n\}$ with each layer defined as

$$L_i = (\vec{F_i}, O_i, T_i, M_i, h_i)$$

where:

- $\vec{F_i}$ is the input vector of state features relevant for learning subtask L_i. $\vec{F_i} = <F_i^1, F_i^2, \ldots>. \forall j, F_1^j \in S$.
- O_i is the set of outputs among which to choose for subtask L_i. $O_n = O$.
- T_i is the set of training examples used for learning subtask L_i. Each element of T_i consists of a correspondence between an input feature vector $\vec{f} \in \vec{F_i}$ and $o \in O_i$.
- M_i is the ML algorithm used at layer L_i to select a hypothesis mapping $\vec{F_i} \mapsto O_i$ based on T_i.
- h_i is the result of running M_i on T_i. h_i is a function from $\vec{F_i}$ to O_i.

As set out in Principle 2 of layered learning, the definitions of the layers L_i are given a priori. Principle 4 is addressed via the following stipulation. $\forall i < n$, h_i directly affects L_{i+1} in at least one of three ways:

- h_i is used to construct one or more features F_{i+1}^k.
- h_i is used to construct elements of T_{i+1}; and/or
- h_i is used to prune the output set O_{i+1}.

It is noted above in the definition of $\vec{F_i}$ that $\forall j, F_1^j \in S$. Since F_{i+1} can consist of new features constructed using h_i, the more general version of the above special case is that $\forall i, j, F_i^j \in S \cup_{k=1}^{i-1} O_k$.

4.3 Instantiation in Simulated Robotic Soccer

One tempting way to approach any new agent-based domain is to try to learn a direct mapping from the agent's sensors to its actuators. However, a quick consideration of the robotic soccer domain is enough to convince oneself that it is too complex for such an approach: the space of possible sensory inputs is huge, there are many possible actions, and there is a large amount of hidden state. Such complexity is an important characteristic of the domain for the purposes of this book, since robotic soccer is meant to represent other domains which are too complex for the straightforward approach.

Table 4.2 illustrates a possible set of learned behavior levels within the simulated robotic soccer domain that correspond to the abstract task decomposition represented in Figure 4.1. We identify a useful low-level skill that must be learned before moving on to higher-level strategies. Then we build upon it to create higher-level multiagent and team behaviors. Using our own experience and insights to help the agents learn, we acted as human coaches do when they teach young children how to play real soccer. Section 4.3 gives an overview of our layered learning implementation in the simulated robotic soccer domain and discusses how the implementation could be extended further.

Table 4.2
Examples of different behavior levels in robotic soccer.

Layer	Strategic level	Behavior type	Example
L_1	robot–ball	individual	ball interception
L_2	one-to-one player	multiagent	pass evaluation
L_3	one-to-many player	team	pass selection
L_4	team formation	team	strategic positioning
L_5	team-to-opponent	adversarial	strategic adaptation

Implemented Learned Layers

Our implementation consists of three learned subtasks, each of which is described more fully in terms of $(\vec{F_i}, O_i, T_i, M_i, h_i)$ along with extensive empirical tests later in the book:

1. Ball Interception — an individual skill (Chapter 5).
First, the agents learn a low-level individual skill that allows them to control the ball effectively. While executed individually, the ability to intercept a moving ball is required due to the presence of other agents: it is needed to block or intercept opponent shots or passes as well as to receive passes from teammates. As such, it is a prerequisite for most ball-manipulation behaviors. We chose to have our agents learn this behavior because it was easier to collect training data than to fine-tune the behavior by hand[1]. Since the skill does not need to change during the course of play, we are able to use off-line learning, specifically a neural network with four inputs.

2. Pass Evaluation — a multiagent behavior (Chapter 6).
Second, the agents use their learned ball-interception skill as part of the behavior for training a multiagent behavior. When an agent has the ball and has the option to pass to a particular teammate, it is useful to have an idea of whether or not the pass will actually succeed if executed: will the teammate successfully receive the ball? Such an evaluation depends on not only the teammate's and opponents' positions, but also their abilities to receive or intercept the pass. Consequently, when creating training examples for the pass-evaluation function, we equip the intended pass recipient as well as all opponents with the previously learned ball-interception behavior. Again, we choose to have our agents learn the pass-evaluation capability because it is easier to collect training data than to construct it by hand. Working under the assumption that the concept would remain relatively constant from game to game, we again use an off-line learning algorithm, namely the C4.5 decision tree training algorithm (Quinlan, 1993). Decision trees are chosen over neural networks because of their ability to ignore irrelevant attributes: in this case, our input representation has 174 continuous attributes.

3. Pass Selection — a collaborative, adversarial team behavior (Chapter 7).
Third, the agents use their learned pass-evaluation capability to create the input space for learning a team behavior. When an agent has the ball, it must decide to which teammate it should pass the ball[2]. Such a decision depends on a huge amount of information including the agent's current location on the field, the current locations of all the teammates and opponents, the teammates' abili-

1 The learning was done in an earlier implementation of the soccer server in which agents did not receive any velocity information when seeing the ball. Thus the ball interception skill described in Appendix B was not applicable.

2 It could also choose to shoot. For the purposes of this behavior, the agents are not given the option to dribble.

ties to receive a pass, the opponents' abilities to intercept passes, teammates' subsequent decision-making capabilities, and the opponents' strategies. The merit of a particular decision can only be measured by the long-term performance of the team as a whole. In this sense, Q-learning, a reinforcement learning method for maximizing long-term discounted reward, seemed applicable. However, Q-learning is known for working poorly with large input representations. Therefore, we drastically reduce the input space with the help of the previously learned decision tree: rather than considering the positions of all of the players on the field, only the pass evaluation for the possible passes to each teammate are considered. The output space is also reduced by pruning some passes based on predictions from the learned pass evaluation that they will fail. Nonetheless, due to the multiagent and opaque transition characteristics of the task, Q-learning does not apply directly. Instead, we create TPOT-RL, a new multiagent reinforcement learning method motivated by Q-learning. Since the learned behavior must adapt to a dynamically changing environment (changing in part because teammates are learning their decision-making policies simultaneously), we need an on-line learning method, which TPOT-RL is.

The learning methods used for each of the above behaviors are summarized in Table 4.3. Possible implementations of the last two layers in Table 4.2 are future work and are described in the next subsection.

Table 4.3
The learning methods used for the implemented layers in the simulated robotic soccer layered learning implementation.

Layer	Learned behavior	Learning method	Training type
L_1	ball interception	neural network	off-line
L_2	pass evaluation	decision tree	off-line
L_3	pass selection	TPOT-RL	on-line

The three learned layers described above illustrate the principles of the layered learning paradigm as laid out in Section 4.1:

• The decomposition of the task into smaller subtasks enables the learning of a more complex behavior than would be possible if learning straight from the agents' sensory inputs (see Section 4.5 for supporting evidence).

• The hierarchical task decomposition is constructed in a bottom-up, domain-dependent fashion.

- Machine learning methods are chosen or created to suit the subtask in question. They exploit available data to train difficult behaviors (ball interception and pass evaluation) or to adapt to changing/unforeseen circumstances (pass selection).
- Learning in one layer feeds into the next layer by providing a portion of the behavior used for training (ball interception – pass evaluation) or by creating the input representation and pruning outputs (pass evaluation – pass selection).

Future Learned Layers

This subsection carries the robotic soccer example of layered learning beyond its implementation in this book, describing how the principles of layered learning could be used to create additional, higher-level learned layers. In particular, I discuss how to implement the last two layers in Table 4.2—strategic positioning and strategic adaptation—on top of the currently-implemented learned layers.

The strategic positioning and strategic adaptation behaviors build upon two characteristics of the implementation of the pass-selection learning that are not described above:

- When using TPOT-RL, the simulated robotic soccer agents stay in a fixed formation and do not switch positions.
- TPOT-RL training is done against a fixed opponent.

In contrast, the following new behaviors would facilitate the learning of the agent positioning which best suits the pass-selection algorithm and the learning of which learned policy to use against a new opponent.

4. Strategic Positioning — a team behavior.
The team of agents could use their pass-selection behavior as part of the training behavior for creating another team behavior. As described in Chapter 3, the team can play in any of a number of different formations. Each player also has some flexibility within its position. Our training of the pass-selection behavior uses players in an arbitrarily chosen fixed formation. However, there is no reason to believe that this formation is the best for learning against a particular opponent. If allowed to use the TPOT-RL learning algorithm while simultaneously adjusting their formation, the team may be able to perform even better. The position adjustments could be done using observational reinforcement learning (RL), another on-line algorithm (Andou, 1998).

5. Strategic Adaptation — an adversarial behavior.
Finally, the agents comprising the team could use their combined strategic-positioning/pass-selection behaviors as the input representation for strategic adaptation. The previous behavior is trained against a fixed opponent. However, there are many different possible opponent strategies. By training the strategic-positioning/pass-selection behavior against a variety of opponents, several different policies could be learned. Then, the opportunity arises to try to match the current opponent with the most similar past opponent as quickly as possible so that the previously learned policy can be adopted. A possible off-line learning approach to this problem would be to characterize teams by a set of performance statistics (e.g. average player location) over the course of a fixed time period. Based on this representation, a memory-based algorithm could be used to match teams with the previously seen opponents that behave most similarly. Then during games, after the fixed evaluation period has identified a similar past opponent, the pass-selection policy that was learned against this similar opponent team could be adopted by the agents.

The learning methods proposed for both of the above behaviors are summarized in Table 4.4. Just as is the case for the implemented behaviors, these new behaviors follow the principles of layered learning as laid out in Section 4.1.

Table 4.4
The proposed learning methods for the future layers in the simulated robotic soccer layered learning implementation.

Layer	Learned behavior	Learning method	Training type
L_4	strategic positioning	observational RL	on-line
L_5	strategic adaptation	memory-based	off-line

4.4 Discussion

In this section I discuss some issues pertaining to layered learning and our implementation thereof as they relate to multiagent learning in general. I begin by bringing up several issues related to the relative merits of, and appropriate times for, off-line and on-line learning. I also frame the above implementation within our team member agent architecture and discuss the possible propagation of errors among the learned behaviors in a layered learning system.

On-line and Off-line Learning

As illustrated in Section 4.3, the type of learning used at each layer in layered learning depends upon the subtask characteristics. We use neural networks and decision trees to learn ball interception and pass evaluation. These off-line approaches are appropriate for fixed tasks that can be trained outside of game situations. In fact, off-line learning is necessary for such basic skills due to the fact that no individual gets enough training examples in game situations to learn them on-line.

This off-line learning of basic skills is similar to chunking (Newell, 1990), something done by human experts in many domains. Performing tasks closely related to simulated robotic soccer, human athletes spend a good deal of time acquiring basic skills so that they can execute them "automatically" during competition. For example, human soccer players, like our robotic soccer agents, learn to control and pass a ball through hours and hours (over many years) of practice outside of game situations.

Similarly, it has been documented that chess experts, rather than reasoning from first principles all the time, learn to recognize common patterns of pieces on the board (Newell and Simon, 1972). Their chunking allows them to quickly eliminate or focus on certain lines of play so that they can efficiently evaluate their options on a given move.

Unlike human learners, when AI agents use off-line learning, there is the opportunity for them to share their learned knowledge with other team members. Rather than each individual agent needing to learn a particular skill, a single agent can do the learning and transfer knowledge to teammates. In fact, we use this method of knowledge sharing for both the ball-interception and pass-evaluation layers.

In PTS domains (see Chapter 3) such as robotic soccer, even on-line learning can be shared to some extent. While the agents may learn different things due to their different experiences during execution, they can still share their experiences completely at the periodic team synchronization opportunities. This approach is the one we take for the learned pass-selection behavior: each agent learns a policy while staying in a fixed position within a fixed formation. However, when given the opportunity, the agents share their learned policies so that they can subsequently switch positions freely.

This sharing of all learned information leads to completely homogeneous agents. It is in contrast with attempts to promote behavioral diversity in learning teams of agents (Balch, 1998). While it is important that not all agents in a team are doing exactly the same thing at the same time, there is no need to enforce difference in behavior *capabilities* or knowledge. Rather than using heterogeneous agents, we have our agents decompose and share their task via their flexible team formations. Although at any given time each agent fills a different role, each agent is capable of switching to any other role.

Two other common issues related to on-line multiagent learning are exploration versus exploitation and the escalating arms race problem. On-line behavior learning methods, whether or not they involve multiple agents, must address the tradeoff between exploration and exploitation. Exploration is acting sub-optimally given the available information in order to gather additional information. On the other hand, exploitation is always taking the best available action given the current state of knowledge at the cost of possibly missing new opportunities. Particularly in simulated robotic soccer, where games last only 10 minutes, agents can only afford to explore on-line briefly. In fact, even our on-line pass-selection training is executed over the course of several games against a fixed opponent using Boltzmann exploration: a probabilistic exploration method that gradually increases the rate of exploitation. And the proposed strategic adaptation learning method is executed off-line with only a brief (perhaps one minute) on-line period to gather performance statistics for the current opponent. In order to adapt on-line within the course of a single game, the learning method must be capable of almost immediate exploitation.

The escalating arms race problem is a phenomenon occurring in on-line multiagent learning systems with concurrently adapting opponents. As one team changes its strategy to counteract the current opponent strategy, the opponent simultaneously alters its strategy to improve its own performance. In this way, the target concept to be learned constantly shifts and neither team is able to converge to a stable strategy. Our layered learning implementation sidesteps this issues by training against fixed opponents. We have not attempted to learn against another adaptive team.

Framing within the Team Member Agent Architecture

In the context of the team member agent architecture presented in Chapter 3, the implemented ball-interception and pass-selection layers are external behaviors, directly affecting the agent's actions. On the other hand, the pass-evaluation layer affects the agent's internal state: it is an internal behavior. Strategic positioning and strategic adaptation are also internal behaviors as they affect aspects of the formation and overall strategy which are components of the internal state via the locker-room agreement.

Error Propagation

An issues that is often raised in regards to layered learning is the problem of error propagation. That is, since the learning at each layer affects the learning at subsequent layers, if something goes wrong, how can we determine which layer is to blame? Or conversely, if the team performs well, which layer deserves the credit? While this question is worth careful examination, such an examination is not a part of this book. When testing the effectiveness of each new learned layer, we isolate it by comparing agent performance with and without the new layer. Thus we validate that the learning does indeed improve performance. However any particular error that does occur with the new layer could be due to that layer or to any previous layer.

One often overlooked fact with regard to error propagation is that each additional layer does not necessarily add to the overall error rate. Instead, it is possible for higher-level behaviors to learn to overcome errors in the underlying layers. For example, in our robotic soccer implementation, the pass-evaluation function may be able learn which passes will be likely failures for the ball-interception function and therefore degrade the predicted likelihood of completing the pass. Similarly, the pass-selection routine may be able to compensate for faulty evaluations by the pass-evaluation layer by, for example, requiring higher success confidences for passes in critical situations.

A detailed study of error propagation and compensation within layered learning implementations is a promising area for future research.

4.5 Related Work

In this section, I briefly discuss some of the most related work to layered learning along three dimensions. (Related work for the book as a whole is discussed in detail in Chapter 9.) First, I substantiate my claim that robotic soccer is too complex a domain for learning straight from sensors to actuators. Second, I present other layered architectures. Third, I bring some other hierarchical learning approaches to attention.

Robotic Soccer

One of the principles of layered learning as laid out in Section 4.1 is that it is to be used in domains that are too complex for learning a mapping directly from sensors to actuators. In general, we assume that any domain that fits the description in Section 1.2—limited communication, real-time, noisy environments with both teammates and adversaries—is such a domain. In particular, empirical evidence indicates that robotic soccer is such a domain: layered learning enables the creation of more successful behaviors than could be achieved if using the agents' sensors as the input representation for a single, all-encompassing learned behavior.

This evidence is based on two attempts to do just that—learn straight from the agents' sensors—in the same robotic soccer domain. First, Luke et al. (1998) set out to create a completely learned team of agents using genetic programming (Koza, 1992). However, the ambition was eventually scaled back and low-level player skills were created by hand as the basis for learning. The resulting learned team won two of its four games at the RoboCup-97 competition, losing in the second round. In that same competition, our CMUnited-97 team, using layered learning, made it to the semi-finals (fourth round) and, although never directly matched against the genetic programming team, was qualitatively clearly a better team.

The following year, at RoboCup-98, another genetic programming attempt at learning the entire team behavior was made (Andre and Teller, 1999). This time, the agents were indeed allowed to learn directly from their sensory input representation. While making some impressive progress given the challenging nature of the approach, this entry was unable to advance past the first round in the tournament.

Given the complex nature of the robotic soccer domain, our initial inclination was that it would be impossible to create successful behaviors by learning straight from sensors to actuators: the space of possible sensory inputs is huge, there are many possible actions, and there is a large amount of hidden state. Combined with the anecdotal evidence provided by the two generally unsuccessful attempts at such learning, we feel confident in our claim that layered learning's decomposition of the robotic soccer task into smaller subtasks enables the creation of more complex and successful learned behaviors than are possible if learning straight from the agents' sensory inputs.

For a further discussion of other learning approaches within the robotic soccer domain, see Chapter 9 (Section 9.2).

Layered Architectures

The layered learning approach is somewhat reminiscent of Brooks' subsumption architecture (Brooks, 1986) which layers reactive control modules, allowing high-level controllers to override lower-lever ones. Each control level is capable of controlling the robot on its own up to a specified level of functionality. Brooks implements his approach on real robots, building controllers for simple tasks such as avoiding collisions and wandering around.

Mataric brings the subsumption architecture to a multiagent learning domain, building controllers on top of a set of learned *basis behaviors* (Mataric, 1995). Mataric's basis behaviors are chosen to be necessary and sufficient for the learning task, while remaining as simple and robust as possible. Since Mataric's robots were to learn social behaviors such as flocking and foraging, they were equipped with basis behaviors such as the ability to follow each other and the ability to wander without running into obstacles.

While layered learning also makes use of multiple behavior layers, the robotic soccer task is much more complex: the agents must be able to generalize across situations, handle adversaries, and achieve complex goals. In order to move quickly to high-level behaviors, the commitment to have every layer be completely able to control the robot is abandoned. Instead, many situation-specific (but as general as possible) behaviors are produced which are then managed by higher-level behaviors. In addition, the robotic soccer behaviors are not entirely reactive, building upon the agents' internal state which changes over time. Nevertheless, the idea of building higher levels of functionality on top of lower levels is retained. It is in producing the situation-specific behaviors that ML techniques are used.

Also building on top of the subsumption architecture, the ALLIANCE systems was built to deal with "loosely-coupled, largely independent tasks" for heterogeneous robots (Parker, 1994). Example tasks are box pushing, janitorial service (dust, empty trash, clean floors), and hazardous waste cleanup. ALLIANCE assumes that the robots have the abilities to do each of the low-level tasks; it provides the coordination mechanism. The L-ALLIANCE variant learns some of the system parameters indicating, for instance, how good each robot is at performing each task. Like in Mataric's work, the learning in L-ALLIANCE is at the level of choosing among hard-wired behaviors: the learning does not cross multiple layers in the architecture. In addition, the tasks considered are neither real-time nor adversarial.

As opposed to the purely reactive subsumption architecture, three-layer architectures include behaviors that refer to an agent's internal state. The three layers are the *controller*, which executes purely reactive behaviors mapping sensors to actuators; the *sequencer*, which references past world states in order to select which reactive behavior to use at a given time; and the *deliberator*, which predicts future states in order to do time-consuming computations such as "planning and other exponential search-based algorithms" (Gat, 1998).

INTERRAP (Mueller, 1996) is a recent example of a three-layer architecture which is designed for multiagent systems. In INTERRAP, the highest layer includes collaborative reasoning using a BDI (Rao and Georgeff, 1995) model to consider other agents' goals and intentions and to resolve conflicts. INTERRAP does not include any machine learning. Indeed, learning is not a consideration in three-layer architectures in general (Gat, 1998).

The layers in layered learning are orthogonal to the layers in a three-layer architecture. Layered learning could easily be used within a three-layer approach with learned layers intersecting the controller, the sequencer, and the deliberator in any way. While our team member agent architecture is not a three-layer approach since there are no purely reactive behaviors (even the lowest-level skills rely on predictions of future world states based on current and past states), robotic soccer could be implemented within the three-layer paradigm while retaining the same learned layers: ball interception would be a part of the controller; pass evaluation and pass selection would be part of the sequencer; and strategic positioning and strategic adaptation would be part of the deliberator.

Layered learning can be used within existing layered architectures or within most other robotic architectures. As long as there are behaviors which build upon each other in some ways, then learning in one behavior can be used to facilitate or influence learning in subsequent behaviors.

Hierarchical Learning

The original hierarchical learning constructs were devised to improve the generalization of a single learning task by running multiple learning processes. Both boosting (Shapire, 1990) and stacked generalization (Wolpert, 1992) improve function generalization by combining the results of several generalizers or several runs of the same generalizer. These approaches contrast with layered learning in that the layers in layered learning each deal with *different* tasks. Boosting or stacked generalization could potentially be used within any given layer, but not across different layers.

More in line with the type of hierarchical learning discussed in this book are hierarchical reinforcement learning algorithms. Because of the well-known "curse of dimensionality" in reinforcement learning—RL algorithms require time that is polynomial in the number of states (Dietterich, 1998)—RL researchers have been very interested in hierarchical learning approaches. As surveyed in (Kaelbling et al., 1996), most hierarchical RL approaches use *gated* behaviors:

> There is a collection of behaviors that map environment states into low-level actions and a gating function that decides, based on the state of the environment, which behavior's actions should be switched through and actually executed. (Kaelbling et al., 1996)

In some cases the behaviors are learned (Mahadevan and Connell, 1991), in some cases the gating function is learned (Maes and Brooks, 1990), and in some cases both are learned (Lin, 1993). In this last example, the behaviors are learned and fixed prior to learning the gating function. On the other hand, feudal Q-learning (Dayan and Hinton, 1993) and the MAXQ algorithm (Dietterich, 1998) learn at all levels of the hierarchy simultaneously. A constant among these approaches is that the behaviors and the gating function are all control tasks with similar inputs and actions (sometimes abstracted). In the RL layer of our layered learning implementation, the input representation itself is learned. In addition, none of the above methods has been implemented in a large-scale, complex domain.

In all of the above RL approaches, like in layered learning, the task decomposition is constructed manually. However, there has been at least one attempt at the challenging task of *learning* the task decomposition. Nested Q-learning (Digney, 1996) generates its own hierarchical control structure and then learns low-level skills at the same time as it learns to select among them. Thus far, like other hierarchical RL approaches, it has only been tested on very small problems (on the order of 100 states in this case).

The hierarchical RL research mentioned in this section is all done with single learning agents. For a full discussion of multiagent learning approaches, see Chapter 9 (Section 9.1).

5 Learning an Individual Skill

As presented in Chapter 4, the initial layer in our simulated robotic soccer layered learning implementation is an individual skill, namely ball interception. In this chapter, I describe our ball-interception learning, the initial learning experiments in the RoboCup soccer server (Stone and Veloso, 1996c, 1998c). In Sections 5.1 and 5.2, I motivate the choice of ball-interception as our initial learned layer and describe the experimental setup. In Section 5.3, I present our detailed empirical results demonstrating the effectiveness of the learned behavior. Sections 5.4 and 5.5 are devoted to discussion and related work.

As the experiments reported in this chapter were carried out in an earlier version of the soccer server—version 2—there were some differences from version 4 as described in Chapter 2. For example, when seeing an object, the agents only received information pertaining to its distance and angle from the agent: never velocity information. I point out this and other differences between server versions when they are relevant to the text.

5.1 Ball Interception in the Soccer Server

Just as young soccer players must learn to control the ball before learning any complex strategies, robotic soccer agents must also acquire low-level skills before exhibiting complex behaviors. In multiagent systems in general, it is crucial that the agents are individually skilled: the most sophisticated understanding of how to act as part of a team is useless without the ability to execute the necessary individual tasks. Therefore, we defined an individual skill as the lower abstraction level to be learned in the layered learning approach.

The low-level skill we identified as being most essential to our soccer server agents was the ability to intercept a moving ball. This skill is ubiquitous in all soccer-type frameworks. Intercepting a moving ball is considerably more difficult than moving to a stationary ball both because of the ball's unpredictable movement (due to simulator noise) and because the agent may need to turn and move in such a direction that it cannot see the ball, as illustrated in Figure 5.1.

Intercepting a moving ball is a task that arises very frequently in the soccer server. Unless the ball has decelerated completely without an agent collecting it, this skill is a prerequisite for any kicking action. It is used by agents filling all the different roles: goaltenders and defenders must intercept shots and opponents' passes, while midfielders and forwards must frequently "intercept," or receive, passes to them from teammates.

Ball interception is a difficult task in the soccer server because of the noise in the ball's motion and because the agents have limited sensing capabilities. As presented in Section 2.2, each agent has a limited visible angle and it gets sensory information at discrete intervals (`send_step` = 250 msec in soccer server version 2). Often when an agent is trying to intercept the ball, the ball is moving roughly in the direction of the agent, the condition which causes the difficulty illustrated in Figure 5.1. The ball can move past the agent as it goes to where the ball used to be. But if the agent turns to move to where the ball *will* be, it may lose sight of the ball. Since the ball's motion is noisy, the agent cannot predict its motion while it is not visible.

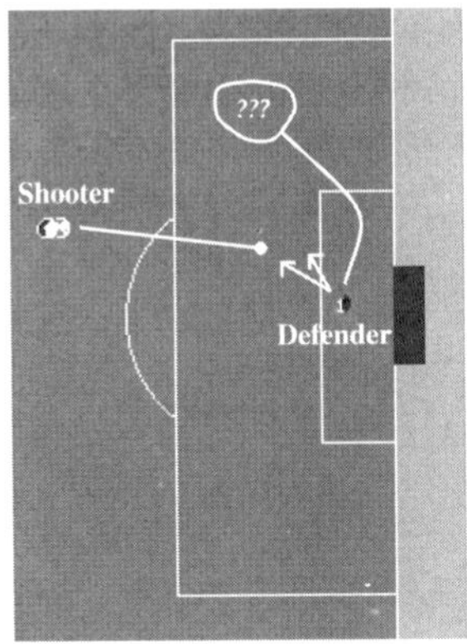

Figure 5.1
The challenge of ball interception. If the defender moves directly towards the ball (left arrow), it will miss entirely. If the defender turns to move in the appropriate direction (right arrow), it may no longer be able to see the ball.

There were two possible methods for equipping our agents with the ability to intercept a moving ball:

Analytically estimating the ball's velocity from its past positions (recall that velocity information was not directly available), and predicting its future motion based on this velocity.

Empirically collecting examples of successful interceptions, and using a supervised learning technique to create a general ball-interception behavior.

We implemented both approaches. For the empirical approach, we used neural networks (NNs) as the supervised learning technique.

As it turns out, the two approaches were roughly equal both in effort of implementation and in effectiveness (see Section 5.3). As the initial learning experiment in our layered learning implementation, we preferred the empirical approach for its appropriateness to our machine learning paradigm. Isolating a situation that requires this skill, we drilled the agents, providing the appropriate reinforcement, until they were able to learn to execute this skill reliably.

5.2 Training

In order to train the ball-interception behavior, we focus on a specific instance of the behavior: a defender blocking a shot from an opponent. The training setup is as follows:

- The *defender* starts at a distance of 4 in front of the center of the goal, facing directly away from the goal.
- The ball and *shooter* are placed randomly at a distance between 20 and 30 from the defender.
- For each training example, the shooter kicks the ball directly towards the defender with maximum power ($Power = 100$).
- The defender's goal is to save the shot. A *save* is a successful ball interception; a *goal* is an unsuccessful attempt in which the ball enters the goal; a *miss* is an unsuccessful attempt in which the ball goes wide of the goal.

Due to the noise in the simulator, the ball does not always move directly at the defender: if the defender remains still, the ball hits it only 35% of the time. Furthermore, if the defender keeps watching the ball and moving directly towards it, it is only able to stop the ball 53% of the time.

The defender's behavior during training is more complex than that of the shooter. As we are using a supervised learning technique, it must first gather training data by acting randomly and recording the results of its actions. As its input representation for learning, the defender notices the ball's distance at time t ($BallDist_t$), the ball's relative angle at time t ($BallAng_t$), and the ball's distance at the time when the previous visual information string was received ($BallDist_{t-1}$): in the context of layered learning, the input vector of state features $\vec{F_1} = \{BallDist_t, BallAng_t, BallDist_{t-1}\}$. As no explicit velocity information is available in version 2 of the soccer server, $BallDist_{t-1}$ serves as an indication of the ball's rate of movement. It would have been possible to base the velocity estimate on several past ball positions. However, we found that a single previous position was sufficient to allow the agent to learn to intercept the ball. Figure 5.2 illustrates the experimental setup, indicating the starting positions of both agents and the ball.

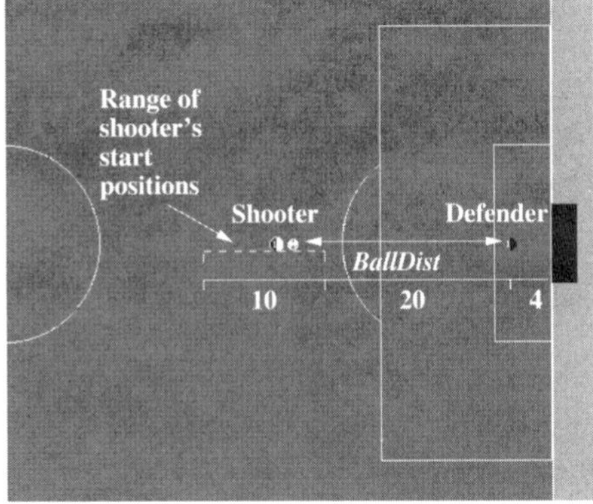

Figure 5.2
The range of training situations for learning ball interception. At the beginning of each trial, the defender starts at a distance of 4 from the goal, while the ball and shooter are placed randomly at a distance between 20 and 30 from the defender. *BallDist* is the distance from the defender to the ball. When the defender is looking straight at the ball, as in this figure, *BallAng* = 0.

The defender's goal is to determine its turn angle $TurnAng_t$ or the angle it should turn at time t relative to the ball's angle in order to intercept the ball: in relation to layered learning, the output for the first layer $O_1 = TurnAng_t$. The defender acts randomly during training according to the following algorithm:

- While $BallDist_t > 14$, Turn($BallAng_t$)
- When $BallDist_t \leq 14$, set $TurnAng_t$ = Random Angle between -45° and 45°.
- Collect the input and output features of the training instance: $BallDist_t$, $BallAng_t$, $BallDist_{t-1}$, and $TurnAng_t$.
- Turn($BallAng_t$ + $TurnAng_t$).
- Dash forward.
- Gather classification as a successful training instance (save) or an unsuccessful instance (goal or miss).

Until the ball is within a given range (14), the defender simply watches and faces the ball, thus ensuring that all of the world features used for training are known. Then, once the ball is in range, the defender turns a random angle (within a range) away from the ball and dashes. This procedure of gathering data does not produce a successful training instance on every trial: only the saves correspond to the correct mapping from world features to the agent's action. Since the defender acts randomly during training, it often misses the ball (76% of the time). However, it can learn based on the successful training examples. These gathered training examples are T_1 in our layered learning implementation.

Our domain is characterized by an agent not always knowing the effects of its actions due to a large amount of hidden state in the world. If the defender is not facing the ball at the end of a trial, it does not know the ball's location, and therefore it does not know whether its interception attempt was successful or not. In order to automate the training process, we use an omniscient, omnipotent centralized agent. The centralized agent classifies each trial as a failure when the ball gets past the defender (a goal or miss) or as a success when the ball starts moving back towards the shooter (a save). Only saves are considered successful training instances and thus used for training. At the end of the trial, the centralized agent resets the positions of the defender, the shooter, and the ball for another trial.

The goal of learning is to allow the defender to choose the appropriate turn angle ($TurnAng_t$) based upon $BallDist_t$, $BallAng_t$, and $BallDist_{t-1}$. In order to learn the $TurnAng_t$, we chose to use a Neural Network (NN). NN's are appropriate for the task because of their ability to learn continuous output values from continuous inputs.

After a small amount of experimentation with different NN configurations, we settled on a fully-connected net with 4 sigmoid hidden units and a learning rate of 10^{-6}. The weights connecting the input and hidden layers used a linearly decreasing weight decay starting at .1%. We used a linear output unit with no weight decay. We trained for 3000 epochs. This configuration proved to be satisfactory for our task with no need for extensive tweaking of the network parameters. The NN training algorithm is the learning algorithm M_1 and the trained NN is the learned hypothesis h_1 in our layered learning implementation.

5.3 Results

Number of Training Examples

In order to test the NN's performance, we ran 1000 trials with the defender using the output of the NN to determine its turn angle. The behaviors of the shooter and the centralized agent are the same as during training. Thus, the testing examples are drawn from the same distribution as the training data. The results for NNs trained with different numbers of training examples are displayed in Figure 5.3. The misses are not included in the results since those are the shots that are far enough wide that the defender does not have much chance of even reaching the ball before it is past. The figure also records the percentage of shots *on-goal* (Saves+Goals) that the defender saved. Reasonable performance is achieved with only 300 training examples, and examples beyond about 750 do not improve performance. The defender is able to save almost all of the shots despite the continual noise in the ball's movement.

Effect of Noise in the Simulation

In order to study the effect of noise in the ball's movement upon the defender's performance, we varied the amount of noise in the soccer server (the `ball_rand` parameter). Figure 5.4 shows the effect of varying noise upon the defender when it uses the trained NN (trained with 750 examples) and when it moves straight towards the ball. The default `ball_rand` value in the soccer server is .05. The "straight" behavior always sets *TurnAng*=0, causing the defender to go directly towards where it last saw the ball. Notice that with no ball noise, both the straight and learned behaviors are successful: the ball and the defender move straight towards each other. As the noise in the ball's motion increases, the advantage of using the learned interception behavior becomes significant. The advantage of the NN can also be seen with no noise if the shooter aims slightly wide (by 4 degrees) of the goal's center. Then the defender succeeds 99% of the time when using the NN, and only 10% of the time when moving straight towards the ball.

Comparison with other Methods

From an examination of the weights of the trained NN, it is apparent that the NN focuses primarily upon the ball's angle ($BallAng_t$). Consequently, we were curious to try a behavior that simply uses a lookup table mapping $BallAng_t$ to the typical output of the NN for that $BallAng_t$. We identified such outputs for

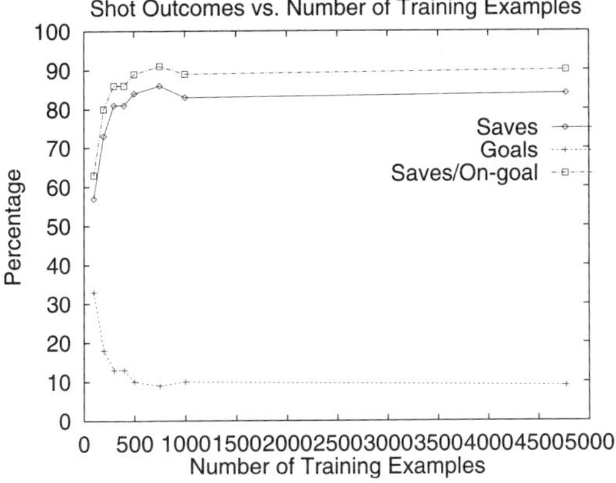

Training Examples	Saves(%)	Goals(%)	Saves / Goals+Saves(%)
100	57	33	63
200	73	18	80
300	81	13	86
400	81	13	86
500	84	10	89
750	**86**	9	**91**
1000	83	10	89
4773	84	9	90

Figure 5.3
The defender's performance when using NNs trained with different numbers of training examples. A "save" is a successful interception of the ball, a "goal" is a failed attempt. The last column of the table indicates the percentage of shots that were "on goal" that the defender saved.

$BallAng_t$ ranging from -7 to 7. Using this one dimensional lookup-table, the defender is able to perform almost as well as when using the full NN (see Table 5.1).

We also were curious about how well the NN would compare to analytical methods. As a basis for comparison, we used a behavior constructed by another student in the project whose goal was to create the best possible analytic behavior[1]. The resulting behavior computes the ball's motion vector from its current and previous positions and multiplies this vector by 3, thus predicting

1 We thank Michael Bowling for creating this behavior. Michael Bowling joined the robotic soccer project as a full-time graduate student in 1998. He now focuses on the real robots (Veloso et al., 1999a).

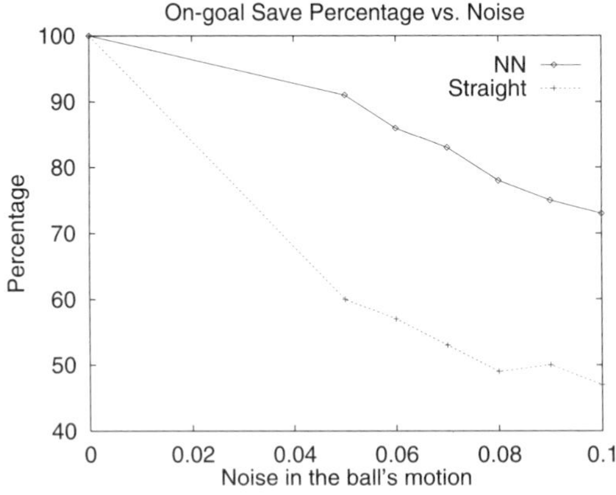

Noise	Behavior	Saves(%)	Goals(%)	$\frac{\text{Saves}}{\text{Goals+Saves}}$(%)
0	NN	100	0	100
	Straight	100	0	100
.05	NN	**86**	9	**91**
	Straight	**53**	35	**60**
.06	NN	75	13	86
	Straight	47	35	57
.07	NN	68	14	83
	Straight	40	36	53
.08	NN	59	16	78
	Straight	34	36	49
.09	NN	53	17	75
	Straight	32	33	50
.1	NN	49	18	73
	Straight	28	32	47

Figure 5.4
The defender's performance when using NNs and moving straight with different amounts of ball noise. A "save" is a successful interception of the ball, a "goal" is a failed attempt.

the ball's position two sensory steps (500 msec) into the future. The defender's $TurnAng_t$ is then the angle necessary to move directly towards the end of the lengthened vector. In particular, if (x_t, y_t) is the ball's current position, and (x_{t-1}, y_{t-1}) was its position at the time of the previous visual input (250 msec in the past), then the agent aims at the point $(x_{t-1}, y_{t-1}) + 3((x_t, y_t) - (x_{t-1}, y_{t-1}))$. Table 5.1 shows the results of the lookup table and analytic methods as compared to the learned NN.

Table 5.1
The defender's performance when using a NN, a one-dimensional lookup table, and an analytic method to determine the $TurnAng_t$.

Defender Behavior	Saves(%)	Goals(%)	Saves/(Goals+Saves) (%)
NN	**86**	9	**91**
Lookup Table	83	8	91
Analytic	82	13	86

5.4 Discussion

In this chapter I presented the initial layer of our layered learning implementation. We used a supervised learning technique to allow agents to learn a useful individual skill in a multiagent domain. In addition to the successful learned method, we investigated other methods of achieving the same behavior functionality, verifying that the learning approach compares favorably with the other options.

Ball interception is a ubiquitous skill in robotic soccer. Not only our agents in the soccer server, but also all other agents in any real-time robotic soccer domain must be able to intercept the ball. Another ball-interception method for the soccer server that relies on knowing the instantaneous ball velocity is used by the AT Humboldt-97 team (Burkhard et al., 1998). It is similar to our own hand-coded ball-interception skill for version 4 of the soccer server described in Appendix B (Section B.1). Also in Appendix B (Section B.2), there is a description of the ball-interception behavior used by our real robotic agents.

As mentioned above, the learning described in this chapter is done in an early implementation of the soccer server in which agents do not receive any velocity information when seeing the ball. Thus the ball interception skill described in Appendix B is not applicable. Although we eventually hand-coded the ball interception skill for use in the new version of the server, the next learned layer—to be described in Chapter 6—uses the learned ball-interception behavior described in this chapter as part of its training behavior. Thus, the two layers link as advocated by the principles of layered learning.

Also in line with the principles of layered learning, the ball-interception subtask is an important initial skill for which it is possible to gather training data. Within the context of layered learning, the subtask is given as part of the task decomposition. We chose the NN machine learning method in order to exploit data to learn a continuous action parameter from three continuous features of the world state as inputs. Both of these choices—the subtask itself and the ML method—are heuristic choices. Other options may have worked equally well.

In summary, layer L_1 of our layered learning implementation is defined concretely as follows:

- $\vec{F}_1 = \{BallDist_t, BallAng_t, BallDist_{t-1}\}$.
- $O_1 = TurnAng_t$.
- T_1 = 750 training examples gathered according to the training procedure laid out in Section 5.2.
- M_1 = a fully-connected neural network with 4 sigmoid hidden units and a learning rate of 10^{-6} trained for 3000 epochs.
- h_1 = a trained ball-interception behavior.

5.5 Related Work

Although the learned ball-interception described in this chapter was the first learning research conducted in the soccer server, individual behaviors had been previously learned in other robotic soccer systems. This section discusses these other early robotic soccer learning systems[2].

Prior to conducting the research reported in this chapter, we used neural networks to teach an agent to shoot a moving ball into a goal in a simulator based closely upon the Dynasim system (Sahota, 1996). The simulator models the non-holonomic wheeled Dynamite robots (Sahota et al., 1995). In this scenario, we were able to use one neural network to time the agent's approach towards the ball, and another to aim the ball. The learned behavior successfully enabled the agent to redirect a moving ball with varying speeds and trajectories into specific parts of the goal. By carefully choosing the input representation to the neural networks so that they would generalize as much as possible, the agent was able to use the learned behavior in all quadrants of the field even though it was trained in a single quadrant (Stone and Veloso, 1998d).

Learning was applied in both simulated and real robotic, to hit a stationary ball into the goal using the concept of learning from easy missions (Asada et al., 1994a). By first placing the ball directly in front of the goal and then

2 A full discussion of related robotic soccer systems, including more recent learning approaches, appears in Chapter 9 (Section 9.2).

gradually moving it farther away, thus making the task harder, the learning time was reduced from exponential to linear in the size of the state space within an RL framework. The robots achieved 70% success in simulation and 40% success in the real world.

Another early example of learning an individual skill in the RoboCup soccer server involved using a neural network to enable an agent to learn when to shoot and when to pass (Matsubara et al., 1996). An agent was given the ball near the opponent's goal with a goaltender blocking the way and a teammate nearby. Based on the positions of the ball, the goaltender, and the teammate, the agent with the ball learned when it was best to shoot directly at the goal and when it was best to pass.

In a similar setup, using the same Dynasim-based simulator mentioned above, we used memory-based learning to allow an agent to learn when to shoot and when to pass the ball (Stone and Veloso, 1996a). This learning was of an individual skill since the goaltender and the teammate used deterministic, fixed behaviors.

6 Learning a Multiagent Behavior

In this chapter I present a learned multiagent behavior, the second layer in our layered learning implementation of simulated robotic soccer agents. Pass evaluation—the estimation of whether or not a pass to a particular teammate will succeed—is a necessary but difficult capability with which to equip our agents. However, by collecting data and using it to train the agents, a successful evaluation function can be constructed (Stone and Veloso, 1998c). As prescribed by the principles of layered learning, this training process incorporates the learned ball-interception skill (see Chapter 5).

Chapter 6 is organized as follows. Section 6.1 describes the motivation for, training of, and testing of the learned multiagent behavior. Section 6.2 verifies that the off-line training can be used in a real-time game situation. In Section 6.3 I describe our use of the learned pass-evaluation capability in a full team behavior. Sections 6.4 and 6.5 are devoted to discussion and related work.

6.1 Decision Tree Learning for Pass Evaluation

Setup and Training

Once young soccer players have learned how to control a ball, they are ready to use their skill to start learning how to make decisions on the field and playing as part of a team. Similarly, our simulated robotic soccer agents can use their learned ball-interception skill to exhibit a more complex behavior: passing. Passing requires action by two different agents. A *passer* must kick the ball towards the *receiver*, who must collect the ball. Since the receiver's task is identical to that of the defender in Chapter 5, the agents can (and do) use the same trained neural network.

Although the execution of a pass in the open field is not difficult given the receiver's ball-interception skill, it becomes more complicated in the presence of opponents that try to intercept the pass. In this section, we assume that the opponents are equipped with the same learned ball-interception skill as the receivers. The passer is faced with the task of assessing the likelihood that a pass to a particular teammate will succeed. For example, in Figure 6.1 teammate 2 may be able to receive a pass from the passer, while teammates 3 and 4 are much less likely to be able to do so. The function that our agents learn evaluates whether or not a pass to a given teammate is likely to succeed.

When deciding whether or not to make a pass, there are many world state features that may be relevant. When many features are available for a machine learning task, it can be very difficult to determine which ones are predictive of the target concept. Therefore, we use a learning method that is capable of determining for itself the features on which to focus. In particular, we use the C4.5 decision tree (DT) training algorithm (Quinlan, 1993).

In order to gather training data, like for the ball-interception behavior, we again define a constrained training scenario and use an omniscient, omnipotent agent to monitor the trials. The training process is illustrated in detail in Figures 6.1–6.5 including their accompanying captions. Table 6.1 specifies the training procedure.

Table 6.1
The training procedure for learning pass evaluation.

1. The players are placed randomly within a region (Figure 6.1).
2. The passer announces its intention to pass (Figure 6.1).
3. The teammates reply with their views of the field when ready to receive (Figure 6.2).
4. The passer chooses a receiver randomly during training, or with a DT during testing (Figure 6.3).
5. The passer collects a large number of features of the training instance (see below).
6. The passer announces to whom it is passing (Figure 6.4).
7. The receiver and four opponents attempt to get the ball **using the learned ball-interception skill** (Figure 6.5).
8. The training example is classified as a *success* if the receiver manages to advance the ball towards the opponent's goal; a *failure* if one of the opponents clears the ball in the opposite direction; or a *miss* if the receiver and the opponents all fail to intercept the ball (Figure 6.5).

Rather than restricting the number of features in the input representation used for learning, we capitalized on the DT's ability to filter out the irrelevant ones. Thus, we gather a total of 174 features for each training example, half from the passer's perspective and half from the receiver's. The features from the receiver's perspective are communicated to the passer before the passer has to decide to which player to pass.

The complete list of features—*all continuous or ordinal*—available to the DT are defined in Table 6.2. These features are the elements of the input vector $\vec{F_2}$ in our layered learning implementation. All of the features starting with "passer" are from the passer's perspective; features starting "receiver" are from the receiver's perspective. For example, `receiver-players-dist8-ang12` is the number of players that the receiver sees within a distance of 8 and angle of

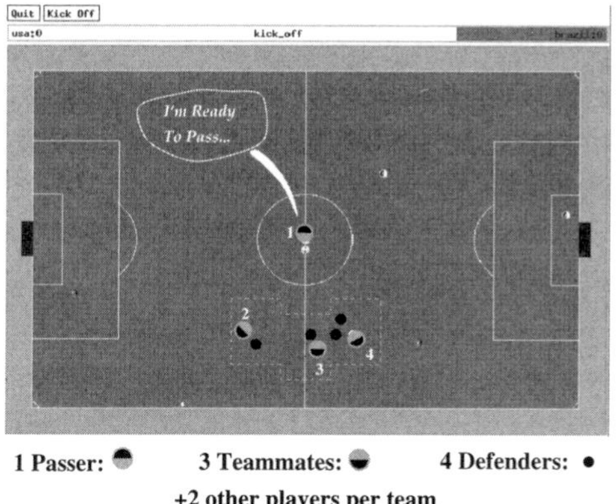

Figure 6.1
The pass evaluation training process, part 1. At the beginning of a trial, the passer is placed behind the ball. 3 teammates and 4 opponents are placed randomly within the region indicated by the dashed line, while 2 other players from each team are placed randomly on the field. In this and the following figures, the players involved in the play are enlarged for presentation purposes. When the passer sees that it has the ball, it announces its intention to pass. Its goal is to assess the likelihood of a pass to a given teammate succeeding.

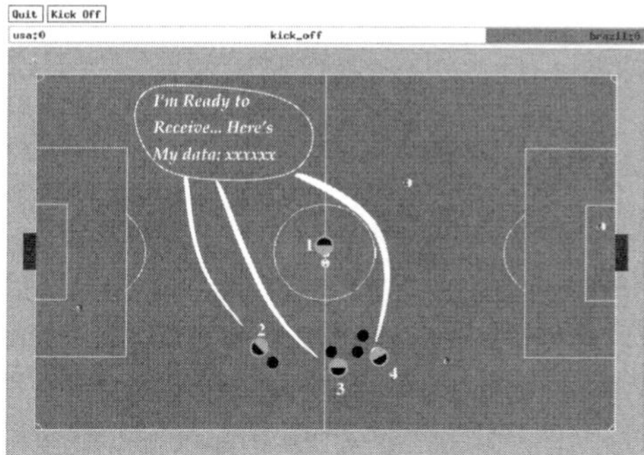

Figure 6.2
The pass evaluation training process, part 2. When the teammates are facing the ball, they tell the passer what the world looks like to them. The passer can use the transmitted data to help it assess the likelihood that each teammate would successfully receive a pass. The data includes distances and angles to the other players as well as some statistics regarding the numbers of players within given distances and angles.

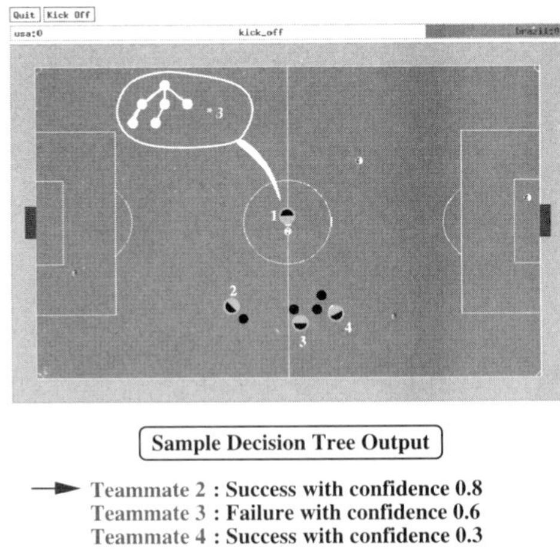

Figure 6.3
The pass evaluation training process, part 3. During training, the passer chooses its receiver randomly. During testing, it uses a DT to evaluate the likelihood that a pass to each of the teammates would succeed. It passes to the one most likely to successfully receive the pass (Teammate 2 in this case).

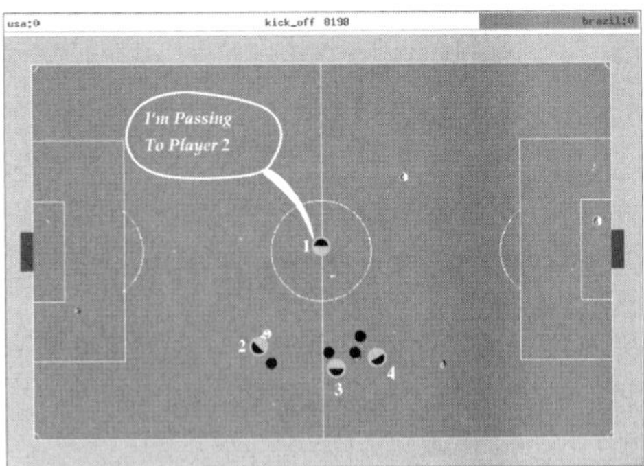

Figure 6.4
The pass evaluation training process, part 4. After choosing its receiver, the passer announces its decision so that the receiver knows to expect the ball and the other teammates can move on to other behaviors. In our experiments, the non-receivers remain stationary.

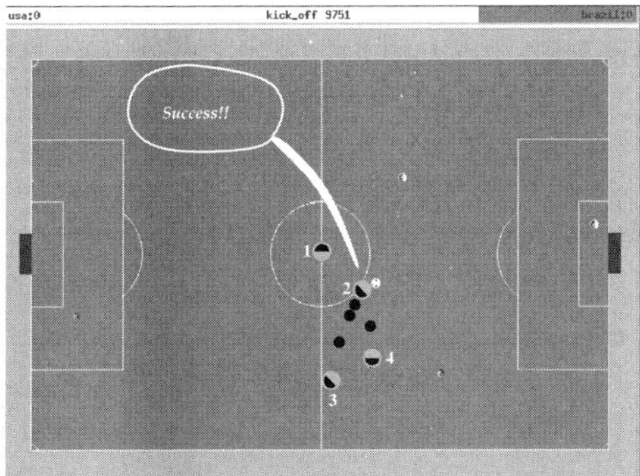

Figure 6.5
The pass evaluation training process, part 5. Finally, the receiver announces the result of the pass.

12 from the passer. The features are defined in the following terms. If x and y are players, then:

- dist(x,y) = the distance between players x and y;
- ang(x,y) = the angle to player y from player x's perspective;
- rel-ang(x,y,z) = |ang(x,y) − ang(x,z)|;
- rel-dist(x,y,z) = |dist(x,y) − dist(x,z)|.

Even though the training examples do not include full teams of players, the features are defined such that they could be used in a game situation. The players whose positions are unknown create missing feature values.

Along with the ability to ignore irrelevant features, another strength of decision trees is their ability to handle missing features. Whenever fewer than the maximum number of players are visible, some features are missing. In addition, if the potential receiver is unable to successfully communicate the data from its perspective, all of the features from the receiver's perspective are missing.

The goal of learning is to use the feature values to predict whether a pass to the given teammate will lead to a success, a failure, or a miss. For training, we use standard off-the-shelf C4.5 code with all of the default parameters (Quinlan, 1993). We gathered a total of 5000 training examples, 51% of which were successes, 42% of which were failures, and 7% of which were misses. In the context of our layered learning implementation, the learning algorithm M_2 is C4.5 and the training set T_2 is the set of 5000 training examples.

Table 6.2
The complete list of 174 continuous and ordinal features available to the decision tree.

- Distance and Angle to receiver (2 features):
  - `passer-receiver-distance` = dist(passer,receiver).
  - `passer-receiver-angle` = ang(passer,receiver).
- Distance and Angle to other teammates sorted by angle from receiver (18 features):
  - Sort the 9 other teammates such that $\forall$i,j, if $i<j$, then rel-ang(passer,teammate-i,receiver) $<$ rel-ang(passer,teammate-j,receiver).
  - For i=1-9, `passer-teammate(i)-distance` = dist(passer,teammate-i).
  - For i=1-9, `passer-teammate(i)-angle` = ang(passer,teammate-i).
- Distance and Angle to opponents sorted by angle from receiver (22 features):
  - Sort the 11 opponents such that $\forall$i,j, if $i<j$, then rel-ang(passer,opponent-i,receiver) $<$ rel-ang(passer,opponent-j,receiver).
  - For i=1-11, `passer-opponent(i)-distance` = dist(passer,opponent-i).
  - For i=1-11, `passer-opponent(i)-angle` = ang(passer,opponent-i).
- Distance and Angle from receiver to teammates sorted by distance (20 features):
  - Sort the 10 teammates (including the passer) such that $\forall$i,j, if $i<j$, then dist(receiver,teammate-i) $<$ dist(receiver,teammate-j).
  - For i=1-10, `receiver-teammate(i)-distance` = dist(receiver,teammate-i).
  - For i=1-10, `receiver-teammate(i)-angle` = ang(receiver,teammate-i).
- Distance and Angle from receiver to opponents sorted by distance (22 features):
  - Sort the 11 opponents such that $\forall$i,j, if $i<j$, then dist(receiver,opponent-i) $<$ dist(receiver,opponent-j).
  - For i=1-11, `receiver-opponent(i)-distance` = dist(receiver,opponent-i).
  - For i=1-11, `receiver-opponent(i)-angle` = ang(receiver,opponent-i).
- Player distribution stats from passer's (45 features) and receiver's (45 features) perspectives:
  - For i=1-6, `passer-teammates-ang(i)` = |{k$\in$teammates | rel-ang(passer,k,receiver) $\leq$ i $\wedge$ dist(passer,k) $\leq$ dist(passer,receiver)}|.
  - For i=1-6, `passer-opponents-ang(i)` = |{k$\in$opponents |rel-ang(passer,k,receiver) $\leq$ i $\wedge$ dist(passer,k) $\leq$ dist(passer,receiver)}|.
  - For i=1-6, `passer-players-ang(i)` = `passer-teammates-ang(i)` + `passer-opponents-ang(i)`.
  - For i=1-3, j=1-3, `passer-teammates-dist(4i)-ang(4j)`= |{k$\in$teammates | rel-ang(passer,k,receiver) $\leq$ 4i $\wedge$ rel-dist(passer,k,receiver) $\leq$ 4j}|.
  - For i=1-3, j=1-3, `passer-opponents-dist(4i)-ang(4j)`= |{k$\in$opponents | rel-ang(passer,k,receiver) $\leq$ 4i $\wedge$ rel-dist(passer,k,receiver) $\leq$ 4j}|.
  - For i=1-3, j=1-3, `passer-players-dist(4i)-ang(4j)`= `passer-teammates-dist(4i)-ang(4j)` + `passer-opponents-dist(4i)-ang(4j)`.
  - For i=1-6, `receiver-teammates-ang(i)` = |{k$\in$teammates | rel-ang(receiver,k,passer) $\leq$ i $\wedge$ dist(receiver,k) $\leq$ dist(passer,receiver)}|.
  - For i=1-6, `receiver-opponents-ang(i)` = |{k$\in$opponents |rel-ang(receiver,k,passer) $\leq$ i $\wedge$ dist(receiver,k) $\leq$ dist(passer,receiver)}|.
  - For i=1-6, `receiver-players-ang(i)` = `receiver-teammates-ang(i)` + `receiver-opponents-ang(i)`.
  - For i=1-3, j=1-3, `receiver-teammates-dist(4i)-ang(4j)`= |{k$\in$teammates | rel-ang(receiver,k,passer) $\leq$ 4i $\wedge$ rel-dist(receiver,k,passer) $\leq$ 4j}|.
  - For i=1-3, j=1-3, `receiver-opponents-dist(4i)-ang(4j)`= |{k$\in$opponents | rel-ang(receiver,k,passer) $\leq$ 4i $\wedge$ rel-dist(receiver,k,passer) $\leq$ 4j}|.
  - For i=1-3, j=1-3, `receiver-players-dist(4i)-ang(4j)`= `receiver-teammates-dist(4i)-ang(4j)` + `receiver-opponents-dist(4i)-ang(4j)`.

Training on this data produces a pruned tree with 87 nodes giving a 26% error rate on the training set. The resulting tree, the learned hypothesis h_2 in our layered learning implementation, is shown in Figure 6.6. The first node in the tree tests for the number of opponents within 6 degrees of the receiver from the passer's perspective. If there are any such opponents, the tree predicts that the pass will fail. Otherwise, the tree moves on to the second node which tests the angle of the first opponent. Since the passer sorts the opponents by angle, the first opponent is the *closest* opponent to the receiver in terms of angle from the passer's perspective. If there is no opponent within 13 degrees of the receiver, the tree predicts success. Otherwise it goes on to deeper nodes in the tree.

Each leaf in the tree shown in Figure 6.6 includes a classification ("S" for success or "F" for failure—no misses are shown) followed by two numbers in parentheses: (N/E). As explained in (Quinlan, 1993, page 42), "N is the number of training examples covered by the leaf. E is just the number of predicted errors if a set of N unseen cases were classified by the tree." Fractional values of N arise when activations are split among branches of the tree due to missing attributes. C4.5 uses N and E to associate a confidence factor $\in [0, 1]$ with each predicted classification (Quinlan, 1993).

We use C4.5's confidence factors to define a function Φ(passer,receiver) $\mapsto [-1, 1]$. Assume that for a pass from passer to receiver the DT predicts class κ with confidence $\gamma \in [0, 1]$. Then

$$\Phi(\text{passer, receiver}) = \begin{cases} \gamma & \text{if } \kappa = \text{S (success)} \\ 0 & \text{if } \kappa = \text{M (miss)} \\ -\gamma & \text{if } \kappa = \text{F (failure)} \end{cases}$$

Thus, in the context of our layered learning implementation, L_2's output set $O_2 = [-1, 1]$.

Results

In order to test the DT's performance, we ran 5000 trials with the passer using the DT to choose the receiver in Step 4 of Table 6.1. All other steps including the placement of players, and consequently the example distribution, are the same during testing as during training. Since the DT returns a confidence estimate in its classification, the passer can choose the best receiver candidate even if more than one is classified as likely to be successful: it passes to the teammate with maximum $\Phi(passer, teammate)$.

We compiled results sorted by the DT's confidence in the success of the pass to the chosen receiver (see Table 6.3). The largest number of passes were

```
C4.5 [release 8] decision tree interpreter
-----------------------------------------
Decision Tree:

passer-opponents-ang6 > 0 : F (1266.0/251.3)
passer-opponents-ang6 <= 0 :
| passer-opponent1-angle > 13 : S (1054.6/290.5)
| passer-opponent1-angle <= 13 :
| | passer-teammates-ang6 <= 0 :
| | | passer-receiver-distance <= 22 :
| | | | passer-opponent1-distance <= 20.9 :
| | | | | passer-players-dist8-ang12 <= 3 : S (162.0/72.9)
| | | | | passer-players-dist8-ang12 > 3 : F (15.0/5.8)
| | | | passer-opponent1-distance > 20.9 :
| | | | | passer-opponent2-distance <= 21.1 :
| | | | | | passer-opponents-dist12-ang8 <= 1 :
| | | | | | | passer-teammates-dist8-ang8 <= 1 :
| | | | | | | | passer-opponents-dist12-ang4 <= 0 :
| | | | | | | | | passer-receiver-distance <= 20.3 : S (52.2/8.6)
| | | | | | | | passer-opponents-dist12-ang4 > 0 :
| | | | | | | | | passer-opponents-dist4-ang12 <= 1 : S (60.5/20.0)
| | | | | passer-opponent2-distance > 21.1 :
| | | | | | receiver-teammates-dist8-ang12 <= 1 : S (704.3/139.6)
| | | passer-receiver-distance > 22 :
| | | | passer-opponent1-distance <= 23.1 :
| | | | | passer-opponents-dist12-ang12 <= 0 :
| | | | | | receiver-players-dist8-ang12 <= 1 : S (87.5/44.7)
| | | | | passer-opponents-dist12-ang12 > 0 :
| | | | | | passer-opponents-dist12-ang8 > 0 : F (191.0/63.0)
| | | | | | passer-opponents-dist12-ang8 <= 0 :
| | | | | | | passer-opponents-dist4-ang12 > 1 : S (14.0/6.8)
| | | | | | | passer-opponents-dist4-ang12 <= 1 :
| | | | | | | | passer-teammate1-distance <= 19.5 : S (15.0/6.8)
| | | | | | | | passer-teammate1-distance > 19.5 : F (234.0/91.7)
| | | | passer-opponent1-distance > 23.1 :
| | | | | passer-opponents-dist12-ang12 <= 1 : S (665.9/259.2)
| | | | | passer-opponents-dist12-ang12 > 1 :
| | | | | | passer-players-dist4-ang12 <= 1 : F (11.0/5.6)
| | | | | | passer-players-dist4-ang12 > 1 :
| | | | | | | passer-opponents-dist4-ang8 <= 0 : S (49.0/19.9)
| | | | | | | passer-opponents-dist4-ang8 > 0 :
| | | | | | | | passer-opponent2-distance <= 23.1 : F (85.0/26.5)
| | | | | | | | passer-opponent2-distance > 23.1 :
| | | | | | | | | passer-opponents-dist12-ang12 <= 2 :
| | | | | | | | | | receiver-opponent3-angle <= 48 : F (9.6/2.2)
| | | | | | | | | | receiver-opponent3-angle > 48 : S (108.4/43.0)
| | passer-teammates-ang6 > 0 :
| | | passer-teammates-ang5 > 0 : F (21.0/7.0)
```

Figure 6.6
The trained decision tree. Some subtrees with fewer cases covered have been removed for purposes of presentation. The features are described in Table 6.2. Predictions are indicated as "S" for success and "F" for failure. The numbers in parentheses indicate the predicted error rates for unseen cases at each leaf.

Table 6.3
The results of 5000 trials during which the passer uses the DT to choose the receiver. Overall results are given as well as a breakdown by the passer's confidence prior to the pass. The passer is forced to pass even if it predicts failures for all 3 teammates. In that case, it passes to the teammate with the lowest likelihood of failure. Results are given in percentages of the number of cases falling within each confidence interval (shown in parentheses).

	Φ(passer,receiver)						
	(success predictions)			(failure predictions)			
	.8–.9	.7–.8	.6–.7	-.6–(-.7)	-.7–(-.8)	-.8–(-.9)	Total
(Number)	(1050)	(3485)	(185)	(34)	(3)	(39)	(5000)
Success (%)	**79**	63	58	44	33	13	65
Failure (%)	15	29	31	53	67	79	26
Miss (%)	5	8	10	3	0	8	8

classified as successes with confidence between .7 and .8, with another large portion classified as successes with confidence between .8 and .9. Overall, the success rate of 65% is much better than the 51% success rate obtained when a receiver is chosen randomly. However, this result is obtained under a condition of forced passing: the passer is *required* to pass the ball during all trials. In a game situation the passer would be given the option to dribble or shoot instead. Notice that if the passer wants to be fairly sure of success, it could pass only when the DT predicted success with confidence greater than .8. The resulting 79% success rate approaches the limit imposed by the success rate of the ball-interception skill. When the testing is repeated with no opponents to intercept the ball, the success rate is 86%.

With all the different features describing each training example, it is not obvious how to construct an analytic heuristic for the passer to use when choosing a receiver. For comparison purposes, we defined a heuristic by which the passer always passes to the closest of the three teammates.

Over 5000 trials, the closest teammate heuristic produces a success rate of 64%. Although this number compares favorably with the overall DT success rate, it is significantly lower than the 79% success rate the passer can achieve with the DT when given the option of not passing. Furthermore, the closest teammate heuristic gives no way of estimating the likelihood that a pass will succeed. It simply postulates that given a choice, the passer should pass to the closest teammate. Since the likelihood estimation is the true goal of our learning in this section, there is a clear advantage to using the DT. As shown in Section 6.3, when deciding whether to pass, dribble, or shoot, the knowledge of whether or not a given pass is likely to succeed is extremely useful.

Summary

In this section, I demonstrated that a higher-level decision can be built upon the low-level skill learned in Chapter 5. Using a DT, our agents learn to judge the likelihood that a pass to a given receiver will be successfully received. This judgment represents the second layer in our layered learning implementation.

Before moving on to the third layer in Chapter 7, I first present some experiments that demonstrate the effectiveness of the learned ball-interception and pass-evaluation capabilities in game situations. Since they are both trained and tested off-line in limited types of situations, their applicability to more realistic scenarios has not yet been established. Section 6.2 presents the initial verification that encourages us to proceed. Section 6.3 presents extensive results demonstrating the utility of the learned behaviors in full game situations.

6.2 Using the Learned Behaviors

Once able to judge the likelihood that a pass will succeed, a human or simulated soccer player is ready to start making decisions in game-like situations. When considering what to do with the ball, the player can pass to a strategically positioned teammate, dribble, or shoot. To verify that the second level of our layered learning implementation can be incorporated into game-like situations, we implemented a play sequence that uses the passing decision described in Section 6.1.

In Figure 6.7 which illustrates the play sequence, the teammates executing the play sequence are shown as white circles and labeled A-G; opponents are shown as black circles. The play sequence is as follows:

- Player A starts with the ball and dribbles towards the opponent's goal.
- When it approaches within 15 of an opponent, it stops dribbling and prepares to pass to one of the two closest teammates: players B and C.
- In accordance with the protocol laid out in Table 6.1, it announces its intention to pass and gets responses from the two nearest players. It then uses the DT to decide which teammate is more likely to successfully receive the pass. In Figure 6.7, player A passes to teammate B ($\Phi(A,B) > \Phi(A,C)$).
- Player B and the adjacent opponent then both try to intercept the ball using the trained ball-interception skill. If the opponent gets the ball, it kicks it back towards the left goal and the play starts over. However, if player B gets the ball, it immediately kicks the ball to player D (if player A had passed to player C,

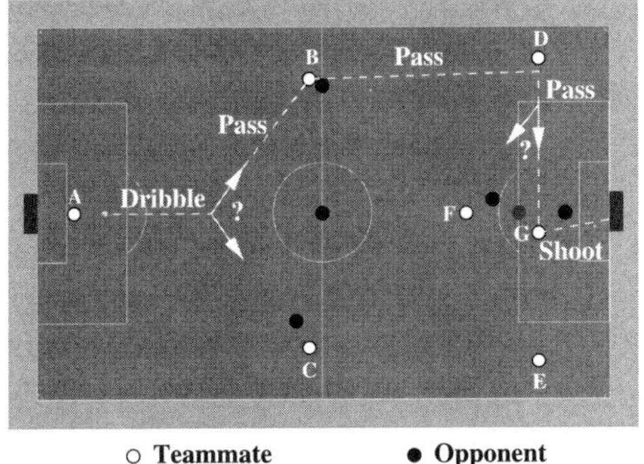

Figure 6.7
An illustration of the implemented play sequence. Players are emphasized for improved visibility. Teammates are labeled A–G. Every player uses at least one of the two learned behaviors: ball interception and pass evaluation.

the ball would have been sent to player E and the play would have continued symmetrically).

- Since player D is not covered, it can easily collect the ball and begin dribbling towards the goal. Using the same behavior as player A, player D stops dribbling when it approaches within 15 of a defender and chooses between passing to teammates F and G. Again, it uses the trained DT.

- If player F or G is able to get to the ball before the opponents, it immediately shoots towards the goal.

We ran this play sequence several times in order to verify that the learned behaviors are both robust and reliable. Since the opponents are all equipped with the same ball-interception skill as the receivers, the opponents are sometimes able to break up the play. However, the fact that the attacking team can sometimes successfully string together three passes and a shot on goal when using the learned behaviors demonstrates that these behaviors are appropriate for game-like situations.

Indeed, in the following section, the learned behaviors are incorporated into a full team of soccer-playing agents. The power of the learned pass evaluation is tested by comparing teams that use it against teams that do not.

6.3 Scaling up to Full Games

As presented in Chapter 5 and above, the ball-interception and pass-evaluation behaviors are both trained and tested in limited, artificial scenarios which do not reflect the full range of game situations. In this section I extend these basic learned behaviors into a full multiagent behavior that is capable of controlling agents throughout an entire game (Stone and Veloso, 1998e). This multiagent behavior is designed for the purposes of testing: it is not the same as the CMUnited-98 behavior specification laid out in Section 3.5.

Since the two learned behaviors defined thus far only apply when a player is in the vicinity of the ball, the player needs to have some other mechanism for acting when it does not have the ball. In addition, when it *does* have the ball, it must decide *when* to pass it: in some cases it may have enough time to execute the ideal pass; however, in other cases it may have to release the ball immediately in order to avoid losing it to an opponent player.

This section is organized as follows. The first subsection defines the mechanism by which the player with the ball chooses its action, either with the aid of the learned DT or without. In the next subsection, I explain how our agents reason about the time available to execute a pass. The following subsection presents the full multiagent behavior including behavior specifications for occasions when the player does not have the ball: it demonstrates how an RCF can be incorporated into such a full behavior. The final subsection demonstrates the effectiveness of the learned pass-evaluation function in the context of full game situations via extensive empirical testing.

Receiver Choice Functions

Recall that the DT estimates the likelihood that a pass to a specific player will succeed. Thus, for an agent to use the DT in a game, the DT must be incorporated into a full *receiver choice function* (RCF). We define an RCF to be a function that determines what the agent should do when it has possession of the ball—when the ball is within `kickable_area` (see Section 2.2)—and it has the opportunity to choose a receiver to which to pass. The input and output of a receiver choice function are as follows.

Input. The input of an RCF is the agent's perception of the current state of the world. This perceived state includes both the agent's latest sensory perception and remembered past positions of currently unseen objects (see Section 3.2).

Output. The output of an RCF is an action from among the options *dribble,* *kick,* or *pass*, and a direction, either in terms of a player (i.e. towards teammate number 4) or in terms of a part of the field (i.e. towards the goal).

First, the RCF identifies a set of candidate receivers given the current world state. Then, the RCF selects a receiver or else indicates that the agent should dribble or kick the ball.

The set of candidate receivers is determined in part by the player's *position*, or role. Each player is assigned a particular position on the field, and the team remains in a constant formation (see Chapter 3). Throughout this section, the team being tested uses the 4-3-3 formation illustrated by the black team in Figure 6.8. The positions in this formation are a goaltender (G), a sweeper (S), three defenders—left (LD), center (CD), and right(RD)—three midfielders (LM, CM, and RM), and three forwards (LF, CF, and RF). The arrows emanating from the players indicate the positions to which each player considers passing when using the RCFs. The options are also apparent in Table 6.5. The position on the left of the field (LD, LM, and LF) consider symmetrical options to their counterparts on the right of the field. The goaltender (G) has the same options as the sweeper (S).

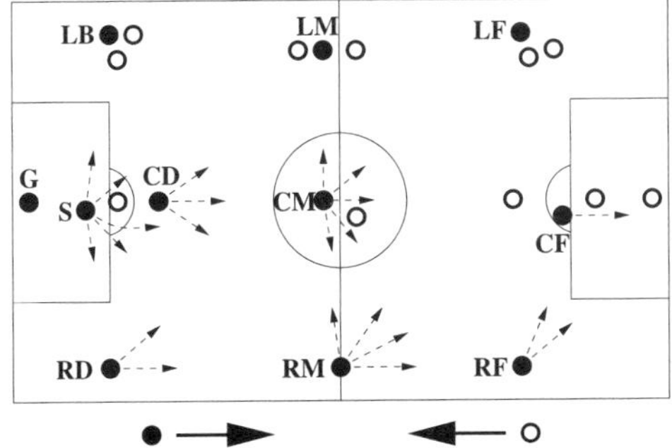

Figure 6.8
Player positions in the 4-3-3 formation used by the behaviors in this section. The black team, moving from left to right, has a goaltender (G), a sweeper (S), three defenders—left (LD), center (CD) right(RD)—three midfielders (LM, CM, and RM), and three forwards (LF, CF, and RF). The arrows emanating from the players indicate the positions to which each player considers passing when using the RCFs. The players on the left of the field (top of the diagram) consider symmetrical options to their counterparts on the right of the field. The goaltender has the same options as the sweeper. The white team has the same positions as the black, except that it has no players on its left side of the field, but rather two in each position on its right.

When a player is near its default position, it periodically announces its position to teammates; when a player leaves its position to chase the ball, it announces this fact and is no longer considered "in position." The agents determine which players are in which positions by listening to their teammates' announcements.

Notice that Figure 6.8 is the same as Figure 3.7, except that an opposing team is also depicted. The white team has the same positions as the black, except that it has no players on its left side of the field. Instead, it has two players in each position on the right side of the field.

Table 6.4 defines three RCFs, one of which uses the DT; the others are defined for the purposes of comparison.

• The PRW—*prefer right wing*—RCF uses a fixed ordering on the candidate receivers for each of the positions on the field. In general, defenders prefer to pass to the wings rather than forward; midfielders prefer to pass forward rather than sideways; and forwards tend to shoot. All players in the center of the field, as indicated by the name, prefer passing to the right rather than passing to the left. The ordered preference lists D_r of the different positions r are specified in Table 6.5. The RCF simply returns the most preferable candidate receiver according to this fixed ordering. Again, if no receivers are eligible, the RCF returns "dribble" or "kick." This RCF was our initial hand-coded behavior for use in games (at Pre-RoboCup-96).

• The RAND—*random*—RCF is the same as the PRW RCF except that it chooses randomly from among all candidate receivers.

• As suggested by its name, the DT—*decision tree*—RCF uses the DT described in Section 6.1 to choose from among the candidate receivers. In particular, as long as the DT predicts a pass to at least one candidate would be successful, the DT RCF indicates that the passer should pass to the teammate with the highest success confidence, breaking ties randomly. If the DT does not predict that any pass would succeed, the RCF specifies that the agent with the ball should dribble or kick the ball forwards (towards the opponent goal or towards one of the forward corners).

Reasoning about Action Execution Time

In the experiments reported in this chapter, the agents are not equipped with the turnball behavior described in Appendix B (Section B.1). Thus, when a player is between the ball and the teammate to which it wants to pass, it must

Table 6.4
Specification of three RCFs: PRW, RAND, and DT.

Let agent $\alpha \in A$ have the ball at time t and be using the RCF. Assume agent α is in position (role) $\rho \in R$ (recall from Chapter 3 that A is the set of agents and R is the set of roles in the team's current formation). First, the RCF determines the set of candidate receivers $C_{\alpha,t} \subseteq A$. Each position $r \in R$ has a set of candidate receiver roles $C_r \subseteq R$, as indicated in Figure 6.8. For example, $C_{\mathrm{CM}} = \{\mathrm{LM,RM,LF,CF,RF}\}$. At time t, α's mapping from agents $A \mapsto R$ specifies which agent is playing which position. Let $a_{r,t}$ be the agent playing position r at time t.

1. Start by setting $C_{\alpha,t} = \{a_{r,t} | r \in C_\rho\}$.
2. Any potential receiver that is too close (closer than d_{min}) or too far away (farther than d_{max}) according to α's world state at time t is eliminated from consideration: set $C_{\alpha,t} = \{a \in C_{\alpha,t} | d_{min} \leq \mathrm{dist}(\alpha, a) \leq d_{max}\}$. We use $d_{min} = 10$ and $d_{max} = 40$.
3. Any player that is out of position (because it was chasing the ball) is eliminated from consideration. Let $A' \subseteq A$ be the set of agents that are currently away from their home positions as determined by the periodic announcements from all teammates. For instance, these agents might be chasing the ball. Set $C_{\alpha,t} = C_{\alpha,t} - A'$.
4. **IF** $\exists i \in$ opponents such that $\mathrm{dist}(\alpha, i) \leq d_{min}$ **THEN** let $C' \subseteq C_{\alpha,t}$ be the set of agents to which α cannot kick the ball directly without the ball hitting α: $C' = \{a \in C_{\alpha,t} | (|\mathrm{ang}(\alpha, a) - \mathrm{ang}(\alpha, \mathtt{ball})|) > c_{ang}\}$. We use $c_{ang} = 130$. Set $C_{\alpha,t} = C_{\alpha,t} - C'$.

After having determined the set of candidate receivers $C_{\alpha,t}$, the RCF specifies which candidate receiver, if any, should receive the pass.

5. **IF** $C_{\alpha,t} = \emptyset$ **THEN**
   - **IF** $\exists i \in$ opponents such that $\mathrm{dist}(\alpha, i) \leq d_{min}$, **THEN** return *kick* to the opponent's goal.
   - **ELSE** return *dribble* to the opponent's goal.
6. **ELSE** ($C_{\alpha,t} \neq \emptyset$) **THEN** pass according to which RCF is being used:

   PRW(*Prefer Right Wing*): Use a fixed ordering on the receivers $D_\rho \subseteq R = (d_1, d_2, \ldots)$ as specified in Table 6.5. Return *pass* to $c \in C_{\alpha,t}$ such that $c = a_{d_i,t} \wedge \forall a_{d_j,t} \in C_{\alpha,t}, j \geq i$.

   RAND(*Random*): Choose randomly among the receivers. Return *pass* to some $c \in C_{\alpha,t}$.

   DT(*Decision Tree*): Set $C_{\alpha,t} = \{a \in C_{\alpha,t} | \Phi(\alpha, a) > 0\}$.
   IF $C_{\alpha,t} = \emptyset$ **THEN** return *kick* or *dribble* as in Step 5.
   ELSE return *pass* to $c \in C_{\alpha,t}$ such that $\forall b \in C_{\alpha,t}, \Phi(\alpha, c) > \Phi(\alpha, b)$.

move out of the ball's path before passing, which empirically takes between 5 and 15 simulator cycles. If there is an opponent in the vicinity, it may be able to steal the ball in that time.

Therefore, the RCF definition (Table 6.4) includes reasoning about the available time to execute an action. In particular, if there is an opponent within d_{min}, there is a danger of losing the ball before being able to pass or shoot it. In this situation, it is to the passer's advantage to get rid of the ball as quickly as possible.

This priority is manifested in the RCFs in two ways:

• In Step 4 of Table 6.4, when there is an opponent within d_{min}, the RCFs only consider passing to players to whom the agent can pass immediately. As mentioned above, this concept is not purely reactive: the positions of opponents that are outside an agent's field of view are remembered.

• In Step 5, when an opponent is within d_{min}, the agent kicks the ball away (or shoots) rather than dribbling. The point of dribbling the ball (kicking the ball a small amount in a certain direction and staying with it) is to keep the ball for a little longer until a good pass becomes available or until the player is in a good position to shoot. However, if there is an opponent nearby, dribbling often allows the opponent time to get to the ball. In this situation, as indicated in Step 5 of Table 6.4, the RCF causes the player to kick the ball forward (or shoot) rather than dribbling.

Thus, the RCF considers whether there is enough time to execute an action without an opponent stealing the ball. The ability to reason about how much time is available for action is an important component of the RCFs and contributes significantly to their success in game situations (see Section 6.3).

Incorporating the RCF in a Behavior

In Section 6.3, the method of using a DT as a part of an RCF is described in detail. However, the RCF is itself not a complete agent behavior: it only applies when the ball is within `kickable_area` of a the player. This subsection situates the RCF within a complete behavior that can then be used throughout

Table 6.5
The ordered preference lists of the positions in the 4-3-3 formation when using the PRW RCF. D_r is the preference list for position r. The positions are indicated as labeled in Figure 6.8. The CF position has no passing options: it always dribbles or shoots.

r	D_r
G	(RD,RM,LD,LM,CM)
S	(RD,RM,LD,LM,CM)
LD	(LM,LF,CM)
CD	(RM,LM,CM)
RD	(RM,RF,CM)
LM	(LF,CF,RF)
CM	(RM,RF,CF,LM,LF)
RM	(RF,CF,LF)
LF	(CF)
CF	—
RF	(CF)

the course of a game. Again, this behavior is not the same as the CMUnited-98 implementation presented in Section 3.5: it is a preliminary version of the full-fledged CMUnited-98 implementation. The complete behavior is laid out in Table 6.6.

Table 6.6
The complete behavior used by the players in game situations to test the different RCFs.

Let α be the agent using this behavior, and ball-dist = dist(α,`ball`).

1. **IF** confidence in the ball's location (see Section 3.5) $< .5$ **THEN** face the ball.
2. **IF** ball-dist $\leq d_{chase}$ or $\forall a \in$ teammates, ball-dist $\leq$ dist(a,`ball`) **THEN**:
   - **IF** ball-dist > `kickable_area` **THEN** move to the ball, using the trained NN when appropriate;
   - **ELSE** pass, dribble, or kick the ball as indicated by the RCF.
3. **ELSE**: (ball-dist $> d_{chase}$ and $\exists a \in$ teammates, ball-dist > dist(a,`ball`))
   - Move within α's home position using ball-dependent flexible positioning (see Section 3.5).

When using this behavior, the player's first priority (Step 1) is always to find the ball's location (only objects in front of the player are seen). If it does not know where the ball is, it turns until the ball is in view. When turning away from the ball, it remembers the ball's location for a short amount of time; however after about three seconds without seeing the ball, its confidence in the ball's location decays enough that it assumes that it no longer knows where the ball is (see Section 3.5).

Once the ball has been located, the agent can carry on with its behavior. As indicated in Step 2 of Table 6.6, the agent chases the ball when either of two conditions is met:

- When the ball is within d_{chase}, the agent always goes towards the ball. We set $d_{chase} = 10$.
- The agent chases the ball whenever it thinks that it is the closest team-member to the ball.

In the second case, notice that the agent may not *actually* be the closest player to the ball if some of its teammates are too far away to see and if they have not announced their positions recently. However, if a player mistakenly thinks that it is the closest player, it will get part of the way to the ball, notice that another teammate is closer, and then turn back to its position.

As required for use of the DT, every player is equipped with the trained neural network (see Chapter 5) which can be used to help intercept the ball. Whenever the ball is within `kickable_area`, the agent uses its RCF to decide whether to dribble, kick, or pass, and to where. Every team member uses the same RCF.

Finally, as described in Section 6.3, each player is assigned a particular position on the field. Unless chasing the ball, the agent goes to its position, moving around within the position's home range using ball-dependent flexible positioning (Step 3).

Results

In this subsection I present the results of empirically testing how the behaviors specified in Section 6.3 perform. Since the behaviors differ only in their RCFs, I refer below to, for example, "the complete behavior using the DT RCF" simply as "the DT RCF." Also presented are empirical results verifying the advantage of reasoning about action-execution time.

In order to test the different RCFs, we created a team formation that emphasizes the advantage of passing to some teammates over others. When both teams use the standard 4-3-3 formation (that of the black team in Figure 6.8), every player is covered by one opponent. However, this situation is an artificial artifact of using the ball-dependent player-positioning algorithm. In reality, the players—using SPAR (Section 3.5)—have the ability to move to open positions on the field. For the purposes of these experiments we use a simpler behavior than the full CMUnited-98 implementation: the players only use ball-dependent positioning. In order to reflect the fact that some players are typically more open than others, we test the RCFs against the OPR—*only play right*—formation which is illustrated by the white team in Figure 6.8. We also use the symmetrical OPL—*only play left*—formation for testing. These behaviors are specified in Table 6.7.

Table 6.7
OPR and OPL behavior specifications.

- The opponent behaviors are exactly the same as the RAND behavior except that the players are assigned to different positions:

OPR(*only play right*): As illustrated by the white team in Figure 6.8, two players are at each position on the right side of the field, with no players on the left side of the field.

OPL(*only play left*): Same as above, except all the players are on the left side of the field.

During testing, each run consists of 34 five-minute games between a pair of teams. We tabulate the cumulative score both in total goals and in games won (ties are not broken) as shown in Table 6.8. Graphs record the *differences* in cumulative goals scored (Figure 6.9) and games won (Figure 6.10) as the runs progress.

Table 6.8
The results of using different RCFs. Results are cumulative over 34 five-minute games: ties are not broken. Unless otherwise indicated, the opponent—whose score always appears second—uses the OPR formation.

RCF (vs. OPR)	Games (W – L)	Overall Score
DT	19 – 9	135 – 97
PRW	11 – 14	104 – 105
PRW (vs. OPL)	8 – 16	114 – 128
RAND	14 – 12	115 – 111

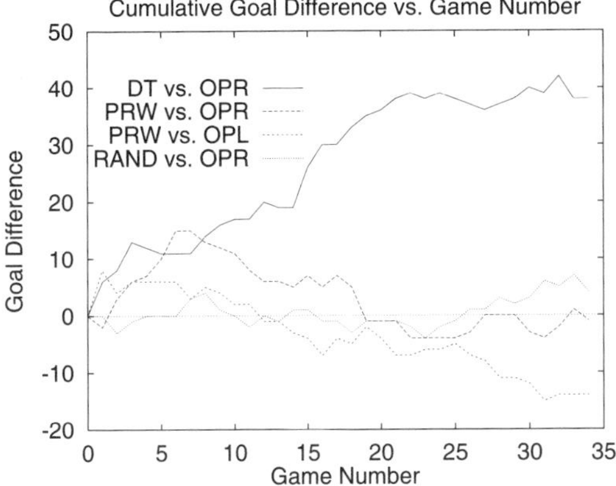

Figure 6.9
The differences in cumulative goals as the runs progress.

In order to test the effectiveness of the DT RCF, we compared its performance against the performance of the PRW and RAND RCFs when facing the same opponent: OPR. While the DT and RAND RCFs are symmetrical in their decision making, the PRW RCF gives preference to one side of the field and therefore has an advantage against the OPR strategy. Thus we also include the

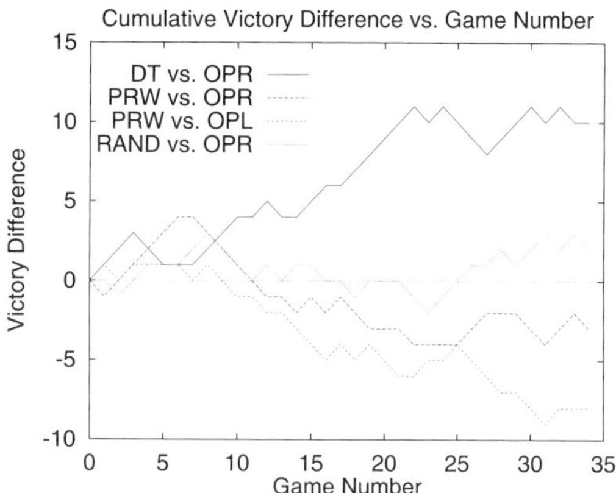

Figure 6.10
The differences in cumulative games won as the runs progress.

results of the PRW RCF when it faces the symmetrical opponent: OPL. From Table 6.8 and Figures 6.9 and 6.10 it is apparent that the DT RCF is an effective method of decision making in this domain.

In order to test the effectiveness of the reasoning about action-execution time, we compare the performance of the standard DT RCF against that of the same RCF with the assumption that there is *never* an opponent within d_{min} ("No-rush DT"): even if there is, the RCF ignores it. This assumption affects Steps 4 and 5 of the RCF specification in Table 6.4 as described in the subsection entitled "Reasoning about Action Execution Time." Both RCFs are played against the OPR behavior. As apparent from Table 6.9, the reasoning about action-execution time makes a significant difference.

Table 6.9
The effect of reasoning about action-execution time within an RCF. No-rush DT is the same RCF as the standard DT RCF except that there is no reasoning about action-execution time. The Standard DT RCF performs significantly better.

RCF (vs. OPR)	Games (W – L)	Overall Score
Standard DT	19 – 9	135 – 97
No-rush DT	13 – 16	91 – 108

Summary

This section demonstrated that, even though trained in a limited, artificial scenario, the learned pass-evaluation capability trained in Section 6.1 generalizes successfully to full games. The players can successfully use it to choose which pass to make from among several options. Combined with some basic reasoning about the action-execution times of different options—necessitated by the real-time nature of this domain—the DT-based control function outperforms both random and hand-coded alternatives. The success of this multiagent behavior encouraged us to incorporate it into a *learned* full team behavior as presented in Chapter 7.

6.4 Discussion

In this section I discuss two aspects of the learned pass-evaluation capability. First, I discuss how it fits within the layered learning context. Then I discuss the use of the decision tree confidence factors for agent control.

Pass Evaluation within Layered Learning

The pass-evaluation capability described in this chapter is the second layer, L_2, of our robotic soccer layered learning implementation:

- $\vec{F_2}$ = a set of 174 continuous and ordinal features enumerated in Table 6.2.
- $O_2 = [-1, 1]$ as determined by the classification and confidence factor of a potential pass as per the function Φ.
- T_2 = 5000 training examples gathered according to the training procedure laid out in Table 6.1. *The training procedure uses h_1, the trained ball-interception skill.*
- M_2 = C4.5 with all of the default parameters.
- h_2 = the trained pass-evaluating decision tree shown in Figure 6.6.

The choice and implementation of the pass evaluation capability follow the principles of layered learning as laid out in Section 4.1:

- It is easier to gather data and to exploit it for training a pass-evaluation function than it is to code such a function by hand. Especially since the question of whether or not a pass will succeed depends on the abilities of players to receive the ball, there is no obvious heuristic that could be used.

• We choose the learning method—the C4.5 decision tree training algorithm—based on the task characteristics. We identify 174 features with potential predictive power for pass evaluation, many of which are frequently unknown. Therefore, the abilities of C4.5 to identify the most relevant features and to handle missing feature values are very important. In addition, the fact that C4.5 provides confidence factors along with its predictions turns out to be very useful.

• The previous learned layer—ball-interception—is used as part of the training behavior: both the intended receiver and all of the opponents use the trained neural network when trying to intercept the moving ball.

Just as this multiagent behavior builds upon the interception skill, higher-level learned behaviors can be built upon the knowledge of when a pass will succeed. Such knowledge can contribute to the decision of to which player to pass or of whether to pass, dribble, or shoot.

The behavior defined in Section 6.3 uses the DT as a part of a hand-coded high-level multiagent behavior. However, the decision function is highly constrained by the limited number of passing options allowed to each player. A behavior that *learns* completely how to map the classifications and confidence factors of the DT to passing/dribbling/shooting decisions may perform better.

Indeed, in Chapter 7, such a learned behavior is created. It uses the learned pass-evaluation function as the input representation to a reinforcement learning algorithm. The result is a completely learned RCF with no limitations on the passing options: players can pass backwards as well as forwards.

Confidence Factors for Agent Control

Although Decision Trees are widely used for classification tasks, they are typically not used for agent control. Nevertheless, the DT RCF uses the confidence factors associated with classifications to differentiate between pass options at a fine-grained level. Rather than just classifying each option as a likely success or likely failure, the RCFs choose the option with the highest confidence of being a success.

The experiments reported Section 6.3 indicate that the confidence factors provided by standard DT software can be used for effective agent control. To my knowledge, this is the first successful use of DT classification confidence factors for agent control. As DT confidence factors are effective tools in this domain, they are potentially useful for agent control in general.

6.5 Related Work

The DT RCF is not the only instance of using tree-like structures for agent control. Specifically, in a multiagent planning context, operator success probabilities have been stored in COBWEB trees (Garland and Alterman, 1996). This multiagent, case-based planning system derives operator success probabilities from the results of past operator executions and uses the success probabilities to guide an agent's future planning choices. If an operator fails to achieve its intended effect due to the non-cooperation of other agents, an agent can adapt by instead using an operator (or operators) that allows it to achieve its goal on its own.

While the COBWEB tree is built with the explicit aim of estimating the success probability of an operator, the DT trained in this chapter was originally intended simply to classify the results of passes into three discrete classes. This classification task is the type of task that DT training algorithms such as C4.5 are typically used for. The confidence factors embedded in the C4.5 algorithm have not been used for control tasks before.

7 Learning a Team Behavior

This chapter serves a dual purpose. It presents the third and final implemented learned layer in our simulated robotic soccer layered learning implementation, and it simultaneously introduces a separate contribution of this book, namely the team-partitioned, opaque-transition reinforcement learning (TPOT-RL) algorithm (Stone and Veloso, 1999d). TPOT-RL is a new machine learning method used to train collaborative and adversarial team behaviors. In the robotic soccer context, we use TPOT-RL to learn pass selection, taking advantage of the learned pass-evaluation capability described in Chapter 6 to construct the input representation for learning.

This chapter is organized as follows. In Section 7.1, I introduce the new collaborative and adversarial robotic soccer behavior and motivate the need for a new multiagent learning algorithm in order to train it. Section 7.2 formalizes the TPOT-RL algorithm in domain-independent terms and Section 7.3 applies it to simulated robotic soccer with extensive empirical testing. In Section 7.4, TPOT-RL is applied in a different multiagent domain—network routing—in order to verify the generality of the new algorithm. Sections 7.5 and 7.6 are devoted to discussion and related work respectively.

7.1 Motivation

In this section, I motivate the need for a new RL algorithm in order to continue our layered learning implementation in the simulated robotic soccer domain. I do so by first describing the task to be learned; then showing that existing RL algorithms cannot be used for this task. I formally define the TPOT-RL algorithm in Section 7.2.

Pass Selection

Once young soccer players have learned how to judge whether a particular pass will succeed, they are ready to learn how to act strategically as part of a team. Based on experience, they can start to estimate the long-term effects of their actions within the context of a game in which the true goal is to help one's team to beat the opponents. Similarly, our simulated robotic soccer agents cooperate to achieve the team's goal by learning pass selection, a team behavior. Good pass selection requires an understanding of the long-term effects of local decisions given the behaviors and abilities of teammates and opponents.

In Section 6.3, I presented a full team behavior based upon the first two learned layers of our layered learning implementation; i.e. ball interception and pass evaluation. Specifically, the learned pass evaluation function was incorporated into the DT (decision tree) receiver choice function (RCF), that determines to which teammate an agent should pass when it has possession of the ball. In the DT RCF, the learned pass-evaluation capability is used in a heuristic, hand-coded function: the potential receivers are limited to those that are at least as close to the opponent's goal as the agent with the ball (C_r), and the agent always passes the ball to the potential receiver to which it can pass with the highest confidence of success according to the trained DT (maximum Φ(passer,receiver)).

While the DT RCF was useful for verifying that the pass-evaluation capability can be used in full-game situations, in reality the choice of where to pass is much more complicated than allowed for by the DT RCF. For one thing, there may be situations in which the best pass is to a receiver that is farther away from the goal than the passer. For another, the receiver that is most likely to successfully *receive* the pass may not be the one that will subsequently act most favorably for the team.

Figure 7.1 illustrates a situation in which the player with the ball, agent b, may want to pass backwards (to the left in the figure). Agent b and its teammates are attacking the right goal. The white arrows emanating from the ball indicate potential passes and their labels indicate the predictions by the DT as to whether or not they will succeed: "S" for success and "F" for failure. In this situation, the DT predicts that all three possible forward passes, to teammates f, g, and h, will fail. However, there are two predicted-successful backwards passes to teammates c and d. If agent b's goal is simply to complete a pass to a teammate, it should clearly pass to teammate c or d.

However, in the context of the team's high-level task of kicking the ball into the opponent's goal, the choice is not so clear:

- Suppose that the opponents are very bad at intercepting the ball. Then the pass to teammate g may be best for the team. Recall that the decision tree is trained off-line in an artificial situation and does not adjust its predictions based on the current opponent. Thus despite the DT's prediction, teammate g may be able to receive the pass. Since it is closest to opponent's goal, the team might be best off if agent b passes *forwards* to teammate g.
- Suppose instead that the opponents are good at intercepting the ball but that teammate c has a poor decision-making policy. Despite the appearance that its

best option would be to pass to teammate f, agent c instead decides to pass to teammate e, which would likely result in the opponents stealing the ball. Again, the team might be better off if agent b passes *forwards* to teammate f, g, or h despite the DT's prediction.

• On the other hand, suppose that the opponents are good at intercepting the ball and that teammate c has a good decision-making policy: it would pass to teammate f after receiving the ball. Then the team will probably be best off in the long run if agent b passes passes *backwards*, away from the goal, to teammate c.

In short, when learning an RCF, the local pass-evaluation information, while helpful, is not enough on which to base a decision. The agent needs to learn *strategic* information which depends on the behaviors of teammates and opponents and which can only be measured by its team's long-term success at achieving its collective goal against an opponent team in a real game. Therefore, as opposed to both lower-level learned behaviors (ball interception and pass evaluation), the pass-selection behavior must be trained *on-line* in a game situation against a particular opponent.

When choosing an ML method for learning an RCF, there are five other task characteristics that are important.

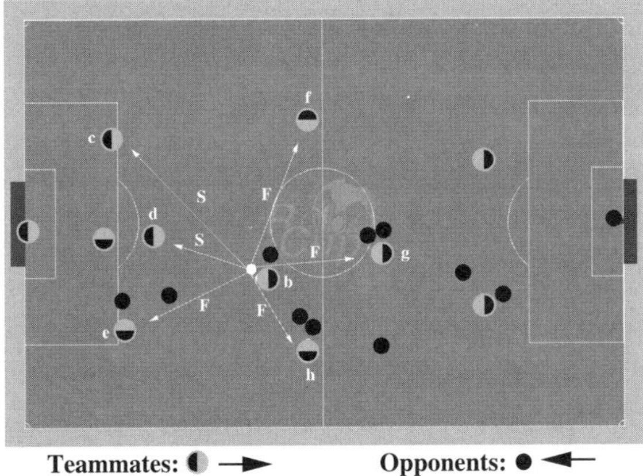

Figure 7.1
An example of when it might be useful to pass backwards. The white arrows emanating from the ball indicate potential passes and their labels indicate predictions by the trained DT as to whether or not they will succeed: "S" for success and "F" for failure. The teammates are attacking the right goal; the opponents, the left.

• The pass-selection decision depends on a *huge amount of information*, including the agent's current location on the field, the current locations of all the teammates and opponents, the teammates' abilities to receive a pass, the opponents' abilities to intercept passes, teammates' subsequent decision-making capabilities, and the possibly-changing opponents' strategies. As presented in Section 2.2, the simulated robotic soccer domain has more than 10^{198} states.

• The agents must learn with *limited training examples*. When running with two full teams of agents, the soccer server is computationally intensive. To run at full speed, the server and the clients must be distributed across at least two 266 MHz computers. And in real games, empirically each agent gets the ball, and therefore the opportunity to collect a training example, about once a minute on average. With additional computational power, the simulation can be sped up somewhat. But unlike most simulations, and more like real robotic domains, training data is relatively difficult and time-consuming to collect.

• The merit of a particular decision can only be measured by the *long-term* performance of the team as a whole and thus only becomes clear over time.

• Since the expected reward for taking a particular action depends on teammates' behaviors, this expected reward changes as teammates simultaneously learn to improve their behaviors. In ML terms, the task to be learned is said to be a *shifting concept*.

• As the teammates each stay in a different geographical region of the field (their positions within the team formation—see Chapter 3), the learning task is *partitioned among the teammates*: each agent only learns how to act when located in a specific part of the field.

In addition to the above task characteristics, recall one important domain characteristic from the presentation of simulated robotic soccer in Chapter 2 that has a bearing on the choice of ML algorithm. In simulated robotic soccer there are *opaque transitions*: when an agent takes an action (passes the ball), the resulting state transition as well as the subsequent actions taken by other agents—both teammates and adversaries—and their resulting state transitions are often unknown.

In summary, the characteristics of an ML algorithm needed for learning pass selection are:

1. on-line;
2. capable of dealing with a large state space despite limited training;
3. capable of learning based on long-term, delayed reward;

4. capable of dealing with shifting concepts;
5. works in a team-partitioned scenario; and
6. capable of dealing with opaque transitions.

Reinforcement Learning for Pass Selection

Although no previously existing ML algorithm has all of the above characteristics, some of the ones that come closest are reinforcement learning (RL) algorithms. RL is an effective paradigm for training an agent to act in its environment in pursuit of a goal. RL techniques rely on the premise that an agent's action *policy* affects its overall reward over time. A policy is defined as an agent's mapping from the state it is in to the action it will take. In robotic soccer, an RCF can be thought of as a policy over the set of states in which an agent has possession of the ball. Throughout this chapter, the RCF is the only part of the agents' policies being learned or otherwise varied in any way.

As surveyed in (Kaelbling et al., 1996), standard RL algorithms are on-line learning algorithms that can learn control policies for Markov decision tasks based on long-term, delayed reward. Whether model-based (e.g. prioritized sweeping (Moore and Atkeson, 1993)) or model-free (e.g. TD(λ) (Sutton, 1988) and Q-learning (Watkins, 1989)), these RL techniques rely on a single agent being able to observe the environmental state transitions in order to propagate reward back from states that generate reward to previous states. In addition, these techniques require time that is polynomial in the number of states. This "curse of dimensionality" typically limits them to relatively small state spaces with abundant training opportunities[1].

In contrast, motivated by the presentation in the previous subsection, we restrict our attention to domains with the following characteristics:

- There are multiple agents organized in a team: they have a common long-term goal.
- There are opaque state transitions: agents cannot observe state transitions when they or other agents act and therefore cannot build a model of transitions in the domain.
- There are too many states and/or not enough training examples for traditional RL techniques to work.

---

1 One notable exception is TD-Gammon (Tesauro, 1994), which achieved champion status in backgammon using RL. It dealt successfully with backgammon's large state space by introducing hand-crafted features and allowing for an extremely large amount of training.

• The target concept can change during the course of learning, for example as a result of other agents in the environment changing their policies. Thus, the Markov property, that the effect of an action depends only on the current state of the world, does not hold.

• There is long-range reward available: agents can notice the long-term effects of their actions by directly observing the environment.

• There are *action-dependent features* available. By "action-dependent," we mean that the feature value depends both on the current world state *and* the action being considered: in a given state, each possible action has its own action-dependent classification.

As opposed to the ultimate learning goal of determining the long-term reward to be expected when executing an action, action-dependent features classify the predicted short-term effects of actions based on local state information.

In order to enable teams of agents to learn in such domains, we introduce team-partitioned, opaque-transition reinforcement learning (TPOT-RL). Like previous RL methods, TPOT-RL allows agents to learn on-line and from delayed rewards. TPOT-RL extends RL to work in domains with the above characteristics.

7.2 TPOT-RL

This section presents TPOT-RL in detail. Like Q-learning, TPOT-RL learns a *value function* that maps state-action pairs to expected rewards. TPOT-RL includes three main adaptations to the standard RL paradigm:

• The value function is partitioned among the team, with each agent only learning for states from which it can act. All agents are trained simultaneously with a gradually decreasing exploration rate and an increasing exploitation rate.

• Action-dependent features are used to produce an aggressively generalized feature space, which is used as the input representation for learning. While other RL approaches aggregate states to reduce the size of the learning task (e.g. (McCallum, 1996)), action-dependent features enable the creation of a particularly small but informative feature space for learning.

• Long-term, discounted rewards are gathered directly from the rewarding states in the environment rather than being propagated back through intermediate states, as the state-transition probabilities are not known. While other RL approaches have learned based on reward from eventual rewarding states (e.g. TD(1) (Sutton, 1988)), none has been applied in a multiagent scenario and they generally do not discount reward based on the time between an action and the eventual reward.

Formally, a policy is a mapping from a state space S to an action space A such that the agent using that policy executes action a whenever in state s. At the coarsest level, when in state s, an agent compares the expected, long-term rewards for taking each action $a \in A$ and chooses an action based on these expected rewards. These expected rewards are learned through experience.

Designed to work in real-world domains with far too many states to handle individually, TPOT-RL exploits action-dependent features to create a small feature space V. V is used as a component of the input representation of the learned value function $Q : V \times A \mapsto \mathbb{R}$.

In short, the policy's mapping from S to A in TPOT-RL can be thought of as a 3-step process:

State generalization: The state s is generalized to a feature vector v using the state generalization function $f : S \mapsto V$.

Value function learning: The feature vector v is used as an input to the learned value function $Q : V \times A \mapsto \mathbb{R}$, which estimates the expected reward for taking each possible action.

Action selection: An action a is chosen for execution and its long-term, observed reward is used to further update Q.

While these steps are common in other RL paradigms, each step has unique characteristics in TPOT-RL. State generalization, value function learning, and action selection in TPOT-RL are further specified in the remainder of this section.

State Generalization

$f : S \mapsto V$ maps the current state of the world, s, to the feature vector used for learning, v. f relies on a unique approach to constructing V. Rather than discretizing the various dimensions of S, it uses an *action-dependent* feature function.

The action-dependent feature function

$$e : S \times A \mapsto U$$

evaluates each possible action $a_i \in A$ based on s. U is a discrete set of features reflecting expected short-term effects of actions. Unlike Q, e does not produce the expected long-term reward of taking an action; rather, it classifies the likely short-term effects of the action. For example, since state transition probabilities are unknown, e might predict the transition to be caused by executing action a_i based on s.

In the multiagent scenario, other than one output of e for each action, the feature space V also involves one coarse component that partitions the state space S among the agents. The partition function

$$P : S \mapsto M$$

breaks the state space into $|M|$ disjoint partitions to be divided among the teammates, with $|M| \geq m$ where m is the number of agents in the team. In particular, if the set of possible actions in state s is $A = \{a_0, a_1, \ldots, a_{n-1}\}$, then

$$\begin{aligned} f(s) &= \langle e(s, a_0), e(s, a_1), \ldots, e(s, a_{n-1}), P(s) \rangle, \text{ and so} \\ V &= U^{|A|} \times M. \end{aligned}$$

Thus, $|V| = |U|^{|A|} * |M|$. Since the goal of constructing V is to create a feature space that is smaller than the original state space, the ranges of the action-dependent feature function and partition function, U and M respectively, are ideally as small as they can be without abstracting away the useful information for learning.

This state generalization process reduces the complexity of the learning task by constructing a small feature space V which partitions S into $|M|$ regions. Each agent need learn how to act only within its own partition(s). Nevertheless, for large sets A, the feature space can still be too large for learning, especially with limited training examples. Our particular action-dependent formulation allows us to reduce the effective size of the feature space in the value-function-learning step. Choosing features for state generalization is generally a hard problem. While TPOT-RL does not specify the function e, our work illustrates effective choices of e.

Value Function Learning

As we have seen, TPOT-RL uses action-dependent features. When using action-dependent features, we can assume (heuristically) that the expected long-term reward for taking action a_i depends only on the feature value related to action a_i. That is,

$$Q(f(s), a_i) = Q(f(s'), a_i) \tag{7.1}$$

whenever $e(s, a_i) = e(s', a_i)$ and $P(s) = P(s')$. Recall that

$$\begin{aligned} f(s) &= \langle e(s, a_1), \ldots, e(s, a_{n-1}), P(s)\rangle \\ f(s') &= \langle e(s', a_1), \ldots, e(s', a_{n-1}), P(s')\rangle \end{aligned}$$

Another way of stating this same assumption is that $Q(f(s), a_i)$ depends upon $e(s, a_i)$ and is independent of $e(s, a_j)$ for all $j \neq i$.

Without this assumption, since there are $|A|$ actions possible for each element in V, the value function Q has $|V| * |A| = |U|^{|A|} * |M| * |A|$ independent values. Under this assumption, however, the Q-table has at most $|U|^1 * |M| * |A|$ entries: for each action possible from state s, only one of the $|A|$ action-dependent feature values $e(s, a_i)$ comprising $f(s)$ is relevant. Therefore, even with only a small number of training examples available, we can treat the value function Q as a lookup-table without the need for any complex function approximation. To be precise, Q stores one value for every possible combination of $a \in A$, $e(s, a) \in U$, and $P(s) \in M$.

For example, Table 7.1 shows the entire feature space for one agent's partition of the state space when $|U| = 3$ and $|A| = 2$. $U = \{u_0, u_1, u_2\}$, $A = \{a_0, a_1\}$. $q_{i,j}$ is the estimated value of taking action a_i when $e(s, a_i) = u_j$. Since this table is for a single agent, $P(s)$ remains constant.

There are $|U|^{|A|} = 3^2$ different entries in feature space with $|A| = 2$ Q-values for each entry: one for each possible action. $|U|^{|A|} * |M|$ is much smaller than the original state space for any realistic problem, but it can grow large quickly, particularly as $|A|$ increases. However, as emphasized by the right side of Table 7.1—which is simply a condensed representation of the left side—under the assumption described above, there are only $3 * 2$ independent Q-values to learn, reducing the number of free variables in the learning problem from 18 to 6, or by 67%, in this case.

The Q-values learned depend on the agent's past experiences in the domain. In particular, after taking an action a while in state s with $f(s) = v$, an agent receives reward r and uses it to update $Q(v, a)$ from its previous value $Q(v, a)$ as follows:

$$Q(v, a) = Q(v, a) + \alpha(r - Q(v, a)) \tag{7.2}$$

where α is the learning rate. Since state transitions are opaque, the agent

Table 7.1
A sample Q-table for a single agent when $|U| = 3$ and $|A| = 2$: $U = \{u_0, u_1, u_2\}$, $A = \{a_0, a_1\}$. $q_{i,j}$ is the estimated value of taking action a_i when $e(s, a_i) = u_j$. Since this table is for a single agent, $P(s)$ remains constant. The table on the right emphasizes that there are only 6 independent q values in the table on the left.

$e(s, a_0)$	$e(s, a_1)$	$Q(f(s), a_0)$	$Q(f(s), a_1)$
u_0	u_0	$q_{0,0}$	$q_{1,0}$
u_0	u_1	$q_{0,0}$	$q_{1,1}$
u_0	u_2	$q_{0,0}$	$q_{1,2}$
u_1	u_0	$q_{0,1}$	$q_{1,0}$
u_1	u_1	$q_{0,1}$	$q_{1,1}$
u_1	u_2	$q_{0,1}$	$q_{1,2}$
u_2	u_0	$q_{0,2}$	$q_{1,0}$
u_2	u_1	$q_{0,2}$	$q_{1,1}$
u_2	u_2	$q_{0,2}$	$q_{1,2}$

$\Longrightarrow$

$e(s, a_i)$	$Q(f(s), a_0)$	$Q(f(s), a_1)$
u_0	$q_{0,0}$	$q_{1,0}$
u_1	$q_{0,1}$	$q_{1,1}$
u_2	$q_{0,2}$	$q_{1,2}$

cannot use the dynamic programming (and Q-learning) approach of updating the value function based on the value of the state that results from executing action a. Instead, the reward r is derived from the observable environmental characteristics—those that are captured in S—over a maximum number of time steps t_{lim} after the action is taken. The reward function

$$R : S^{t_{lim}} \mapsto \mathbb{R}$$

returns a value at some time no further than t_{lim} in the future. The reward is discounted based on the amount of time between acting and receiving the reward. During that time, other teammates (or opponents, if any) can act in the environment and affect the action's outcome, but the agent may not be able to observe these actions. In practice, the range of R is $[-Q_{max}, Q_{max}]$ where Q_{max} is the reward for immediate goal achievement. In order to associate the eventual reward with the action it took, the agent must keep track of the last action taken a_i and the feature vector v at that time.

Notice from Equation 7.2 that in TPOT-RL, the updated action value depends only on the previously stored action value in the same state as opposed to chains of learned state values. That is, when updating $Q(v, a)$ TPOT-RL does not reference any $Q(v', a')$ such that $v \neq v'$ or $a \neq a'$. If the actual value of executing action a from state s with $f(s) = v$ changes, the agent can adjust by simply executing a in such a state several times: no other states-action pairs need to be updated first. Therefore, TPOT-RL is able to adopt relatively quickly to shifting concepts.

The reward function, including t_{lim} and Q_{max}, is domain-dependent. One possible type of reward function is based entirely upon reaching the ultimate goal. In this case, an agent charts the actual (long-term) results of its policy in the environment. However if goal achievement is infrequent, a reward function based on *intermediate reinforcement*, which provides feedback based on intermediate states towards the goal, may be needed.

Action Selection

As in all RL techniques, the issue of exploration vs. exploitation is important for TPOT-RL. Particularly since the target concept can shift due to teammates learning and changing their policies, or due to changes in policies of opponents (if any), it is important for agents to gather information about the value of actions that are currently considered sub-optimal by the value function. Any standard exploration heuristic, such as the randomized Boltzmann exploration strategy (Kaelbling et al., 1996), could be used.

Informative action-dependent features can be used to reduce the free variables in the learning task still further at the action-selection stage if the features themselves discriminate situations in which actions should not be used. For example, suppose we can define a set $W \subseteq U$ such that if $e(s, a) \notin W$, then a should not be considered as a potential action from state s.

Formally, consider $W \subseteq U$ and $B(s) \subseteq A$ with $B(s) = \{a \in A | e(s, a) \in W\}$. When in state s, the agent then chooses an action from $B(s)$ instead of from the entire action set A, either randomly when exploring or according to maximum Q-value when exploiting. In effect, W acts in TPOT-RL as an action filter which reduces the number of options under consideration at any given time. Again, any standard exploration heuristic can be used over the possible actions in $B(s)$. Of course, exploration at the filter level can also be achieved by dynamically adjusting W.

For example, Table 7.2, illustrates the effect of varying $|W|$. Notice that when $W \neq U$, it is possible that $B(s) = \emptyset$: $\forall a_i \in A, e(s, a_i) \notin W$. In this case, either a random action can be chosen, or rough Q-value estimates can be stored using sparse training data. This condition becomes rarer as $|A|$ increases. For example, with $|U| = 3$, $|W| = 1$, and $|A| = 2$ as in Table 7.2(b), 4/9 = 44.4% of feature vectors have no action that passes the W filter. However, with $|U| = 3$, $|W| = 1$, and $|A| = 8$ only 256/6561 = 3.9% of feature vectors have no action that passes the W filter. If $|U| = 3$, $|W| = 2$ and $|A| = 8$, only 1 of 6561 feature vectors fails to pass the filter. Thus using W to filter action selection can reduce the number of free variables in the learning problem

Table 7.2
The resulting Q-tables when $U = \{u_0, u_1, u_2\}$, $A = \{a_0, a_1\}$, and (a) $W = \{u_0, u_2\}$, or (b) $W = \{u_2\}$.

$e(s, a_0)$	$e(s, a_1)$	$Q(f(s), a_0)$	$Q(f(s), a_1)$
u_0	u_0	$q_{0,0}$	$q_{1,0}$
u_0	u_1	$q_{0,0}$	—
u_0	u_2	$q_{0,0}$	$q_{1,2}$
u_1	u_0	—	$q_{1,0}$
u_1	u_1	—	—
u_1	u_2	—	$q_{1,2}$
u_2	u_0	$q_{0,2}$	$q_{1,0}$
u_2	u_1	$q_{0,2}$	—
u_2	u_2	$q_{0,2}$	$q_{1,2}$

(a)

$e(s, a_0)$	$e(s, a_1)$	$Q(f(s), a_0)$	$Q(f(s), a_1)$
u_0	u_0	—	—
u_0	u_1	—	—
u_0	u_2	—	$q_{1,2}$
u_1	u_0	—	—
u_1	u_1	—	—
u_1	u_2	—	$q_{1,2}$
u_2	u_0	$q_{0,2}$	—
u_2	u_1	$q_{0,2}$	—
u_2	u_2	$q_{0,2}$	$q_{1,2}$

(b)

without significantly reducing the coverage of the learned Q-table. However, there is always the danger that the best possible action from a particular state could be filtered out: an informed, heuristic choice of W is required.

Summary

By partitioning the state space among teammates, by using action-dependent features to create a coarse feature space and to filter actions, and with the help of a reward function based entirely on individual observation of the environment, TPOT-RL enables team learning in complex multiagent, non-stationary environments even when agents cannot track state transitions.

In order to apply TPOT-RL to particular learning problems, as we do in Sections 7.3 and 7.4, the following functions and variables must be specified within the domain:

- The action-dependent feature function e and its range U.
- The partition function P and its range M.
- The reward function R including variables Q_{max} and t_{lim}.
- The learning rate α.
- The action-filtering set $W \subseteq U$.

In the two TPOT-RL implementations reported in Sections 7.3 and 7.4, the specifications of these variables are all set apart for emphasis.

7.3 TPOT-RL Applied to Simulated Robotic Soccer

In this section, I describe our application of TPOT-RL to a complex multiagent learning task, namely pass selection in simulated robotic soccer. Pass selection is the third layer in our layered learning implementation.

In the soccer domain, we apply TPOT-RL to enable each teammate to simultaneously learn a high-level action policy, or receiver choice function (RCF). The RCF is a function that determines what an agent should do when it has the opportunity to kick the ball. When it does not have the ball, the agent acts according to a manually created behavior as defined in Section 6.3.

As also presented in Section 6.3, the input of the RCF is the agent's perception of the current world state; the output is a target destination for the ball in terms of a location on the field, e.g. the opponent's goal. In our experiments reported in this section, each agent has 8 possible actions in A: it can pass towards either of the two goals, towards any of the four corners of the field, or to either side of the midfield line. Notice that in this case, the agents consider passing to *locations* on the field rather than to actual players. Nonetheless, the trained pass-evaluation DT can be used *as if* there were a teammate in the proposed field location. The action space is illustrated in Figure 7.2. In the context of our layered learning implementation, this action space is O_3, the set of outputs from which to choose for subtask L_3.

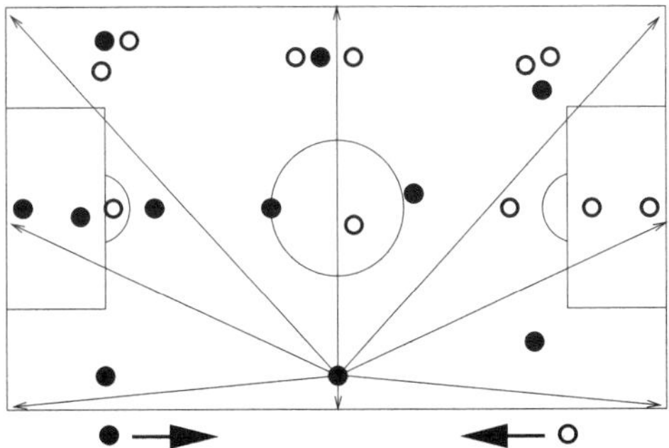

Figure 7.2
The action space used in this chapter. The black and white dots represent the players attacking the right and left goals respectively. Arrows indicate a single player's (the player from which the arrows emanate) action options when in possession of the ball. The player kicks the ball towards a fixed set of markers around the field, including the corner markers and the goals.

We extend the definition of Φ first presented in Section 6.1 to cover the action space used in this section as follows. Assume that for the action $a \in A$ (a kick to a location on the field), the DT predicts class κ with confidence $\gamma \in [0, 1]$ when the agent is in state s. The DT is evaluated as if there were a teammate at the kick destination corresponding to action a. Then[2]

$$\Phi(s, a) = \begin{cases} \gamma & \text{if } \kappa = \text{S (success)} \\ 0 & \text{if } \kappa = \text{M (miss)} \\ -\gamma & \text{if } \kappa = \text{F (failure)} \end{cases}$$

The two previously-learned behaviors (see Chapters 5 and 6) are both trained off-line in limited, controlled training situations. They can be trained in such a manner due to the fact that they only involve a few agents: ball interception only depends on the ball's and the agent's motions; passing only involves the passer, the receiver, and the agents in the immediate vicinity. On the other hand, deciding where to pass the ball during the course of a game requires training in real games since the value of a particular action can only be judged in terms of how well it works when playing with particular teammates against particular opponents. For example, as presented in Section 7.1, passing backwards to a defender could be the right thing to do if the defender has a good action policy, but the wrong thing to do if the defender is likely to lose the ball to an opponent.

Although our trained DT accurately predicts whether a player can execute a pass, it gives no indication of the strategic value of doing so. But the DT reduces a detailed state description to a single continuous output. It can then be used to drastically reduce the complex state and provide a useful state generalization. In this work we use the DT to define the crucial action-dependent feature function e in TPOT-RL. Thus, in the context of our layered learning implementation, the new learned layer (pass selection) uses the previous layer (pass evaluation) as part of its input representation.

State Generalization Using a Learned Feature

As is the case throughout this book and as illustrated in Figure 7.2, the team formation is divided into 11 positions. Thus,

$$\begin{aligned} M &= \text{the team's set of positions (roles) } (|M| = 11) \\ P(s) &= \text{the player's own current position} \end{aligned}$$

2 In Chapter 6, the parameter s was implicit for consistency of notation within the chapter. Similarly, for notational consistency within this chapter, the fact that Φ is evaluated from the perspective of the "passer"—the agent that is acting—is implicit.

Using the layered learning approach, we use the previously trained DT to define e, which is the main component of the input representation used to learn Q. In particular, we use Φ to cluster actions into two sets indicating predicted success or failure:

$$\begin{aligned} U &= \{Success, Failure\} \\ e_\Phi(s,a) &= \begin{cases} Success & \text{if } \Phi(s,a) \geq C \\ Failure & \text{if } \Phi(s,a) < C \end{cases} \end{aligned}$$

In our experiments reported in this section, we use $C = .734$ as the threshold for clustering action. We find that this threshold clusters the predictions into classes of roughly equal size.

With these definitions, $|U| = 2$ and $V = U^8 \times \{PlayerPositions\}$ so $|V| = |U|^{|A|} * |M| = 2^8 * 11$. Under the assumption that $Q(s, a_i)$ depends only on $e(s, a_i)$, the total number of independent Q-values is $|U| * |M| * |A| = 2 * 8 * 11$. In the context of our layered learning implementation, L_3's input vector $\vec{F}_3 = V = U^8 \times \{PlayerPositions\}$. Note that U is derived from O_2, the output of learned layer L_2.

This feature space is immensely smaller than the original state space, which has more than 10^{198} states (see Section 2.2). Since e indicates the likely success or failure of each possible action, at action-selection time, we only consider the actions that are likely to succeed:

$W = \{Success\}$.

Therefore, each agent learns $|W| * |A| = 8$ Q-values, with a total of 88 ($|W| * |A| * |M|$) learned by the team as a whole. Even though each agent only gets about 10 training examples per 10-minute game and the reward function shifts as teammate policies improve, such a learning task is tractable.

In addition to e_Φ, we define two other action-dependent feature functions for the purpose of comparison:

- e_r is a random function, returning *Success* or *Failure* randomly.
- e_h is a hand-coded heuristic pass-evaluation function based on one defined in Appendix B (Section B.2) that we successfully used on our real robot team.

Value Function Learning via Intermediate Reinforcement

As in any RL approach, the reward function plays a large role in determining what policy is learned when using TPOT-RL. One possible reward function, R_g is based entirely upon reaching the ultimate goal. In the soccer domain, we define R_g in terms of goals scored. If a goal is scored t time steps after action a is taken ($t \leq t_{lim}$), then the reward is $\pm Q_{max}/t$ depending on whether the goal is scored for or against. In this way, an agent charts the actual (long-term) results of its policy in the environment. Notice that the reward is discounted based on how long after acting the rewarding state is achieved.

Although goals scored are the true rewards in this domain, such events are very sparse. In order to increase the feedback from actions taken, it is useful to use an intermediate reinforcement function, which provides feedback based on intermediate states towards the goal (Mataric, 1994a). Without exploring the space of possible such functions, we created one reward function R_i using intermediate reinforcement.

Like R_g, R_i gives rewards for goals scored. However, agents also receive rewards if the ball goes out of bounds, or else after a fixed period of time t_{lim} based on the ball's average lateral position on the field. In particular, when an agent takes action a_i in state s such that $e(s, a_i) = u$, the agent notices the time t at which the action was taken as well as the x-coordinate of the ball's position at time t, x_t. The reward function R_i (like R_g) takes as input the observed ball position over time t_{lim} (a subset of $S^{t_{lim}}$) and outputs a reward r. Since the ball position over time depends on other agents' actions, the reward is stochastic and non-stationary. When one of the following conditions is met, the agent fixes the reward r:

1. if the ball goes out of bounds (including a goal) at time $t + t_o$ ($t_o < t_{lim}$);
2. if the ball returns to the agent at time $t + t_r$ ($t_r < t_{lim}$);
3. if the ball is still in bounds at time $t + t_{lim}$.

In case 1, the reward r is based on the value r_o as indicated in Figure 7.3:

$$r = \frac{r_o}{1 + (\phi - 1) * t_o/t_{lim}}. \tag{7.3}$$

Thus, the farther in the future the ball goes out of bounds (i.e. the larger t_o), the smaller the absolute value of r. This scaling by time replaces the discount factor used in Q-learning. We use:

$$\begin{aligned} t_{lim} &= 30 \text{ seconds (300 simulator cycles)} \\ Q_{max} &= 100 \\ \phi &= 10 \end{aligned}$$

In cases 2 and 3, the reward r is based on the average x-position of the ball

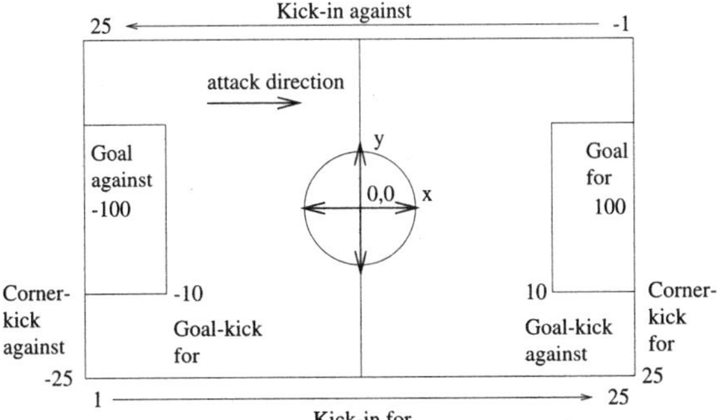

Figure 7.3
The component r_o of the reward function R_i based on the circumstances under which the ball goes out of bounds. For kick-ins, the reward varies linearly with the x-position of the ball.

over the time t to the time $t+t_r$ or $t+t_{lim}$. Over that entire time span, the agent samples the x-coordinate of the ball at fixed, periodic intervals and computes the average x_{avg} over the times at which the ball position is known. Then if x_{og} is the x-coordinate of the opponent goal (the right goal in Figure 7.3) and x_{lg} is the x-coordinate of the learner's goal:

$$r = \begin{cases} \phi * \frac{x_{avg}-x_t}{x_{og}-x_t} & \text{if } x_{avg} > x_t \\ -\phi * \frac{x_t-x_{avg}}{x_t-x_{lg}} & \text{if } x_{avg} \leq x_t \end{cases} \tag{7.4}$$

Thus, the reward is the fraction of the available field by which the ball is advanced, on average, over the time-period in question. Note that a backwards pass can lead to positive reward if the ball then moves forward in the near future and conversely, a forwards pass can lead to a negative reward. The use of parameter ϕ in both Equations 7.3 and 7.4 insures that intermediate rewards cannot override rewards for attaining the ultimate goal, Q_{max} which is the maximum value of r_o in Equation 7.3.

When using either R_g or R_i, the reward r is based on direct environmental feedback. R_g passes discounted reward back to the agents only when the world enters a state with which some reward is associated. R_i is a domain-dependent intermediate reinforcement function based upon heuristic knowledge of progress towards the goal.

Notice that R_i relies solely upon the agent's own impression of the environment. If it fails to notice the ball's position for a period of time, the intermediate reward is affected (the agents always notice when the ball goes out of bounds or into a goal via an aural message from the referee). However, agents can track the ball much more easily than they can deduce the internal states of other agents as they would have to do were they to determine future team state transitions.

Finally, after taking action a_i and receiving reward r, $Q(e(s, a_i), a_i)$ is updated according to equation 7.2 with the learning rate

$\alpha = .02$

Thus, even though we average all reward values achieved as a result of taking an action in a given state, each new example accounts for 2% of the updated Q-value: rewards achieved further in the past are weighted less heavily.

In the context of our layered learning implementation, T_3, the training examples used in layer L_3, is the set of action-reinforcement pairs gathered by the agents during the course of play and used to update the function Q.

Action Selection for Multiagent Training

One characteristic of some multiagent domains that makes them non-stationary is the fact that multiple agents are concurrently learning. Thus, from each individual's perspective, the environment is not a stable system. In order to deal with this challenge, we adopt two action strategies:

- Each agent stays in the same state partition throughout training;
- Exploration rate is very high at first and gradually decreases simultaneously for all agents;

By having each agent remain in the same partition throughout training, we are, in effect, distributing training into $|M|$ partitions, each with a lookup-table of size $|A| * |U|$. After training, each agent can be given the trained policy for all of the values of M, enabling the agents to move through the entire state space. Were each agent required to learn the policies of all positions, training would take at least $|M|$ times longer[3].

As in all RL paradigms, the tradeoff between exploration and exploitation is potentially problematic. Especially since rewards in our case are stochastic and feature values encode large numbers of states, early exploitation runs the risk of ignoring the best possible actions in certain states. As a result, when in state s, our agents choose the action with the highest Q-value—action a_i such

3 Training would likely take even longer than that. Since teammates would all be learning more slowly as well, it would take longer for the agents to receive informative reinforcement values.

that $\forall j,\ Q(f(s), a_i) \geq Q(f(s), a_j)$—with probability p, and a random action with probability $1 - p$. In all of our training runs, p gradually increases from 0 to .99.

Results

Empirical testing demonstrates that TPOT-RL can effectively learn multiagent control policies with few training instances in a complex, dynamic domain. Unless otherwise noted, for all experiments reported in this section:

- The learning agents start out acting randomly and with empty Q-tables: $\forall v \in V, a \in A,\ Q(v, a) = 0$.
- Over the course of learning, the probability of acting randomly, p, decreases linearly over periods of 40 games from 1 to .5 in game 40, to .1 in game 80, to .01 in game 120 and thereafter.
- The learning agents use the intermediate reward function R_i.

Figure 7.4 plots cumulative goals scored by a learning simulated soccer team playing against an otherwise equally-skilled team that passes to random destinations over the course of a single long run equivalent in time to 160 10-minute games. As apparent from the graph, the team using TPOT-RL learns to vastly outperform the randomly passing team. Other than the pass decisions, the behaviors of the agents on the randomly passing team are identical to those on the learning team. During this experiment, $|U| = 1$, thus rendering the function e irrelevant: the only relevant state feature is the player's own position on the field.

A key characteristic of TPOT-RL is the ability to learn with minimal training examples. During the run graphed in Figure 7.4, the 11 players get an average of 1490 action-reinforcement pairs over 160 games. Thus, players only get reinforcement an average of 9.3 times each game, or less than once every minute. Since each player has 8 actions from which to choose, each action is only tried an average of 186.3 times over 160 games, or just over once every 10-minute game. Under these training circumstances, very efficient learning is clearly needed.

TPOT-RL is effective not only against random teams, but also against goal-directed, hand-coded teams. For testing purposes, we construct an opponent team which plays with all of its players on the same side of the field, leaving the other side open as illustrated by the white team in Figure 7.2. The agents use a hand-coded RCF which directs them to pass the ball up the side of the

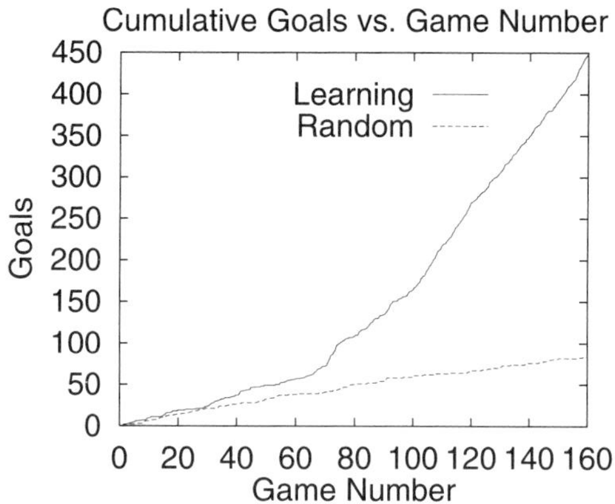

Figure 7.4
Total goals scored by a learning team playing against a randomly passing team. The independent variable is the number of 10-minute games that have elapsed.

field to the forwards who then shoot on goal. The team switches from one side of the field to the other every 5 minutes of simulation (half of a game). We call this team the *switching team*. Note that the switching team is similar to a team that switches between the OPR and OPL (only play right/left) strategies defined in Chapter 6. The only difference is that the switching team uses a goal-directed, rather than a random, RCF.

Were the opponent team to always stay on the same side of the field, as is the case with the goal-directed OPR team, the learning team could advance the ball up the other side of the field without any regard for current player locations. Thus, TPOT-RL could be run with $|U| = 1$, which renders e inconsequential. Indeed, we verified empirically that TPOT-RL is able to learn an effective policy against the OPR team using $|U| = 1$. After 160 games of learning, the learning team is able to beat the OPR team by a cumulative score of 259–124 over the course of 40 test games (Figure 7.5(b)). As a point of comparison, Figure 7.5(a) shows the result of always shooting towards the opponent goal—a reasonable heuristic—when playing against the OPR team.

Also against the OPR team, we tested the effect of training time on the effectiveness of the learned policy. The results can be seen by comparing Figures 7.5(b) and 7.5(c). These two trials are identical except that the latter used an accelerated training schedule: The exploration rate was decreased over 20-game intervals for a total of 80 games rather than 40-game intervals for a total of 160 games. The reduced training leads to worse performance over

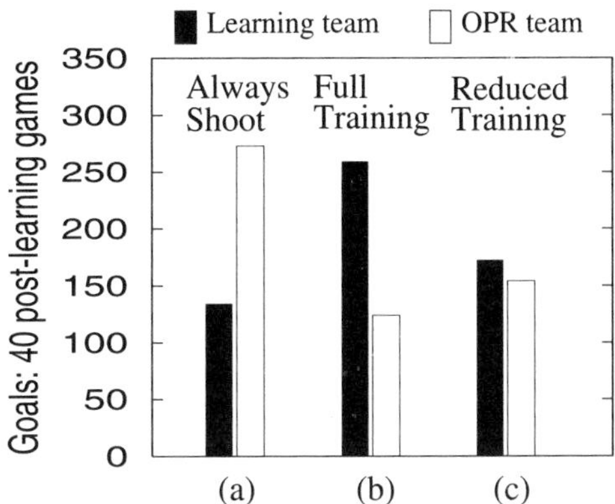

Figure 7.5
The results after training of 3 different runs against the OPR team (always shown as the white bar). (a) shows the result of always executing the shoot action. (b) and (c) show the results when training for 160 and 80 games respectively when using TPOT-RL with $|U| = 1$.

40 subsequent test games. The purpose of this experiment was to verify the need for on the order of 160 training games to adequately evaluate TPOT-RL's performance. Further testing indicated that training beyond 160 games does not significantly affect performance. All other trials reported below use 160 games of training.

Exploiting the Previously Learned Features

Against the switching team, an agent's best action depends on the current state: in general, the agent should pass away from the side of the field on which the opponents are located. Thus an action-dependent feature function that discriminates among possible actions dynamically can help TPOT-RL. Figure 7.6 compares TPOT-RL with different functions e and different sets W when learning against the switching team.

With $|U| = 1$ (Figure 7.6(a)), the learning team is unable to discriminate among states in which passes are likely to succeed or fail since each agent has only one Q-value associated with each possible action[4]. With $|U| = 1$, it loses 139–127 (cumulative score over 40 games after 160 games of training).

In contrast, with the previously trained DT classifying passes as likely successes or failures (e_Φ) and with filtering out the failures ($W = \{Success\}$), the learning team wins 172–113 (Figure 7.6(b)). Therefore the learned pass-

4 Notice that whenever $|U| = 1$, it must be the case that $W = U$.

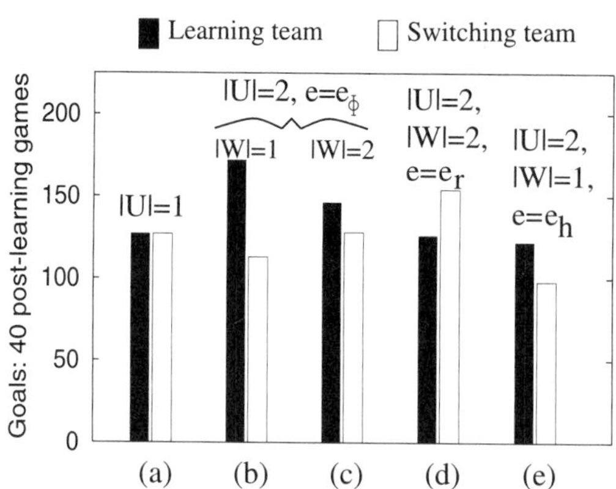

Figure 7.6
The results after training of 5 different TPOT-RL runs against the switching team.

evaluation feature is able to usefully distinguish among possible actions and help TPOT-RL to learn a successful action policy. The DT also helps learning when $W = U$ (Figure 7.6(c)), but when $W = \{Success\}$ performance is better.

Figure 7.6(d) demonstrates the value of using an informative action-dependent feature function e. When a random function e_r is used, TPOT-RL performs noticeably worse than when using e_Φ. For e_r we show $|W| = 2$ because it only makes sense to filter out actions when e contains useful information. Indeed, when $e = e_r$ and $|W| = 1$, the learning team performs even worse than when $|W| = 2$ (it loses 167–60). The DT even helps TPOT-RL more than a hand-coded heuristic pass-evaluation function (e_h) based on the one defined in Appendix B (Section B.2) that we successfully used on our real robot team (Figure 7.6(e)).

Final score is the ultimate performance measure. However, we examined learning more closely in the best case experiment ($e = e_\Phi$, $W = \{Success\}$—Figure 7.6(b)). Recall that the learned feature provides no information about which actions are *strategically* good. TPOT-RL must learn that on its own. To test that it is indeed learning to advance the ball towards the opponent's goal (other than by final score), we calculated the number of times each action is predicted to succeed ($e_\Phi(s, a) = Success$) and the number of times it was actually selected by TPOT-RL after training. Throughout the entire team, the 3 of 8 (37.5%) actions towards the opponent's goal were selected 6437/9967 = 64.6% of the times that they were predicted to succeed. Thus TPOT-RL learns that it is, in general, better to advance the ball towards the opponent's goal.

Verifying that the filter is eliminating action choices based on likelihood of failure, we found that 39.6% of action options were filtered out when $e = e_\Phi$ and $|W| = 1$. Out of 10,400 action opportunities, it was never the case that all 8 actions were filtered out: in all cases, $B(s) \neq \emptyset$.

Comparing Reward Functions

The reward function R_i, used in all the experiments reported above, is engineered to increase the amount of reinforcement information available to the agents as opposed to the extremely sparse reinforcements available from goals scored (R_g). Nevertheless, while not as effective as R_i, R_g does provide enough reinforcement for agents to learn effective policies. Using the same 160-game training paradigm and using $|U| = 1$, a team learning with R_g is able to beat the OPR team (Figure 7.7(a)), though by considerably less than the team using R_i in otherwise identical circumstances (Figure 7.7(b)—the same trial as shown in Figure 7.5(b)). Therefore, the intermediate reinforcement reward function, R_i is a key component to achieving successful results with TPOT-RL.

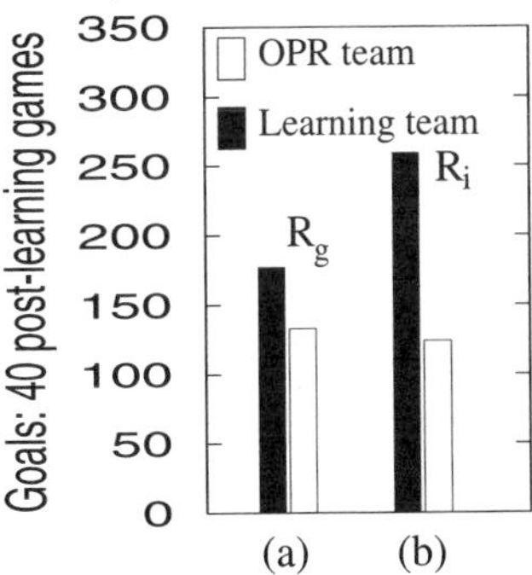

Figure 7.7
The results after training of 2 different runs against the OPR team. (a) shows the result of learning with the R_g reward function. (b) shows the result of training with the R_i reward function. In both cases, $|U| = 1$.

7.4 TPOT-RL Applied to Network Routing

Section 7.3 demonstrates that TPOT-RL can be used to learn effective behaviors in one team-partitioned, opaque-transition domain. However, in creating TPOT-RL, we intend it as a new general multiagent learning algorithm. This section demonstrates that it can indeed apply beyond simulated robotic soccer.

We identify network routing as another team-partitioned, opaque transition domain. As presented in Section 2.4, in our formulation of network routing, each network node is considered as a separate agent. The agents act as a team as they try to cooperate in sending packets through the network as efficiently as possible. The domain is team-partitioned since each agent learns only a policy at its own node: the function P partitions the state space based, in part, on the node at which each agent is situated. Prior research indicates that distributed network control is advantageous even in high-speed networks (such as ATM networks) in which centralized control is possible (Horikawa et al., 1996).

Network routing is opaque-transition because agents cannot see a packet's route after sending it along a link. Like in robotic soccer, agents' actions are chained, with each agent able to affect which agent will act *next*, but with no control beyond that. Agents get no short-term reward for their actions and cannot track the transitions in the environment.

Nonetheless, the team of agents can learn to effectively route packets by observing local state information (network traffic). The action-dependent feature function e in our implementation of TPOT-RL for network routing provides useful local information that correlates with the long-term reward: e returns the amount of recent network traffic on the links leading from an agent's node. In our experiments, we assume that the agents get intermittent long-term performance statistics transmitted back to them. Thus they are able to learn to collaborate.

Aside from being team-partitioned and opaque-transition, network routing is also similar to robotic soccer in that the world changes dynamically in a manner beyond the team's control. In robotic soccer, opponents can change their strategies; in network routing the distribution of packets introduced into the network can change.

In this section, I present in detail our application of TPOT-RL to network routing, a second multiagent learning task. In the first three subsections, I provide the algorithmic details of our implementation of TPOT-RL. The next subsection specifies our experimental methodology including the parameters used in the network routing simulator and the last subsection presents detailed empirical results demonstrating the effectiveness of TPOT-RL in the network routing domain.

State Generalization

As defined in Section 7.2, the function $f : S \mapsto V$ generalizes the state space based on two components: an action-dependent feature function $e : S \times A \mapsto U$ and a coarse partitioning function $P : S \mapsto M$. Given a state $s \in S$ from which the agent at node n_i is faced with the decision of routing packet k_j:

$$\begin{aligned} M &= N \times N \;\; (|M| = m^2) \\ P(s) &= (n_i, k_{j_{dest}}) \end{aligned}$$

Recall that, as defined in Section 2.4, m is the number of nodes in the network: $|N| = m$. Using this partitioning function P, the agent at node n_i learns to act only in the cases that $P(s) = (n_i, k_{j_{dest}})$ for some j: the space is partitioned evenly among the m agents, with each getting m partitions.

The action-dependent feature function $e : S \times A \mapsto U$ is defined as follows. A is the set of actions available and is represented in terms of the nodes to which a packet can be sent. Thus $A = N$. However, the agent at node n_i may only use the actions in $L_{n_i} \subseteq N$—the set of links from node n_i. The elements of

$$U = \{high, low\}$$

reflect the network activity over a particular link in the last `activity_window` time units. An agent can store the link activity along all of the links from its node since it is either the sender or the recipient of all packets sent along these links.

Define $\tau(s, a, \texttt{activity\_window})$ as the number of packets sent along the link corresponding to action a in the last `activity_window` time units divided by `activity_window`. Then if action a is the act of sending a packet along link l,

$$e(s, a) = \begin{cases} high & \text{if } \tau(s, a, \texttt{activity\_window}) \geq C \\ low & \text{if } \tau(s, a, \texttt{activity\_window}) < C \end{cases}$$

We use `activity_window` = 100 and $C = .5$. Notice that e is an action-dependent function since it depends on the proposed action of sending a packet along link l. It is also based entirely upon local information available to agents that maintain internal state, collecting traffic statistics over time.

Like in the robotic soccer example, this state generalization drastically reduces a huge state space to the point that agents can store Q-values in a lookup table. In our implementation, according to Equation 2.2, the entire state space in our experiments has more than 10^{3000} states ($m = 12, C_{net} = 1000$). However, with $|U| = 2$, $|A| \leq 3$, and $|M| = m^2$ the total number of Q-values for the team to learn is at most $6m^2$, with each agent learning no more than $6m$ values. In our experiments reported below, $m = 12$. Therefore each agent must learn only 72 Q-values.

Value Function Learning

As per equation 7.2, agents learn $Q(v, a)$—the value of taking action a when in a state s such that $f(s) = v$—by receiving a reward r via a reward function R. In this case, if v indicates that node n is trying to send a packet k on its way to node k_{dest} ($P(s) = (n, k_{dest})$), then $Q(v, a)$ is meant to estimate the time that it will take for the packet to reach node k_{dest}. Thus agents aim to take actions that will lead to *minimal* r.

Unlike the soccer domain, in which agents can observe the ball's progress over time, network routing does not provide much opportunity for intermediate reinforcement. R is almost entirely based on the actual time that the packet k takes to travel from node n_i to its destination k_{dest}.

When k successfully arrives at k_{dest}, the agent at node k_{dest} can examine the times at which it left each node along its path from k_{source} as stored in k_{path}. From this information, it can deduce the time taken from each node along the path given the action taken at that node. Then periodically, every `update_interval` seconds, the nodes in the network update each other on the long-term results of their actions.

Thus, after the agent at node n_i sends a packet k_i along link l at time $t_{k_i,l}$, the agent at node n_i receives reward r equal to the time it took for the packet to eventually reach its destination $k_{i_{dest}}$:

$$r = k_{i_{dtime}} - t_{k_i,l}$$

In this case, the goal of each node is to minimize its reward r. Notice that this formulation of the reward function R is entirely goal oriented—in general, there is no opportunity for the agent at node n_i to observe a packet's progress on the way to its destination.

However, there *is* one exception. Especially at the early stages of learning when actions are mostly random, a packet often returns to a node from whence it came at some interval t later than it last left the node. In this situation, the agent at the node in question infers that the previous action a taken on this packet was ineffective and generates an intermediate reward signal $r = Q(v, a) + t$, thus increasing the cost estimate $Q(v, a)$.

To put a bound on the amount of time it takes to receive a reward, the maximum reward is defined to be Q_{max}. That is, if a node takes longer than Q_{max} to arrive, then $r = Q_{max}$. A node can assume that the packet did not arrive in this time if it has not heard about its arrival after $Q_{max}+$ `update_interval` simulated seconds. Therefore, $t_{lim} = Q_{max}+$ `update_interval`. In our experiments, we use

$$\begin{aligned} Q_{max} &= 2000 \\ \texttt{update\_interval} &= 10 \\ t_{lim} &= 210 \end{aligned}$$

Finally, just as in the robotic soccer implementation of TPOT-RL, after the agent at node n takes action a on a packet k destined for node k_{dest} and receives reward r, $Q((e(s, a), (n, k_{dest})), a)$ is updated according to equation 7.2 with the learning rate

$\alpha = .02$

Thus, again, even though we average all reward values achieved as a result of taking an action in a given state, each new example accounts for 2% of the updated Q-value: rewards achieved further in the past are weighted less heavily.

Action Selection

In our network routing implementation of TPOT-RL, Q-values are all initialized to low values (0 or the shortest path length between nodes) before learning and agents always choose the action with the lowest Q-value. Thus, each action is tried at least once, but there is no deliberate exploration. We find this total exploitation strategy to be effective, presumably because as unsuccessful actions are repeated, their costs increase due to network congestion, thus naturally causing agents to try the other alternatives periodically. However, should exploration become necessary, we could easily switch to a probabilistic action-selection strategy similar to the one we use in the robotic soccer implementation.

We do not experiment with action filtering in this domain, finding that it is not necessary to achieve good results. Thus, in all of our experiments,

$W = U$

Experimental Setup

In this subsection I lay out the details of our experimental setup for testing the effectiveness of TPOT-RL in the network routing domain. The detailed empirical results are then reported in the next subsection.

All of the experiments use a network architecture (node and link patterns) as shown in Figure 7.8. The nodes are numbered for reference in the text. Packets are injected into the network at random intervals according to a Poisson distribution at an average rate of c per simulated second. In our experiments, we use $c = 3$. We create three different traffic patterns within this network by controlling the distributions of sources and destinations of injected packets. Our traffic patterns are controlled by two variables: p_6, the probability that a new packet is destined for node 6 (see Figure 7.8); and f_s, the frequency with which the traffic patterns switches (i.e. number of simulated seconds between pattern switches). In our experiments, we use $p_6 = .25$ and $f_s = 10{,}000$. The three traffic patters we define are:

Top-heavy: With probability p_6, the injected packet has node 6 as its destination and a random source; with probability $1 - p_6$, the injected packet has source and destination chosen randomly (without replacement) from the set of nodes {1,2,3,4,5}.

Bottom-heavy: With probability p_6, the injected packet has node 6 as its destination and a random source; with probability $1 - p_6$, the injected packet has source and destination chosen randomly from the set of nodes {7,8,9,10,11}.

Switching: Every f_s simulated seconds, the traffic pattern switches between the top-heavy and bottom-heavy patterns.

As laid out in Section 2.4, there are several parameters governing the timing and capacities of network traffic. We use $C_{node} = C_{net} = 1000$, $t_n = t_l = 1.0$.

In our experiments, we test several different packet routing strategies under the different traffic patterns defined above. I define the strategies in terms of what the agent at node n does when trying to route packet k to its destination k_{dest}. It must choose from among the possible links in L_n.

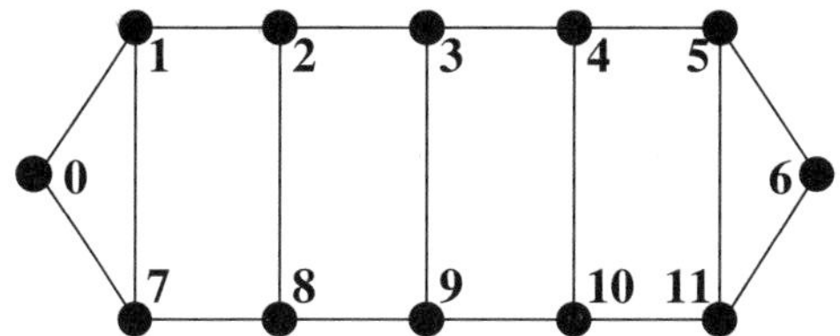

Figure 7.8
The network architecture used for our experiments. The nodes are numbered for reference in the text.

Random (RAND): k is sent along a random link $l \in L_n$.

Shortest (SHRT): k is sent along the link that would get it to k_{dest} in the fewest number of hops. Shortest paths are precomputed and stored based on the network topology. If more than one link would lead along paths of the same shortest length, one such link is chosen randomly.

Hand-coded (HAND): We created a policy by hand designed to work well with the top-heavy traffic pattern.

- When $k_{dest} = 6$, if $n \in \{7, 8, 9, 10, 11\}$, k is sent along the shortest path towards node 6 (along the bottom of the network in Figure 7.8). Otherwise, ($n \in \{0, 1, 2, 3, 4, 5\}$) k is sent to a node in the set $\{6, 7, 8, 9, 10, 11\}$ from where it can then continue along the shortest path to node 6. Note that in all cases k can be sent to a node in this set in one hop.
- When $k_{dest} \in \{1, 2, 3, 4, 5\}$, k is sent along the shortest path (along the top of the network).
- Similarly, when $k_{dest} \in \{7, 8, 9, 10, 11\}$, k is sent along the shortest path (along the bottom of the network).

We expect this policy to do fairly well with the top-heavy traffic pattern since the traffic is distributed fairly evenly among the top and bottom portions of the network. Packets headed for node 6 ($p_6 = 25\%$ of the packets) use the bottom, while other packets use the top of the network.

Q-routing (QROUT): This strategy is the Q-routing algorithm introduced in (Littman and Boyan, 1993). We use exactly the same implementation for testing. There are two variants. One that starts with all Q-values initialized to 0, and another that initializes all Q-values to be the shortest distance between nodes. In the former case, the policy at the beginning is equivalent to RAND; in the latter, it is equivalent to SHRT. In both cases, the Q-values can change freely during learning. We use the default learning rate of $\eta = 0.7$.

TPOT-RL: This strategy is the one described in detail in the beginning part of this section. Like QROUT, TPOT-RL can be initialized with Q-values at 0 or with the length of the shortest path between nodes. In the latter case, the initialization is immediately overwritten by the first real reward signal. However, the initialization guides the initial agent decisions.

In addition, stored Q-routing and TPOT-RL policies can be loaded and used with no further learning allowed. We use this technique for testing purposes.

A major difference between Q-routing and TPOT-RL is that when using Q-routing, neighboring nodes send back their own value estimates after every packet transfer. Thus Q-routing generates a considerable amount of additional traffic. On the other hand, we assume that agents do not know anything about the network beyond their own nodes and links. Performance statistics are propagated through the network in batches periodically, allowing for a tradeoff between overhead packets and learning rate. However, unlike Q-routing agents, TPOT-RL agents are unable to use dynamic programming.

Results

This subsection presents detailed empirical results verifying the effectiveness of TPOT-RL in the network routing domain. First I present comparisons of the different routing strategies in a top-heavy traffic pattern. Then I describe the effects of testing the resulting policies on the bottom-heavy traffic pattern. Finally, I present our results from training policies on the switching traffic and testing their generalization across the three traffic patterns.

Top-Heavy Traffic

First, we tested the five different routing strategies under top-heavy network traffic conditions. I chart both the average delivery time of the packets and the average number of hops per packet. Results are tabulated over intervals of 100 simulated seconds. Because of the difference in scales of the performance of, on the one hand RAND and SHRT, and on the other hand HAND, QROUT, and TPOT-RL, I break the results into two sets of graphs. Figures 7.9 and 7.10 compare the results of using the RAND, SHRT, and TPOT-RL routing strategies in terms of average delivery time and average number of hops respectively. Notice that as the network fills up, the RAND performs worse and worse in both respects. By definition, SHRT produces the minimum possible number of hops per packet, but again exhibits a continual increase in average delivery time as the nodes' packet queues lengthen.

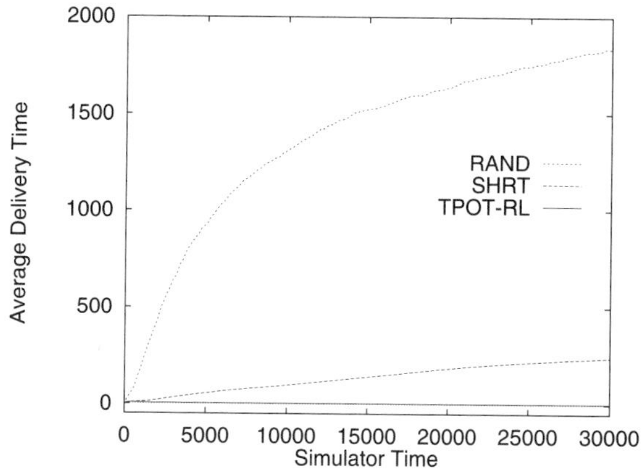

Figure 7.9
Average delivery time of packets in a network with the top-heavy traffic pattern when using three different routing strategies: RAND, SHRT, and TPOT-RL.

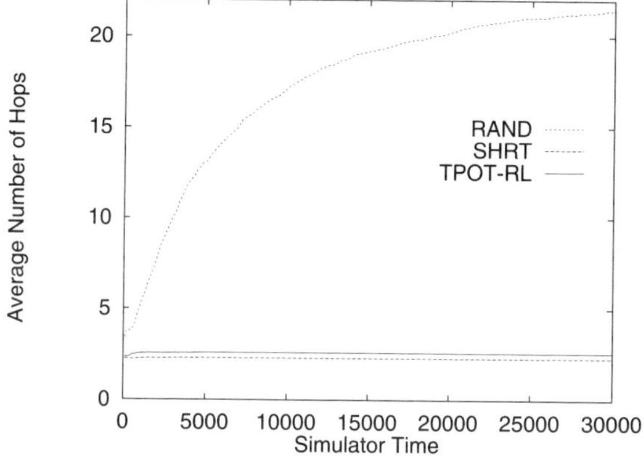

Figure 7.10
Average number of hops for packets in a network with the top-heavy traffic pattern when using three different routing strategies: RAND, SHRT, and TPOT-RL.

In this and all other TPOT-RL runs, unless specified otherwise, `update_interval = 10`, $Q_{max} = 2000$, and $|U| = 1$: like in robotic soccer, under constant conditions, TPOT-RL can be effective even without the help of action-dependent features.

Figures 7.11 and 7.12 are drawn on smaller y-axis scales, as the HAND, QROUT, and TPOT-RL strategies all vastly outperform the other two (at least

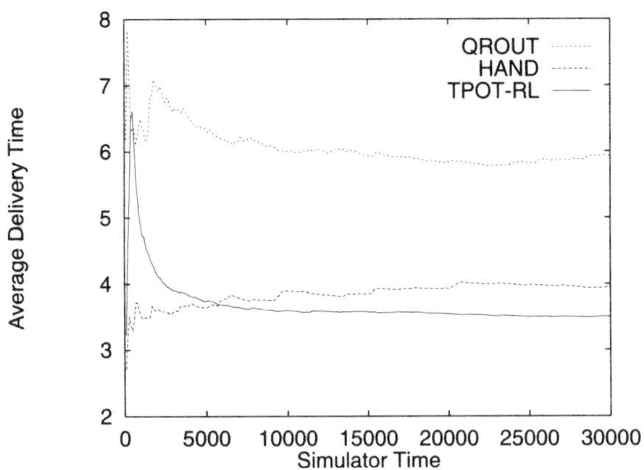

Figure 7.11
Average delivery time of packets in a network with the top-heavy traffic pattern when using three different routing strategies: QROUT, HAND, and TPOT-RL.

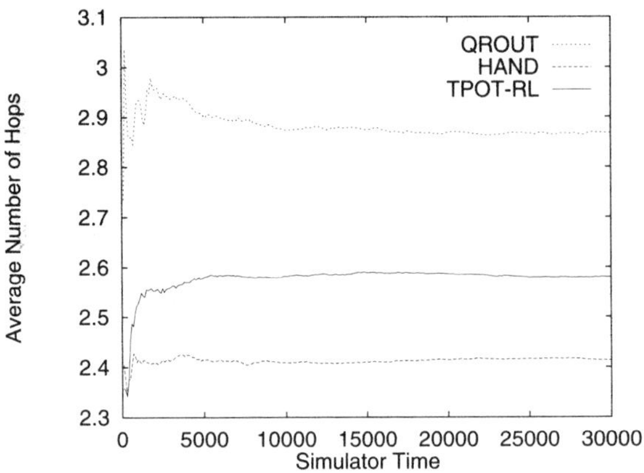

Figure 7.12
Average number of hops for packets in a network with the top-heavy traffic pattern when using three different routing strategies: QROUT, HAND, and TPOT-RL.

in terms of average delivery time). In these runs, QROUT and TPOT-RL are initialized with the shortest paths to eliminate the big spike that would otherwise throw off the scale at the beginning of the graphs as the algorithms begin acting randomly. When these algorithms start out with Q-values initialized to 0, the right hand parts of the curves look qualitatively the same.

Again, the average number of hops does not correlate with the average delivery time, the real measure of interest. TPOT-RL outperforms both HAND and QROUT by sending some packets along longer, but less congested paths. The remainder of the results in this section are presented only in terms of average packet delivery time.

Bottom-Heavy Traffic

Figure 7.13 illustrates the results of running policies designed for top-heavy traffic under bottom-heavy conditions. The solid bars show average traffic delivery time for SHRT, HAND, QROUT, and TPOT-RL under top-heavy traffic. These numbers are the same as the end-results shown in Figures 7.9 and 7.11. As noticed above, the HAND, QROUT, and TPOT-RL strategies all perform well, having been designed or trained for these conditions.

However, when the resulting policies are tested under bottom-heavy traffic conditions, none of them perform well. In these runs, shown with hollow bars, the policies from the ends of the previous runs are used with no additional learning. Of course the SHRT and HAND policies, which do not learn, are constant throughout both runs.

I use a logarithmic scale on the y axis in Figure 7.13 in order to accommodate the large discrepancy in values while still illustrating the differences.

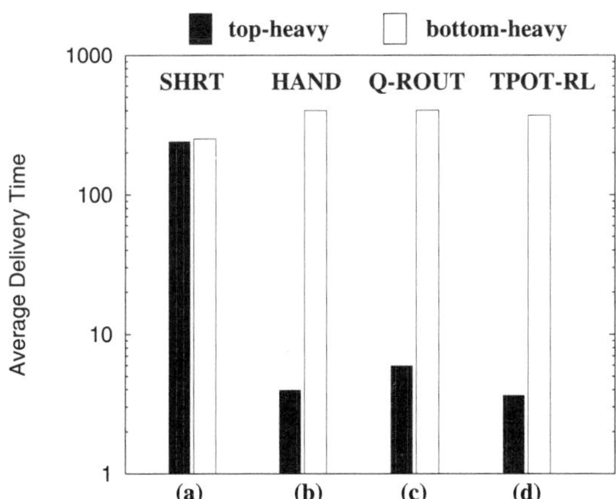

Figure 7.13
Fixed policies running in the top-heavy and bottom-heavy traffic patterns. The QROUT and TPOT-RL policies are both trained under top-heavy conditions. Note the log scale on the y axis.

Switching Traffic

While we would not expect a policy trained exclusively under top-heavy network traffic conditions to generalize to bottom-heavy conditions, we would like a policy trained under switching conditions, since it includes periods of both of the other traffic patterns, to generalize across all three. Figure 7.14 shows the results of HAND, QROUT, and two variants of TPOT-RL under all three traffic patterns. In all of the learning cases, the policy is first trained under switching network traffic for 30,000 simulated seconds and then fixed for testing. In all cases, the solid bar shows results for top-heavy traffic, the hollow bar for bottom-heavy traffic, and the striped bar for switching traffic. Again, I use a logarithmic scale on the y axis for presentation purposes.

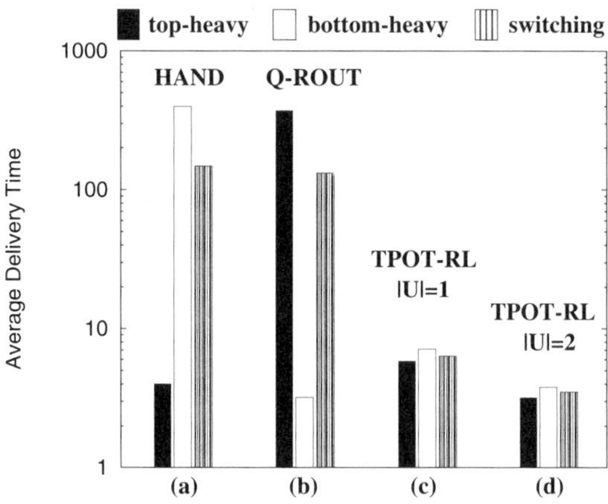

Figure 7.14
Fixed policies running in the top-heavy, bottom-heavy, and switching traffic patterns. The QROUT and TPOT-RL policies are both trained under switching conditions. Note the log scale on the y axis.

The two TPOT-RL runs differ only in the set U used. When $|U| = 1$, no difference is made based on local traffic conditions: routing decisions are based entirely upon the packet's destination. When $|U| = 2$, agents can implement different policies based on different local traffic conditions. Note that Q-routing always routes packets based solely on their destinations.

Figure 7.14 clearly shows the advantage of TPOT-RL. Since HAND is designed explicitly for top-heavy traffic, it fails as expected in other conditions (Figure 7.14(a)). Similarly, QROUT is forced to adapt to one traffic pattern at the expense of the other (Figure 7.14(b)). In this case, it clearly optimizes its performance under bottom-heavy conditions, sacrificing its performance under top-heavy conditions, and thus under switching conditions as well.

On the other hand, TPOT-RL with $|U| = 1$ (Figure 7.14(c)) finds a middle ground in which the network performs fairly well under all traffic conditions, but never as well as possible. It is when $|U| = 2$ (Figure 7.14(d)) that TPOT-RL can take advantage of its action-dependent feature function to find correlations between local information and long-term reward. In this case, TPOT-RL is able to perform well under all traffic conditions with a single policy.

This last result repeats the result reported in the simulated robotic soccer domain in Section 7.3. Namely, TPOT-RL is capable of learning an effective policy under dynamic conditions in a team-partitioned, opaque-transition domain.

7.5 Discussion

As mentioned at the outset, this chapter serves a dual purpose. First, it represents the final layer in our layered learning implementation in the simulated robotic soccer domain. Second, it defines a new multiagent learning technique that generalizes outside of the robotic soccer domain.

Pass Selection within Layered Learning

Pass selection represents the third and highest-level behavioral layer, L_3, within our layered learning implementation:

- $\vec{F}_3 = U^8 \times \{PlayerPositions\}$, as defined in Section 7.3. There is one action-dependent feature input (U) for each of the 8 possible actions in O_3. *The action-dependent features are derived from the result of h_2 executed for each possible pass target.*
- $O_3 =$ the set of 8 target locations indicated in Figure 7.2.
- $T_3 =$ on-line training examples gathered by individual team members during real games as prescribed in Section 7.3. *For each particular action decision, the eligible members of O_3 are pruned based on h_2: only passes predicted to succeed are considered* ($W = \{Success\}$).
- $M_3 =$ TPOT-RL.
- $h_3 =$ a distributed pass-selection policy. Several learned policies are presented in Section 7.3.

Our implementation of pass selection follows the principles of layered learning as laid out in Section 4.1:

• Pass selection is a behavior that must be adaptable. Since it depends on the behaviors of teammates and opponents, agents must be able to adjust their decisions based on the empirical results of past decisions. Thus, pass selection is an appropriate behavior for learning because of the possibility of exploiting data to adapt to a shifting concept.

• We chose the machine learning method for pass selection based on the task characteristics. As presented in Section 7.1, no pre-existing machine learning method is suitable for learning pass selection in simulated robotic soccer. Therefore, we introduce a new multiagent reinforcement learning algorithm, TPOT-RL, to accomplish this task.
Low-level learning in complex domains can be well-defined with easy-to-isolate problems that allow agents to gather extensive training examples. However, when learning high-level multiagent behaviors, training opportunities can be sparse and agents cannot be trained in isolation since agent policies are interdependent. Although RL typically suffers from the "curse of dimensionality," the use of TPOT-RL to learn a successful pass-selection behavior indicates that it can be used to learn complex multiagent behaviors with few training examples in very large state spaces.

• The previous learned layer—pass evaluation—is used as part of the input space for TPOT-RL. In particular, the trained DT for pass evaluation is used to define the crucial action-evaluation function e when using TPOT-RL for learning pass selection. The previously-trained DT gives an indication of the likelihood that a given pass will succeed based on the configuration of teammates and opponents, but regardless of the receiver's position on the field. The trained RCF then maps the collection of feature values (decision tree classifications) to a Q-value for each action. A key assumption is that the Q-value of a particular action does not depend on the feature values for the other actions. The Q-values indicate the long-term strategic value of taking a particular action given the predicted short-term effect of that action in the current state.

In this chapter, TPOT-RL is used to learn pass selection, the third layer of our layered learning implementation. When learning pass selection, the team of agents uses a fixed formation against a fixed opponent. As presented in Section 4.3, our layered learning implementation could be extended by incorporating pass selection within higher-level learned behaviors. For example, the team might learn to adjust its formation against a fixed opponent. It might also learn to switch among pass selection policies when facing different opponents.

TPOT-RL

TPOT-RL is an effective technique for enabling a team of agents to learn to cooperate towards the achievement of a specific goal. It is an adaptation of traditional RL methods that is applicable in complex, non-stationary, multiagent domains with large state spaces and limited training opportunities. TPOT-RL enables teams of agents to learn effective policies with very few training examples even in a large state space with large amounts of hidden state.

In short, TPOT-RL applies in domains with the following characteristics:

- There are multiple agents organized in a team.
- There are opaque state transitions.
- There are too many states and/or not enough training examples for traditional RL techniques to work.
- The target concept is non-stationary.
- There is long-range reward available.
- There are action-dependent features available.

There are several such domains. As seen in Sections 7.3 and 7.4, simulated robotic soccer and network packet-routing are two such team-partitioned, opaque-transition domains. Other domains to which TPOT-RL could potentially be applied are information networks, distributed logistics, and rescue missions. For example, an information agent may broadcast a message without any knowledge of who will receive and react to it.

In all of these team-partitioned, opaque-transition domains, a team of agents works together towards a common goal, but each individual agent only executes a portion of the actions along the path to the goal. Agents can control their own destinies only intermittently and at irregular intervals. While not in full control of the team's goal achievement, they must still learn how to act so as to *help* their team achieve its goal. These domains are in contrast with, for example, grid world domains in which a single agent moves from some initial location to some final goal location; domains where agents take actions in parallel though also possibly in coordination—two robots executing tasks in parallel; and game domains where the rules of the game require that an agent and its opponent alternate actions.

One main contribution of this book is the adaptation of the RL paradigm to a non-stationary, opaque-transition multiagent domain with a huge state space and extremely limited training examples. TPOT-RL succeeds in this challenging domain by:

- Partitioning the value function among multiple agents.
- Training agents simultaneously with a gradually decreasing exploration rate.
- Using action-dependent features to aggressively generalize the state space.
- Gathering long-term, discounted reward directly from the environment.

7.6 Related Work

The use of machine learning in multiagent systems has recently been receiving a good deal of attention. For a detailed discussion, see Chapter 9. This section highlights some of the prior RL research that is most related to TPOT-RL.

TPOT-RL mixes characteristics of different RL approaches. From a team perspective, there are a series of action opportunities resulting in state transitions and occasionally leading to rewards. In this sense, it is similar to Q-learning. However, from an individual agent's perspective, since transitions are opaque, TPOT-RL is more like a Monte Carlo system in which actions are rewarded for their eventual outcomes without any regard for the path of states traversed between the action and the reward. In this sense, TPOT-RL is similar to TD(1) (Sutton, 1988) [5].

One method of dealing with large state spaces in RL is approximation of the function Q. There has been much research into function approximation techniques in which the value function is a neural network or perhaps a decision tree (e.g. (Boyan and Moore, 1995)—see (Kaelbling et al., 1996) for a survey). In contrast to TPOT-RL's construction of a small feature space prior to learning, function approximators generalize large state spaces during learning.

When using a feature space V, the definition of V can have a huge effect on the nature of Q. For example, in (Salustowicz et al., 1998), a grid-like discretization is used for V. Since too many states result for a lookup-table, a neural network is used as the value function approximator. This approach is shown not to work very well, and the authors conclude that a more complex function approximator might work better. In contrast, we take the approach of using a smaller feature space and the simplest possible evaluation function: a lookup-table.

5 TD(1) is equivalent to a form of Monte Carlo learning (Singh and Sutton, 1996).

One RL application that has some similar characteristics to simulated robotic soccer is distributed elevator control (Crites and Barto, 1996). In this domain, a team of RL agents—each responsible for one of four elevator cars—in a large, partially hidden, continuous state space. Since the four agents learn simultaneously, the reinforcement to each individual agent is non-stationary: it depends on the policies of the other agents. Crites and Barto report very good results in comparison with heuristic control policies.

Elevator control as presented in (Crites and Barto, 1996) differs in two main ways from the problems with which we are concerned. First, the approach is not team-partitioned since each agent learns to operate in the entire state space. Second, it is not opaque-transition. After taking an action in a state, an elevator agent knows the subsequent state that it enters and is able to update its value function based on the value of this subsequent state.

TPOT-RL is able to learn with very few training examples. Prioritized sweeping (Moore and Atkeson, 1993) is another method for learning with limited training examples. However, like many other RL techniques, it relies on being able to store trajectories of state transitions in the environment.

Even the partially observable Markov decision process (POMDP) (Kaelbling et al., 1994) framework, which is designed for problems with hidden state, relies on agents having some knowledge of state transitions: POMDPs assume that the agent knows when the system has transitioned to a new state and a new action can be taken. Thus reward can still be propagated back through the state-action trajectory. Without access to future action opportunities agents must accumulate their rewards directly from the environment.

Although the use of the environment for reward accumulation is a necessity in this domain, it has also been shown to be an advantage in similar situations. Searching in stochastic policy space and using an average payoff for evaluating observation-action pairs can produce successful policies without relying on the Markov property (Singh et al., 1994). As in our case, the work reported there involves a domain in which several states are in the same observation class due to the use of coarse features.

The intermediate reinforcement in the reward function R is similar to *progress estimators* (Mataric, 1994a). Progress estimators use the short-term real-world effects of actions as intermediate rewards to help robots reach their ultimate goal location. Mataric's *conditions* also play a similar role to the features used here, reducing the size of the domain of the value function. This work was done using a reactive approach, as opposed to our more deliberative approach which takes into account past world states and agents' internal states.

Previous multiagent reinforcement learning systems have typically dealt with much simpler tasks than the one presented here. Littman uses Markov games to learn stochastic policies in a very abstract version of 1-on-1 robotic soccer (Littman, 1994). There have also been a number of studies of multiagent reinforcement learning in the pursuit domain with four predators chasing a single prey in a small grid-like world. For example, Tan (1993) compares situations in which predator agents are allowed to share reinforcement information and/or policies; Arai (1997) provides agents with reinforcement for enabling successful actions by teammates; and Ono (1997) equips each predator agent with different behavior modules based on how many teammates are closer than it is to the prey. Even the relatively complex backgammon (Tesauro, 1994) and elevator control (Crites and Barto, 1996) domains have much smaller state space than the simulated robotic soccer domain.

In another predator-like task, Zhao and Schmidhuber (1996) use a single run to deal with the opponents' shifting policies and ignore the opponents' policies just as we do. The effects of opponent actions are captured in the reward function.

In robotic soccer, a reinforcement learning approach has been used for strategic positioning (Andou, 1998) in the soccer server. Introducing *observational reinforcement learning*, this system allows players to notice where the ball has traveled most often in the past and to adjust their positions such that they are closer to the ball's path in the future.

Within network routing, Q-routing (Boyan and Littman, 1994) is discussed in detail above as it is one of the benchmarks against which we compare TPOT-RL. Another approach to network routing in the same simulator is inspired by an ant metaphor (Subramanian et al., 1997). Ants crawl backwards over the network to discover link costs and shortest paths. This system rests on the assumption that link costs are the same for packets going in either direction. It also adds an overhead cost of sending the ant packets through the network.

Similarly inspired by the ant metaphor, AntNet (Caro and Dorigo, 1998) agents traverse a routing network and write information at the nodes reflecting their experience of the current network status. Within the framework presented in (Caro and Dorigo, 1998), TPOT-RL is a distributed, adaptive, non-minimal (i.e. packets do not necessarily always go along minimal cost paths), and optimal (i.e. the objective is to optimize the entire network's performance as opposed to any individual packet's traversal time) routing algorithm.

8 Competition Results

In Chapters 3–7, I presented the main contributions of this book along with extensive controlled experiments empirically validating each individual contribution. However, since the overall goal is to a create a complete team of agents that can operate in an adversarial environment, it is also interesting and informative to note how the team performs against a wide range of previously-unseen adversaries.

This chapter documents our experiences at several robotic soccer competitions in which we have participated over the years. Since competitions are not controlled experiments, their results are not presented as scientific validation of our individual techniques. Such validation is presented in the previous chapters. However, I believe that competition results provide useful evaluations of complete systems. In addition, I believe that qualitative evaluations and anecdotes from these competitions teach some valuable lessons and provide insights into the strengths and weaknesses of various approaches.

We named all of the teams that we entered in competitions "CMUnited." In this chapter, I differentiate among the teams based on the year and platform in which they competed. For example, the "CMUnited-96 simulator team" competed in the simulator competition in 1996; the "CMUnited-97 small-robot team" competed in the small-robot competition in 1997.

No individual team that we entered in a competition embodies all of the research contributions of this book. The team member agent architecture is used in several of the teams, while TPOT-RL is used in none: it requires more training against an opponent than is possible in competitions. Throughout this chapter, I indicate which techniques are used by each team and Table 8.1 summarizes the correspondence between teams and techniques. Although set-plays (Section 3.3) and SPAR (Section 3.5) are presented in Chapter 3 as part of the flexible teamwork structure, they are given separate entries in the table since they are both used outside of the teamwork structure by at least one team.

Sections 8.1–8.5 provide match results and anecdotes from 5 competitions in which we participated. Section 8.6 concludes with the most important lessons learned from these competitions.

Table 8.1
The research techniques used by the various CMUnited teams which we entered in competitions.

CMUnited Team (year/platform)	Team Member Agent Arch.	Comm. Paradigm	Teamwork Struct.	Set-Plays	SPAR	Learned Ball Intcpn. (NN)	Learned Pass Eval. (DT)
96/simulator						+	
96/robots				+			
97/simulator	+	+	+	+		+	+
97/robots	+		+	+			
98/simulator	+	+	+	+	+		+
98/robots	+				+		
99/simulator	+	+	+	+	+		+

8.1 Pre-RoboCup-96

The first robotic soccer competition of any sort was held on November 5–7, 1996 in Osaka, Japan (Kitano, 1996). In conjunction with the IROS-96 conference, Pre-RoboCup-96 was meant as an informal competition to test the RoboCup soccer server in preparation for RoboCup-97. Most of the entrants were from the Tokyo region and were in frequent contact with the developer of the soccer server.

At the time of the competition, we had only begun our agent development, having created nothing more than the learned ball-interception behavior described in Chapter 5. In last-minute preparation for the event, we developed a static team formation and a fixed, hand-coded receiver choice function (RCF) similar to the prefer right wing (PRW) RCF defined in Section 6.3. The player closest to the ball always moved towards it and then passed to a pre-determined teammate, with one designated player shooting towards the goal.

We were aware that our CMUnited-96 simulator team implementation was preliminary, but we entered the competition in order to obtain a feeling for what areas needed the most attention, and to help test the soccer server. Table 8.2 shows the results of the games in which CMUnited-96 participated.

An important lesson learned at this competition was that it is very important to be able to get to the ball quickly and efficiently. The two top teams, Ogalets and Sekine, each had several players quickly moving towards the ball, thus increasing the likelihood that they would retain possession. Our preliminary strategy of having a single player moving slowly and deliberately towards the ball proved to be ineffective. The trained neural network was good at block-

Table 8.2
The scores of CMUnited-96's games in the simulator league of Pre-RoboCup-96. CMUnited-96 won 2 of its 5 games, finishing in 4th place out of 8 teams.

Opponent	Affiliation	Score (CMU–Opp.)
Oota	Tokyo Institute of Technology, Japan	4 – 1
ETL	Electrotechnical Laboratory, Japan	7 – 0
Sekine	Tokyo Institute of Technology, Japan	1 – 13
Ogalets	Tokyo University, Japan	1 – 9
Waseda	Waseda University, Japan	3 – 4
TOTAL		16 – 27

NOTE: The last game was lost by one goal in overtime.

ing the ball, but there was no incentive built into the training regime to get to the ball quickly. We learned at this competition that robot soccer teams must have either very efficient ball-interception, or several players moving towards the ball at once. In later competitions, we aimed to improve ball-interception efficiency, while also occasionally sending multiple players towards the ball.

8.2 MiroSot-96

The first robotic soccer competition involving real robots was held immediately after Pre-RoboCup-96, on November 9–12, 1996 in Taejon, South Korea (Kim, 1996). Called MiroSot-96, this tournament included 19 robotic teams. As a single elimination tournament, it provided for only a single game for many of the teams, including CMUnited-96, which was matched in its first game against the eventual runner-up.

MiroSot-96 required smaller robots than the ones described in Section 2.3 (7.5cm^3 maximum). In addition, there were only three allowed per team. The robots we used in this competition were a preliminary version of those described in Section 2.3 (Achim et al., 1996). Although they did not use the team member agent architecture or any of the machine learning techniques described in this book, they did include complex set-plays.

Table 8.3 shows the result of our single game at the MiroSot-96 competition. The Miro team ended up losing in the finals 20–0 to the team from NewtonLabs, USA.

The winner of MiroSot-96, NewtonLabs, dominated at this tournament due mostly to the speed of its vision system and robots (Sargent et al., 1997). At

Table 8.3
The score of CMUnited-96's game in the robot league of MiroSot-96. CMUnited-96 lost its only game.

Opponent	Affiliation	Score (CMU–Opp.)
Miro	Korean Advanced Institute of Science and (KAIST)	3 – 7
TOTAL		3 – 7

this tournament we learned the importance of the vision component of robotic soccer systems.

In addition to the 3-robot competition, MiroSot-96 also included a single robot competition: each team was allowed just a single robot on the field. In this competition, the CMUnited-96 robot lost in the finals by one goal. Table 8.4 shows the results of the two games in which it competed.

Table 8.4
The scores of CMUnited-96's games in the single robot league of MiroSot-96. CMUnited-96 won 1 of its 2 games, finishing in 2nd place out of 4 teams.

Opponent	Affiliation	Score (CMU–Opp.)
Rogi	University of Girona, Catalonia, Spain	4 – 2
Lami	Federal Institute of Technology, Switzerland	4 – 5
TOTAL		8 – 7

8.3 RoboCup-97

RoboCup-97 was the first formal RoboCup championship. It was held on August 23–29, 1997 in Nagoya, Japan in conjunction with the IJCAI-97 conference (Kitano, 1998). At RoboCup-97, we entered teams in both the simulator competition and the small-robot competition.

Simulator Competition

The RoboCup-97 simulator competition was the first formal simulated robotic soccer competition. With 29 teams entering from all around the world, it was a very successful tournament.

It was in preparation for this competition that the team member agent architecture, including both the flexible teamwork structure and the inter-agent communication paradigm, described in Chapter 3 was developed. In addition to the team member agent architecture, the CMUnited-97 simulator team which we entered in this competition used the learned ball-interception and pass-evaluation skills. In particular, the decision tree (DT) RCF presented in Section 6.3 was used.

Table 8.5 shows the results of CMUnited-97's games in this tournament. CMUnited-97 won 3 of its first 4 matches by wide margins, with the other match being a close victory. Its 5th opponent, FCMellon, was also our own team and was identical to CMUnited except that it did not use a flexible teamwork structure: players did not switch positions, did not use flexible positioning of any sort, and did not use set-plays. Our goal in entering FCMellon in the competition was to highlight the impact of our research contributions in CMUnited. Due to the results reported in Section 3.6, we expected CMUnited to win this game. Before the game between CMUnited and FCMellon, FCMellon won its 4 games by a combined score of 49–4.

Table 8.5
The scores of CMUnited-97's games in the simulator league of RoboCup-97. CMUnited-97 won 5 of its 7 games, finishing in 4th place out of 29 teams.

Opponent	Affiliation	Score (CMU–Opp.)
LAI	Universidad Carlos III De Madrid, Spain	9 – 1
RM Knights	Royal Melbourne Inst. of Tech., Australia	16 – 0
Kinki	Kinki University, Japan	6 – 5
Team Garbage Collectors	Justsystem, Japan	24 – 0
FCMellon	Carnegie Mellon University, USA	6 – 0
AT-Humboldt	Humboldt University of Berlin, Germany	0 – 6
ISIS	Information Sciences Institute (USC), USA	1 – 2
TOTAL		62 – 14

NOTE: The last game was lost by one goal in overtime.

The subsequent game was against the eventual tournament champion AT-Humboldt. As described in Section 3.6, CMUnited-97 used a 4-4-2 formation in general, switching to an 8-2-0 formation if winning near the end of the game, or a 3-3-4 formation if losing. The triggers for these formation switches were defined as part of the locker-room agreement. However, by the time CMUnited-97 played against them, it was clear from watching other games that

AT-Humboldt was the team to beat. Therefore, we altered the team's locker-room agreement so that it would adopt a more conservative, defensive strategy at the beginning of the game. As a result, AT-Humboldt scored fewer goals against CMUnited-97 than it did against any of its other competitors. The 6–0 result might have been closer had CMUnited-97 not automatically switched to the more offensive 3-3-4 formation near the end of the game when it was losing in an attempt, though unsuccessful, to score some goals.

One of the main advantages of AT-Humboldt was its ability to kick the ball harder than any other team. Its players did so by kicking the ball around themselves, continually increasing its velocity so that it ended up moving towards the goal faster than was imagined possible. Since the soccer server did not enforce a maximum ball speed, a property that was changed immediately after the competition, the ball could move arbitrarily fast, making it impossible to stop. With this advantage at the low-level behavior level, no team, regardless of how strategically sophisticated, was able to defeat AT-Humboldt.

Having lost in the semi-finals, CMUnited-97 then played in the 3rd-place game against ISIS. CMUnited-97 scored first in this game off of a corner-kick set-play. However, ISIS equalized near the end of the game and the game went to overtime. ISIS scored to win in what proved to be one of the more exciting matches of the tournament.

The RoboCup-97 simulator competition was won by the team that found the best domain-dependent solutions, moving and kicking better than the other teams. However, this team's success alerted other teams to the necessity of solving the low-level problems. At the subsequent competition, RoboCup-98, there were several teams with roughly equal low-level skills, thus allowing the high-level, more MAS-research-based solutions to make the key differences.

Small-Robot Competition

As described in Section 3.7, our team member agent architecture—including the teamwork structure and set-plays— while developed in simulation, was also used by the CMUnited-97 real robots which won the RoboCup-97 small-robot competition (Veloso et al., 1998a). Table 8.6 shows the results of the games at RoboCup-97.

In total, CMUnited-97 scored thirteen goals, allowing only one against. The one goal against was scored by the CMUnited goaltender against itself, though under an attacking situation from MICROB. We refined the goaltender's behavior as presented in Appendix B (Section B.2), following the observation of our goaltender's error.

Table 8.6
The scores of CMUnited-97's games in the small-robot league of RoboCup-97. CMUnited-97 won all 4 games, finishing in 1st place out of 4 teams.

Opponent	Affiliation	Score (CMU–Opp.)
NAIST	Nara Institute of Science and Technology, Japan	5 – 0
MICROB	University of Paris VI , France	3 – 1
Girona U.	University of Girona, Catalonia, Spain	2 – 0
NAIST	Nara Institute of Science and Technology, Japan	3 – 0
TOTAL		13 – 1

As the CMUnited-97 small-robot matches proceeded, spectators noticed many of the team behaviors described in Chapter 3. The robots switched positions during the games, and there were several successful passes. The most impressive goal of the tournament was the result of a 4-way passing play: robot 1 passed to robot 2, which passed back to robot 1; then robot 1 passed to a third robot, robot 3, which shot the ball into the goal.

Like in the simulator competition, this first RoboCup small-robot competition was won by the team with the best low-level sensing and acting abilities. No other team had the reliable vision or skills exhibited by the CMUnited-97 robots. However, also like in the simulator competition, CMUnited-97's success alerted other teams to the importance of these low-level abilities, leading to a competition among several more equally-skilled teams the following year.

8.4 RoboCup-98

The second international RoboCup championship, RoboCup-98, was held on July 2–9, 1998 in Paris, France (Asada and Kitano, 1999). It was held in conjunction with the ICMAS-98 conference. As mentioned in Section 8.3, the winners of both the simulator and small-robot competitions at RoboCup-97 had much better low-level skills than the other teams and won easily. At RoboCup-98, both the simulator and small-robot competitions had much closer matches among the best teams. CMUnited-98 won both of these competitions due to a combination of good low-level and high-level strategic reasoning.

Simulator Competition

As one of the main contributions of this book, The CMUnited-98 simulator team is fully specified in Section 3.5 and Appendix B, Section B.1. It uses the team member agent architecture, including the teamwork structure, communication paradigm, set-plays, and SPAR, and a trained decision tree for pass evaluation. At the RoboCup-98 simulator competition, CMUnited-98 won all 8 of its games by a combined score of 66–0, finishing 1st in a field of 34 teams. Table 8.7 details the game results.

Table 8.7
The scores of CMUnited-98's games in the simulator league of RoboCup-98. CMUnited-98 won all 8 games, finishing in 1st place out of 34 teams.

Opponent	Affiliation	Score (CMU–Opp.)
UU	Utrecht University, The Netherlands	22 – 0
TUM / TUMSA	Technical University Munich, Germany	2 – 0
Kasuga-Bitos II	Chubu University, Japan	5 – 0
Andhill'98	NEC, Japan	8 – 0
ISIS	Information Sciences Institute (USC), USA	12 – 0
Mainz Rolling Brains	Johannes Gutenberg-University Mainz, Germany	13 – 0
Windmill Wanderers	University of Amsterdam, The Netherlands	1 – 0
AT-Humboldt'98	Humboldt University of Berlin, Germany	3 – 0
TOTAL		66 – 0

From observing the games, it was apparent that the CMUnited-98 low-level skills were superior in the first 6 games: CMUnited-98 agents were able to dribble around opponents, had many scoring opportunities, and suffered few shots against.

However, in the last 2 games, the CMUnited-98 strategic formations, communication, and ball-handling routines were tested as the Windmill Wanderers (3rd place) and AT-Humboldt'98 (2nd place) had similar low-level capabilities. In these games, CMUnited-98's abilities to use set-plays to clear the ball from its defensive zone, to get past the opponents' offsides traps, and to maintain a cohesive defensive unit became very apparent. Many of the goals scored by CMUnited-98 were a direct result of the opponent team being unable to clear the ball from its own end after a goal kick: a CMUnited-98 player would intercept the clearing pass and quickly shoot it into the goal. In particular, two of the goals in the final game against AT-Humboldt'98 were scored in this manner. On the other hand, the CMUnited-98 simulator team was able to clear the ball successfully from its own zone using its ability to execute set-plays, or pre-compiled, multiagent plans (see Section 3.5). Rather than kicking the ball up the middle of the field, one player would pass out to the sideline to a second player that would then clear the ball up the field. After a series of 3 or 4 passes, the ball was usually safely in the other half of the field.

Another strategic advantage that was clear throughout CMUnited-98's games was the players' abilities to maintain a coherent defensive unit exploiting the offsides rule, and conversely, its ability to get through the defense of other teams. Often, the opposing teams were unable to get anywhere near the CMUnited-98 goal because of the defenders' ability to stay in front of some of the opposing forwards, thus rendering them offsides and prohibiting them from ever successfully receiving the ball.

In order to deal with opposing teams that tried to use a similar technique, the CMUnited-98 forwards would kick the ball towards the offensive corners of the field (the "sending" skill described in Appendix B, Section B.1, in the subsection on "Clearing") and then either get to the ball before the defenders or intercept defenders' clearing passes. CMUnited-98 scored several goals after such kicks to the corners.

In addition to the strategic reasoning that helped the team win its final two games, the fine points of the dribbling and goaltending skills also came into play. Using their predictive, locally optimal skills (PLOS—see Section 3.5), the CMUnited-98 players were occasionally able to dribble around opponents for shots. At a crucial moment against the Windmill Wanderers, the CMUnited-98 goaltender made a particularly important save: while winning 1–0 near the end of the game, a shot got past the goaltender, but it was able to turn and catch the ball before the ball entered the goal.

Small-Robot Competition

Like in the simulator competition, the RoboCup-98 small-robot competition featured matches against several teams with similar low-level sensing and acting abilities. Since the CMUnited-97 small-robot team is more reflective of the contributions of this book than the CMUnited-98 small-robot team, it is the CMUnited-97 small-robot team that is described in Section 3.7 and Appendix B, Section B.2. However, CMUnited-98 uses both the team member agent architecture and SPAR (see Section 3.5, which was developed in parallel both in simulation and on the real robots. Table 8.8 shows the scores of the games of the CMUnited-98 small-robot team.

In the second match, against 5DPO, we experienced the brittleness of low-power radio communication in public places. In this match, CMUnited-98 performed miserably, often just turning in circles. We think that this failure occurred because of radio interference. After identifying and eliminating a

Table 8.8
The scores of CMUnited-98's games in the small-robot league of RoboCup-98. CMUnited-98 won 4 of its 5 games, finishing in 1st place out of 11 teams.

Opponent	Affiliation	Score (CMU–Opp.)
iXS	iXs Inc.	16 – 2
5DPO	University of Porto, Portugal	0 – 3
Paris-8	University of Paris-8	3 – 0
Cambridge	University of Cambridge, UK	3 – 0
Roboroos	University of Queensland, Australia	3 – 1
TOTAL		25 – 6

possible source of interference, CMUnited-98 was able to resume its successful performance.

The final two games, against Cambridge and Roboroos, were both close matches against teams with similar sensing and acting capabilities to those of CMUnited-98. The key to CMUnited-98's success was its strategic play, including sophisticated goaltending, defending, and collaborative attacking using SPAR.

8.5 RoboCup-99

The research and history reported in this book culminate with the RoboCup-98 competition. In particular, version 4 of the soccer server which is described in Section 2.2 was used at RoboCup-98; the implementation details given in Section 3.5 and Appendix B are those of the CMUnited-98 team; and the references to related work in the robotic soccer domain include work reported before and including the RoboCup-98 Workshop (Asada and Kitano, 1999). However, in that the results of the RoboCup-99 simulator competition are relevant to this book, I briefly summarize them in this Section.

The third international RoboCup championship, RoboCup-99, was held on July 28–August 4, 1999 in Stockholm, Sweden in conjunction with the IJCAI-99 conference (Veloso et al., 2000). As the defending champion team, the CMUnited-98 simulator team was entered in the competition. Its code was left unaltered from that used at RoboCup-98 except for minor changes necessary to update to version 5 of the soccer server[1] In addition, the

1 Some of the differences between version 5 and version 4 of the soccer server are noted in Section 2.2. Server parameter changes that reduced player size, speed, and kickable area required

CMUnited-99 simulator team is based closely upon CMUnited-98. In particular, like CMUnited-98, CMUnited-99 uses the team member agent architecture, including the teamwork structure, communication paradigm, set-plays, and SPAR, and a trained decision tree for pass evaluation.

The CMUnited-98 team became publicly available soon after RoboCup-98 so that other people could build upon our research. Thus, we expected there to be several teams at RoboCup-99 that could beat CMUnited-98, and indeed there were. Nonetheless, CMUnited-98 performed respectably, winning 3 games, losing 2, and tying 1 and outscoring its opponents by a combined score of 29–3. Table 8.9 presents the details of CMUnited-98's matches.

Table 8.9
The scores of CMUnited-98's games in the simulator league of RoboCup-99. CMUnited-98 won 3, lost 2, and tied 1 game.

Opponent	Affiliation	Score (CMU–Opp.)
Kasuga-Bitos III	Chubu University, Japan	19 – 0
Karlsruhe Brainstormers	University of Karlsruhe, Germany	1 – 0
Cyberoos	CSIRO, Australia	1 – 0
Essex Wizards	University of Essex, UK	0 – 0
Mainz Rolling Brains	University of Mainz, Germany	0 – 2
Gemini	Tokyo Institute of Technology, Japan	8 – 0
11 Monkeys	Keio University, Japan	0 – 1
TOTAL		29 – 3

NOTE: The last game was lost by one goal in overtime.

Meanwhile, the CMUnited-99 team was even more successful at the RoboCup-99 competition than was its predecessor at RoboCup-98. It won all 8 of its games by a combined score of 110–0, finishing 1st in a field of 37 teams. While CMUnited-99 includes several improvements over CMUnited-98[2], in the context of this book it is significant to note that all of the main research contributions from CMUnited-98 remain intact in the CMUnited-99 team (see Table 8.1). Table 8.10 shows CMUnited-99's game results.

adjustments in the CMUnited-98 code. However CMUnited-98 did not take advantage of additions to the players' capabilities such as the ability to look in a direction other than straight ahead (simulation of a neck).

2 The most significant improvements are the introduction of teammate and opponent modeling for improved decision making, particularly when near the opponent's goal; and the optimization of several low-level behaviors through automatic training. These improvements, joint work with Patrick Riley and Manuela Veloso, will be the subjects of future publications.

Table 8.10
The scores of CMUnited-99's games in the simulator league of RoboCup-99. CMUnited-99 won all 8 games, finishing in 1st place out of 37 teams.

Opponent	Affiliation	Score (CMU–Opp.)
Ulm Sparrows	University of Ulm, Germany	29 – 0
Zeng99	Fukui University, Japan	11 – 0
Headless Chickens III	Linköping University, Sweden	17 – 0
Oulu99	University of Oulu, Finland	25 – 0
11 Monkeys	Keio University, Japan	8 – 0
Mainz Rolling Brains	University of Mainz, Germany	9 – 0
Magma Freiburg	Freiburg University, Germany	7 – 0
Magma Freiburg	Freiburg University, Germany	4 – 0
TOTAL		110 – 0

8.6 Lessons Learned from Competitions

Robotic soccer competitions have the potential to accelerate scientific progress within the robotic soccer domain. However, there are also many potential hazards that can render them detrimental to progress. By participating in the competitions described in Sections 8.1–8.4, we learned many things, both about competitions themselves and about our own research.

RoboCup, one of the main robotic soccer organizations and the one with which I am most closely associated, is primarily a research initiative. As such, the goal of the entire organization is to help advance the state of the art. It has certainly done so by providing new and challenging domains for studying issues within robotics and AI, such as "design principles of autonomous agents, multiagent collaboration, strategy acquisition, real-time reasoning and planning, intelligent robotics, sensor-fusion, and so forth" (Kitano et al., 1997).

However, the domains exist without the competitions. In this section, I examine the potential hazards and potential benefits of having periodic large-scale robotic soccer competitions, drawing on our experiences as participants. I operate under the premise that scientific progress (as opposed to, for example, entertainment) is the primary goal.

I start by examining the potential hazards of competitions; then I point out the potential benefits. As many potential hazards and benefits are quite similar, it is up to the participants and organizers to sway the balance towards the benefits.

Hazards

There are many potential hazards to scientific progress involved in holding organized robotic soccer competitions. However, many can be avoided through careful organization of the competitions along with an engineered social climate within the community. Here, I list the possible hazards while, where possible, indicating how RoboCup has tried to avoid them.

Obsession with winning. One of the most obvious potential hazards of competitions is that people try to win them at the expense of all else, including science. Especially if there are monetary prizes involved, many people will focus only on winning and there is a potential incentive to keep successful techniques secret from year to year. RoboCup does its best to avoid this hazard by not awarding any monetary prizes. In addition, "scientific challenge" awards are given to teams who, in the opinions of the organizers, have demonstrated the best scientific contributions in their teams. In comparison with the competition winners, winners of these scientific challenge awards are given equal, if not greater, status at the awards ceremonies and within the community. Thus, there is explicit incentive given to deemphasize winning in favor of focusing on scientific contributions. Nonetheless, competitive spirit can easily take over.

Domain-dependent solutions. Another potential hazard of competitions, particularly within complex domains, is that it can be difficult to avoid getting bogged down in the low-level details of the domain. If the competition is to serve scientific interests, the winning solutions should be ones that are generally applicable beyond the particular domain in question. Of course, it is impossible to avoid requiring some domain-dependent solutions. However, while necessary, they should not be sufficient to produce a winning team. One way to encourage an emphasis on high-level, generalizable solutions is to repeat the same competition several times. While the first iteration is likely to be won by the best domain-dependent solution, subsequent events are more likely to find several teams using the same low-level approach that has already been proven effective. Then the difference among the teams will be more at the general levels. For example, at RoboCup-97, the winning teams in both the simulator and small-robot competitions were the ones that had the best low-level sensing and acting capabilities. However at RoboCup-98, there were several teams with similar low-level capabilities. Instead, the crucial differences were at the level of collaborative and adversarial strategic reasoning using techniques, such as those described in this book, that are not limited to the robotic soccer domain.

Cost escalation. Especially in the robot competitions, there is the potential to have increasingly expensive solutions. If an expensive technology provides a significant advantage at one competition, then it might become a prerequisite for success in future years. If the expense is prohibitive to academic researchers, then the competition could die out. This issue has not yet been addressed in RoboCup. One possible solution would be to require that all teams use a common hardware platform, restricting the differences to the software. In fact, the RoboCup-98 legged robot competition used this approach as the only robots meeting the competition specifications were the Sony legged robots (Veloso et al., 1998c). However, in general, this is not a satisfactory approach for RoboCup given that some of the interesting research issues are in the creation of the hardware itself. Another possible solution would be to enforce cost limits on entrants. However, such a restriction would be very difficult to define and enforce adequately. Cost escalation may become a serious issue for RoboCup in the near future.

Restrictive rules. While it is important to have well-defined rules for competitions, there is a potential to discourage research innovations via these rules. Especially for competitions involving robots, it is difficult to create rules that have no loopholes but are not overly restrictive. RoboCup's approach has been to make the rules flexible enough to allow for a wide variety of robot-design decisions. The inevitable rules disputes are handled as amicably as possible in a spirit of cooperation at the competitions. While this approach has the potential to lead to some heated arguments, it is the best from a research perspective.

Invalid evaluation conclusions. There is the potential at competitions to conclude that if team A beats team B, then all of the techniques used by team A are more successful than those used by team B. However, this conclusion is invalid. Unless the teams are identical except in one respect, no individual aspect of either team can conclusively be credited with or blamed for the result. Indeed, the CMUnited team won several of the competitions described above, but I do not present this chapter as an evaluation of any of the general contributions of this book other than the team as a whole. Instead, we conduct extensive controlled experiments to validate our research contributions.

Benefits

While there are many potential hazards to holding robotic soccer competitions, there are also many potential benefits. Here I list the possible benefits, again illustrating them with specific examples from RoboCup whenever possible.

Research Inspiration. While one potential hazard of competitions stemming from peoples' competitive spirit is an obsession with winning, a related benefit is that competitions are a great source of research inspiration. Several of the innovations reported in this book, most significantly the entire team member agent architecture, are the direct result of preparations for one of the above competitions. While they started as innovative solutions to challenging specific problems, we were then able to abstract their contributions into general frameworks. The natural desire to win is a strong motivation to create a good team by solving the challenging aspects of the domain.

Deadlines for creating complete agents. Competitions create hard deadlines for the creation of *complete* working systems. In order to compete, it is not sufficient for any one component of the system to be operational. Therefore, entrants must confront the challenging issues of "closing the loop," i.e. getting all components working from sensing, to acting, to strategic reasoning. They must create complete agents. No matter how sophisticated a team's high-level strategic reasoning, if it does not solve the low-level issues, some other team will easily win. Our experience has been that these deadlines have forced us to solve difficult holistic problems that we might have otherwise overlooked: these problems have been a source of research inspiration for us.

Common platform for exchanging ideas. Robotic soccer competitions can bring together a group of people who have all tried to solve the same problems in the same domain. Unlike in many research communities, there is a common substrate system and a common language among participants. For example, in the planning community (Simmons et al., 1998), researchers use a wide variety of planning systems, each with its own properties and idiosyncrasies, sometimes making it difficult to directly compare approaches and technique. In RoboCup, on the other hand, everyone implements their ideas in the same underlying architecture. Consequently, it is relatively easy to compare the various systems.

Continually improving solutions. When holding repeated competitions with the same platform, there is likely to be a continual improvement in solutions from event to event. All entrants know that in order to have a chance of winning a competition, they must be able to outperform the previous champion. Therefore, they are motivated to find some method of improving over the previous solutions. Of course, this benefit only applies if the same, or similar, rules are used as the basis for competition year after year. For example, in the AAAI robot competitions (Arkin, 1998), there are new tasks to be solved every year. While the new tasks encourage new entrants, there is no basis for directly measuring improvement from year to year.

Excitement for students at all levels. The inherent excitement of the robotic soccer competitions encourages students at all levels to become involved in serious research. Competition entries often come from large teams of professors, graduate students, and undergraduates working together. By encouraging more people to become involved in the research, the competitions can speed up progress.

Wide pool of teams created. After each competition, all of the entrants have created teams capable of performing in the given domain. If these teams are made available in some way, they can subsequently be used for controlled testing of research contributions. For example, in order to test technique x that is a single aspect of one's team, one could play the team against another team first with technique x active, and then without, thus establishing the effects of technique x. While such testing could be done against any team, it is often up to the researchers themselves to create the team against which to test. As a result the comparison is often done against a trivial or simple team. The competition can provide several teams against which to test, each of which is the result of serious effort by an independent group of researchers.

Encourage flexible software and hardware. Taking a system out of one's own lab and into a new setting, whether it be a software system that is to be run on different computers or a robotic system that is to be run under different environmental conditions, requires a certain degree of flexibility in the system's creation. For example, rather than creating a vision system that works only in the lighting conditions in one's own lab, researchers must create a system that is easily adaptable to new conditions. Thus, the competition encourages general solutions that are more likely to apply in a wide variety of circumstances.

It has been our experience so far that the benefits of robotic soccer competitions outweigh the hazards. Most significantly as a strong source of inspiration, robotic soccer competitions have played an important role in my research. Again, the competition results themselves are not scientifically conclusive. But the process of competition, including the lessons learned, can be scientifically valuable.

9 Related Work

This book contributes to the fields of Multiagent Systems (MAS), Machine Learning (ML), and a subfield of ML, Reinforcement Learning (RL). In each of these areas, there is an immense body of literature. The book also contributes to the growing body of research within the robotic soccer domain.

In this chapter, I review the prior work in these areas that is most related to my research which is reported in this book. In Section 9.1, I review the intersection of MAS and ML. In particular, I give an overview of MAS with emphasis on multiagent learning approaches (Stone and Veloso, 1997). In Section 9.2, I review research within the robotic soccer domain.

Note that Chapters 3–7 each contain discussions of the related work that most closely pertains to their individual topics. This chapter does not repeat those discussions.

9.1 MAS from an ML Perspective

There are many possible ways to divide MAS and the related field of Distributed Artificial Intelligence (DAI). Overviews and taxonomies are numerous (Decker, 1987; Bond and Gasser, 1988; Durfee et al., 1989; Durfee, 1992; Lesser, 1995; Parunak, 1996; Stone and Veloso, 1997; Jennings et al., 1998; Sycara, 1998), each with its own way to organize the field. This chapter is organized along two main dimensions: agent heterogeneity and amount of communication among agents. Agents are *homogeneous* if they are physically and behaviorally identical; they are *heterogeneous* if they differ in some way. *Communication* is direct interaction among agents in the world. Beginning with the simplest multiagent scenario, homogeneous non-communicating agents, the full range of possible multiagent systems, through highly heterogeneous communicating agents, is considered.

Because of the inherent complexity of MAS, there is much interest in using ML techniques to help deal with this complexity (Weiß and Sen, 1996; Sen, 1996; Weiß, 1997). Many existing ML techniques can be directly applied in multiagent scenarios by delimiting a part of the domain that only involves a single agent. However *multiagent learning* is more concerned with learning issues that arise because of the multiagent aspect of a given domain. As described by Weiß, multiagent learning is "learning that is done by several agents and that becomes possible only because several agents are present" (Weiß, 1995).

In this section, I consider MAS from an ML perspective. Specifically, I consider the primary research topics in MAS, giving examples of ML approaches to these topics when possible. The first subsection is devoted to multiagent systems with homogeneous non-communicating agents; The next considers multiagent systems with heterogeneous non-communicating agents; The next examines multiagent systems with homogeneous communicating agents; and the last subsection focuses on multiagent systems with heterogeneous communicating agents. Many of the issues that arise in the earlier scenarios also apply in the later scenarios. Nevertheless, they are only mentioned again in the later scenarios to the degree that they differ or become more complex. The multiagent scenarios along with the issues that arise therein are summarized in Table 9.1.

Table 9.1
Issues arising in the various MAS scenarios as reflected in the literature.

Homogeneous non-communicating	**Heterogeneous non-communicating**
• Reactive vs. deliberative agents	• Benevolence vs. competitiveness
• Local or global perspective	• Stable vs. evolving agents
• Modeling other agents' states	• Modeling others' goals, actions, and knowledge
• How to affect others	• Resource management (interdependent actions)
	• Social conventions
	• Roles
Homogeneous communicating	**Heterogeneous communicating**
• Distributed sensing	• Understanding each other
	• Planning communicative acts
	• Benevolence vs. competitiveness
	• Negotiation
	• Resource management (schedule coordination)
	• Commitment/decommitment

In multiagent systems, there are multiple agents which model each other's goals and/or actions. In the fully general multiagent scenario, there may be direct interaction among agents via communication. Although this interaction could be viewed as environmental stimuli, we present inter-agent communication as being separate from the environment. From an individual agent's perspective, the environment's dynamics can be affected by other agents. In addition to the uncertainty that may be inherent in the domain, other agents intentionally affect the environment in unpredictable ways. Thus, all multiagent systems can be viewed as having dynamic environments.

Figure 9.1 illustrates the view that each agent is both part of the environment and modeled as a separate entity. There may be any number of agents, with different degrees of heterogeneity and with or without the ability to communicate directly. From the fully general case depicted here, I begin by eliminating both the communication and the heterogeneity to present homogeneous, non-communicating MAS. Then, the possibilities of agent heterogeneity and inter-agent communication are considered one at a time. Finally, at the end of this section, we arrive back at the fully general case by considering heterogeneous agents that can interact directly.

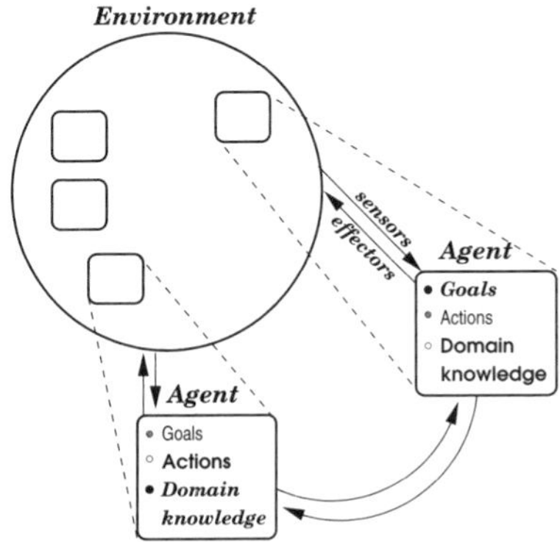

Figure 9.1
The general multiagent scenario. Agents model each other's goals, actions, and domain knowledge, which may differ as indicated by the different fonts. They may also interact directly (communicate) as indicated by the arrows between the agents.

For each of these scenarios, I present the research issues that arise and the existing techniques to deal with them. The issues may appear across scenarios, but they are presented and discussed in the first scenario to which they apply. When possible, ML approaches are emphasized.

The simulated robotic soccer domain can be used to study all of the different multiagent scenarios presented in this section. Throughout the section, I discuss how the different issues are reflected in this domain. Section 9.2 presents related robotic soccer research in detail.

Homogeneous, Non-Communicating MAS

In homogeneous, non-communicating multiagent systems, all of the agents have the same internal structure including goals, domain knowledge, and *pos-*

sible actions. They also have the same procedure for selecting among their actions. The only differences among agents are their sensory inputs and the actual actions they take: they are situated differently in the world. Having different effector output is a necessary condition for MAS: if the agents all act as a unit, then they are essentially a single agent. In order to realize this difference in output, homogeneous agents must have different sensor input as well. Otherwise they will act identically. For this scenario, in which I consider non-communicating agents, assume that the agents cannot communicate directly. Figure 9.2 illustrates the homogeneous, non-communicating multiagent scenario, indicating that the agents' goals, actions, and domain knowledge are the same by representing them with identical fonts.

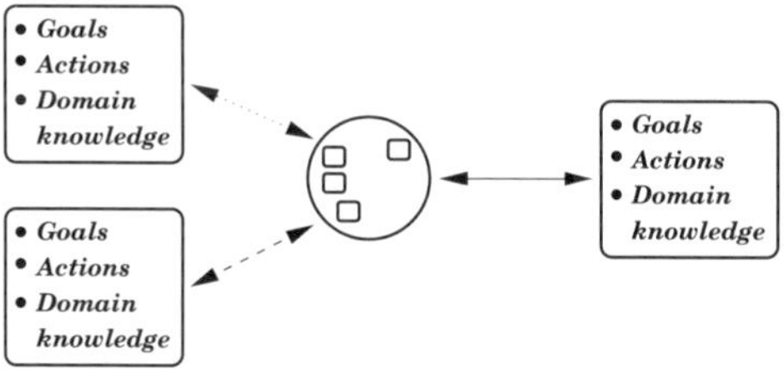

Figure 9.2
MAS with homogeneous, non-communicating agents. Only the sensor input and effector output of agents differ, as represented by the different arrow styles. The agents' goals, actions, and domain knowledge are all identical as indicated by the identical fonts.

Even in this most restrictive of multiagent scenarios, there are several issues with which to deal. The techniques provided here are representative examples of ways to address the presented issues. The issues and techniques are summarized in Table 9.2.

Reactive vs. Deliberative agents

When designing any agent-based system, it is important to determine how sophisticated the agents' reasoning will be. Reactive agents simply retrieve preset behaviors similar to reflexes without maintaining any internal state. On the other hand, deliberative agents behave more like they are thinking, by searching through a space of behaviors, maintaining internal state, and predicting the effects of actions. Although the line between reactive and deliberative agents can be somewhat blurry, an agent with no internal state is certainly reactive, and one which bases its actions on the predicted actions of other agents is de-

Table 9.2
The issues and techniques for homogeneous, non-communicating multiagent systems as reflected in the literature.

Homogeneous, Non-Communicating MAS

Issues

- Reactive vs. deliberative agents
- Local or global perspective
- Modeling other agents' states
- How to affect others

Techniques

- Reactive behaviors for formation maintenance. (Balch and Arkin, 1995)
- Deliberative behaviors for pursuit. (Levy and Rosenschein, 1992)
- Mixed reactive and deliberative behaviors. (Sahota, 1994; Rao and Georgeff, 1995)
- Local knowledge sometimes better. (Roychowdhury et al., 1996)
- (limited) Recursive Modeling Method (RMM). (Durfee, 1995)
- Don't model others–just pay attention to reward. (Schmidhuber, 1996)
- Stigmergy. (Goldman and Rosenschein, 1994; Holland, 1996)
- Q-learning for behaviors like foraging, homing, etc. (Mataric, 1994a)

liberative. Here we describe one system at each extreme as well as two others that mix reactive and deliberative reasoning.

Balch and Arkin (1995) use homogeneous, reactive, non-communicating agents to study formation maintenance in autonomous robots. The robots' goal is to move together in a military formation such as a diamond, column, or wedge. They periodically come across obstacles which prevent one or more of the robots from moving in a straight line. After passing the obstacle, all robots must adjust in order to regain their formation. The agents reactively convert their sensory data (which includes the positions of the other robots) to motion vectors for avoiding obstacles, avoiding robots, moving to a goal location, and formation maintenance. The actual robot motion is a simple weighted sum of these vectors. Military formations differ from the formations introduced as part of our flexible teamwork structure in Section 3.3. In our case, a "formation" refers to a decomposition of the team's overall task as opposed to a geometrical configuration of agents.

At the deliberative end of the spectrum is some research in the pursuit domain (Benda et al., 1986), a multiagent domain in which several independent predators try to catch a prey. Levy and Rosenschein (1992) create agents that each act in service of its own goals. They use game theoretic techniques to find equilibrium points and thus to decide how to act. These agents are clearly deliberative, considering that they search for actions rather than simply retrieving them.

There are also several existing systems and techniques that mix reactive and deliberative behaviors. One example is the OASIS system which reasons about when to be reactive and when to follow goal-directed plans (Rao and Georgeff, 1995). Another example is *reactive deliberation* (Sahota, 1994). As the name implies, it mixes reactive and deliberative behavior: an agent reasons about which reactive behavior to follow under the constraint that it must choose actions at a rate of 60 Hz. Reactive deliberation was developed on the first robotic soccer platform (Barman et al., 1993).

The agents developed in this book also mix reactive and deliberative behaviors. Internal behaviors in the team member agent architecture are exclusively deliberative as they rely upon the locker-room agreement and past internal states. In our soccer implementation, the top-level external behavior which chooses the agent's behavior mode is also deliberative, whereas some of the low-level external behaviors, such as turning to face the ball when it is visible, are purely reactive. When turning to face the ball, an agent refers only to the ball's current relative angle and turns in that direction.

Local or global perspective

Another issue to consider when building a multiagent system is how much sensor information should be available to the agents. Even if it is feasible within the domain to give the agents a global perspectives of the world, it may be more effective to limit them to local views.

As presented in Chapter 2, agents in the simulated robotic soccer and network routing domains are restricted to local perspectives by the nature of their sensory inputs: they can only see a portion of the world. In the real robotic soccer domain, our agents have a global world view.

Roychowdhury et al. consider a case of multiple agents sharing a set of identical resources in which they have to learn (adapt) their resource usage policies (Roychowdhury et al., 1996). Since the agents are identical and do not communicate, if they all have a global view of the current resource usage, they will all move simultaneously to the most under-used resource. However, if they each see a partial picture of the world, then different agents gravitate towards different resources: a preferable effect. Better performance by agents with less knowledge is occasionally summarized by the cliche "Ignorance is Bliss."

Modeling other agents' states

Durfee (1995) provides another example of "Blissful Ignorance," mentioning it explicitly in the title of his paper: "Blissful Ignorance: Knowing Just Enough to Coordinate Well." Now rather than referring to resource usage, the saying applies to the limited recursive modeling method (RMM). When using RMM, agents explicitly model the belief states of other agents, including what they know about each others' beliefs. If agents have too much knowledge, RMM could recurse indefinitely. Even if further information can be obtained by reasoning about what agent A thinks agent B thinks agent A thinks . . . , endless reasoning can lead to inaction. Durfee contends that for coordination to be possible, some potential knowledge must be ignored.

Although it may be useful to build models of other agents in the environment, agent modeling is not done universally. A form of multiagent RL is defined in which agents do not model each other as agents (Schmidhuber, 1996). Instead they consider each other as parts of the environment and affect each other's policies only as sensed objects. The agents pay attention to the reward they receive using a given policy and checkpoint their policies so they can return to successful ones. Schmidhuber shows that the agents can learn to cooperate without modeling each other.

Similarly, the agents developed in this book learn to act in an environment involving adversaries without explicitly modeling the adversaries' intentions. They do, on the other hand, model the goals and internal states of teammates.

How to affect others

When no communication is possible, agents cannot interact with each other directly. However, since they exist in the same environment, the agents can affect each other indirectly in several ways. They can be sensed by other agents, or they may be able to change the state of another agent by, for example, pushing it. Agents can also affect each other by one of two types of *stigmergy* (Holland, 1996). First, *active stigmergy* occurs when an agent alters the environment so as to affect the sensory input of another agent. For example, a robotic agent might leave a marker behind it for other agents to observe. Goldman and Rosenschein (1994) demonstrate an effective form of active stigmergy in which agents heuristically alter the environment in order to facilitate future unknown plans of other agents. Second, *passive stigmergy* involves altering the environment so that the effects of another agent's actions change. For example, if one agent turns off the main water valve to a building, the effect of another agent subsequently turning on the kitchen faucet is altered.

Holland (1996) illustrates the concept of passive stigmergy with a robotic system designed to model the behavior of an ant colony confronted with many dead ants around its nest. An ant from such a colony tends to periodically pick up a dead ant, carry it for a short distance, and then drop it. Although the behavior appears to be random, after several hours, the dead ants are clustered in a small number of heaps. Over time, there are fewer and fewer large piles until all the dead ants end up in one pile. Although the ants behave homogeneously and, at least in this case, we have no evidence that they communicate explicitly, the ants manage to cooperate in achieving a task.

Holland (1996) models this situation with a number of identical robots in a small area in which many pucks are scattered around. The robots are programmed reactively to move straight (turning at walls) until they are pushing three or more pucks. At that point, the robots back up and turn away, leaving the three pucks in a cluster. Although the robots do not communicate at all, they are able to collect the pucks into a single pile over time. This effect occurs because when a robot approaches an existing pile directly, it adds the pucks it was already carrying to the pile and turns away. A robot approaching an existing pile obliquely might take a puck away from the pile, but over time the desired result is accomplished. Like the ants, the robots use passive stigmergy to affect each other's behavior.

Mataric (1994a) explores a similar scenario with more deliberative robots. In this case, the robots use Q-learning to learn behaviors including foraging for pucks as well as homing and following. Mataric's robots actively affect each other through observation: a robot learning to follow another robot can base its action on the relative location of the other robot.

Our small-robots use active stigmergy. When a robot that does not have the ball is filling a forward role and it moves to a new location on the field, it changes the result of the pass evaluation function used by the robot that does have the ball. As presented in Section B.2 of Appendix B, the robot with the ball bases its action on the perceived locations of teammates and opponents.

Similarly, our simulated robotic soccer agents use active stigmergy when they change their locations in the environment. Particularly when using the SPAR variant of flexible positioning (see Section 3.5), teammate positions affect an agent's behavior.

Heterogeneous, Non-Communicating MAS

The multiagent scenario with heterogeneous, non-communicating agents is depicted in Figure 9.3. As in the homogeneous case (Figure 9.2), the agents are situated differently in the environment which causes them to have different sensory inputs and necessitates their taking different actions. However in this scenario, the agents have much more significant differences. They may have different goals, actions, and/or domain knowledge, as indicated by the different fonts in Figure 9.3.

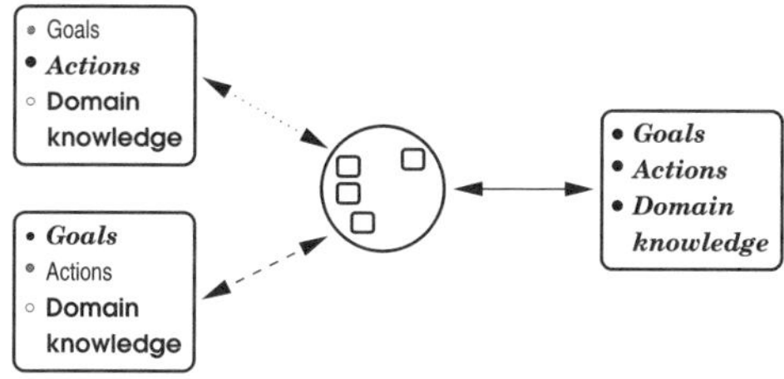

Figure 9.3
MAS with heterogeneous, non-communicating agents. Now agents' goals, actions, and/or domain knowledge may differ as indicated by the different fonts. The assumption of no direct interaction remains.

To this point, we have only considered agents that are homogeneous. Adding the possibility of heterogeneous agents in a multiagent domain adds a great deal of potential power at the price of added complexity. Agents might be heterogeneous in any of a number of ways, from having different goals to having different domain models and actions. An important sub-dimension of heterogeneous agent systems is whether agents are benevolent or competitive. Even if they have different goals, they may be friendly to each others' goals or they may actively try to inhibit each other. This aspect of heterogeneous systems, along with several others summarized in Table 9.3, is described below.

Benevolence vs. competitiveness

One of the most important issues to consider when designing a multiagent system is whether the different agents will be benevolent or competitive. Even if they have different goals, the agents can be benevolent if they are willing to help each other achieve their respective goals (Goldman and Rosenschein,

Table 9.3
The issues and techniques for heterogeneous, non-communicating multiagent systems as reflected in the literature.

Heterogeneous, Non-Communicating MAS

Issues

- Benevolence vs. competitiveness
- Stable vs. evolving agents
- Modeling others' goals, actions, and knowledge
- Resource management (interdependent actions)
- Social conventions
- Roles

Techniques

- Game theory, iterative play. (Mor and Rosenschein, 1995; Sandholm and Crites, 1996)
- Minimax-Q. (Littman, 1994)
- Competitive co-evolution. (Rosin and Belew, 1995; Haynes and Sen, 1996; Grefenstette and Daley, 1996)
- Deduce intentions, abilities through observation. (Huber and Durfee, 1995; Wang, 1996)
- Autoepistemic reasoning (ignorance). (Permpoontanalarp, 1995)
- Model as a team (individual → role). (Tambe, 1995, 1996b)
- Social reasoning: depend on others for goal (≠ game theory). (Sichman and Demazeau, 1995)
- GAs to deal with Braes' paradox (more resource → worse). (Glance and Hogg, 1995; Arora and Sen, 1996)
- Multiagent RL for adaptive load balancing. (Schaerf et al., 1995)
- Focal points/emergent conventions. (Fenster et al., 1995; Walker and Wooldridge, 1995)
- Agents filling different roles. (Prasad et al., 1996; Tambe, 1997; Balch, 1998)

1994). On the other hand, the agents may be selfish and only consider their own goals when acting. In the extreme, the agents may be involved in a zero-sum situation so that they must actively oppose other agents' goals in order to achieve their own.

Mor and Rosenschein (1995) illustrate the benevolent scenario in the context of the prisoner's dilemma. In the prisoner's dilemma, two agents try to act so as to maximize their own individual rewards. They are not actively out to thwart each other since it is not a zero-sum game, yet they place no inherent value on the other receiving reward. The prisoner's dilemma is constructed so that each agent is given two choices: defect or cooperate. No matter what the other agent does, a given agent receives a higher reward if it defects. Yet if both agents cooperate, they are better off than if they both defect. In any given play, an agent is better off defecting. Nevertheless, Mor and Rosenschein show that if the same agents come up against each other repeatedly (the iterated prisoner's dilemma), cooperative behavior can emerge. In effect, an agent can serve its own self-interest by establishing a *reputation* for being cooperative. Then when coming up against another cooperative agent, the two can benefit from a sense of trust for each other: they both cooperate rather than both defecting. Only with repeated play can cooperation emerge among the selfish agents in the prisoner's dilemma.

In the prisoner's dilemma, the agents are selfish but not inherently competitive: in specific circumstances, they are willing to act benevolently. However, when the agents are actually competitive (such as in zero-sum games), cooperation is no longer sensible. For instance, Littman considers a zero-sum game in which two agents try to reach opposite ends of a small discrete world. The agents can block each other by trying to move to the same space. Minimax-Q is a variant of Q-learning which is designed to work on Markov games as opposed to Markov decision processes (Littman, 1994). The competitive agents learn probabilistic policies since any deterministic policy can be completely counteracted by the opponent. Minimax-Q is applied to a simplified soccer simulation. Like in this application, the robotic soccer domains considered in this book are zero-sum games at the team level: the two teams are in direct competition with one another.

STABLE VS. EVOLVING AGENTS

Another important characteristic for consideration when designing multiagent systems is whether the agents are stable or evolving. Evolving agents can be useful in dynamic environments. But particularly when using competitive agents, allowing them to evolve can lead to complications. Such systems that use competitive evolving agents are said to use a technique called *competitive co-evolution*. Systems that evolve benevolent agents are said to use *cooperative co-evolution*.

The evolution of both predator and prey agents in the pursuit domain qualifies as competitive co-evolution (Haynes and Sen, 1996). When just the predators are evolved together, it is cooperative co-evolution (Haynes et al., 1995). Rather than evolving predator agents in a single evolutionary pool and then combining them into teams to test performance, this approach considers each individual in the population as a team of four agents already specifically assigned to different predators. Thus the predators can evolve to cooperate. This co-evolution of teammates is one possible way around the absence of communication in a domain. In place of communicating planned actions to each other, the predators can evolve to *know*, or at least act as if knowing, each other's future actions.

Grefenstette and Daley (1996) conduct a preliminary study of competitive and cooperative co-evolution in a domain that is loosely related to the pursuit domain. Their domain has two robots that can move continuously and one morsel of (stationary) food that appears randomly in the world. In the cooperative task, both robots must be at the food in order to "capture" it.

One problem to contend with in competitive rather than cooperative co-evolution is the possibility of an escalating "arms race" with no end. Competing agents might continually adapt to each other in more and more specialized ways, never stabilizing at a good behavior. In a dynamic environment, it may not be feasible or even desirable to evolve a stable behavior. Applying RL to the iterated prisoner's dilemma, it has been demonstrated that a learning agent is able to perform optimally against a fixed opponent (Sandholm and Crites, 1996). But when both agents are learning, there is no stable solution.

Another issue in competitive co-evolution is the credit-assignment problem. When performance of an agent improves, may not be clear whether the improvement is due to an improvement in that agent's behavior or a negative change in the opponent's behavior. Similarly, if an agent's performance gets worse, the blame or credit could belong to that agent or to the opponent.

One way to deal with the credit-assignment problem is to fix one agent while evolving the other and then switch. This method encourages the arms race more than ever. Nevertheless, Rosin and Belew (1995) use this technique, along with an interesting method for maintaining diversity in genetic populations, to evolve agents that can play TicTacToe, Nim, and a simple version of Go. When it is a given agent's turn to evolve, it executes a standard Genetic algorithm (GA) generation. Individuals are tested against individuals from the competing population, but a technique called "competitive fitness sharing" is used to maintain diversity. When using this technique, individuals from agent X's population are given more credit for beating opponents (individuals from agent Y's population) that are not beaten by other individuals from agent X's population. More specifically, the reward to an individual for beating individual y is divided by the number of other individuals in agent X's population that also beat individual y. Competitive fitness sharing shows much promise for people building systems that use competitive co-evolution.

TPOT-RL (Chapter 7) implements cooperative co-evolution. The individual agents learn their policies simultaneously, eventually creating a compatible set of policies. Competitive co-evolution is not considered in this book.

Modeling others' goals, action, and knowledge

For the case of homogeneous agents, it was useful for agents to model the internal states of other agents in order to predict their actions. With heterogeneous agents, the problem of modeling others is much more complex. Now the goals, actions, and domain knowledge of the other agents may also be unknown and thus need modeling.

Without communication, agents are forced to model each other strictly through observation. Huber and Durfee (1995) consider a case of coordinated motion control among multiple mobile robots under the assumption that communication is prohibitively expensive. Thus the agents try to deduce each other's plans by observing their actions. In particular, each robot tries to figure out the destinations of the other robots by watching how they move. Plan recognition of this type is also useful in competitive domains, since knowing an opponent's goals or intentions can make it significantly easier to defeat.

In addition to modeling agents' goals through observation, it is also possible to learn their actions. The OBSERVER system (Wang, 1996) allows an agent to incrementally learn the preconditions and effects of planning actions by observing domain experts. After observing for a time, the agent can then experimentally refine its model by practicing the actions itself.

When modeling other agents, it may be useful to reason not only about what is true and what is false, but also about what is not known. Such reasoning about ignorances is called *autoepistemic reasoning* (Permpoontanalarp, 1995).

Just as RMM is useful for modeling the states of homogeneous agents, it can be used in the heterogeneous scenario as well. Tambe (1995) takes it one step further, studying how agents can *learn* models of teams of agents. In an air combat domain, agents can use RMM to try to deduce an opponents' plan based on its observable actions. For example, a fired missile may not be visible, but the observation of a preparatory maneuver commonly used before firing could indicate that a missile has been launched.

When teams of agents are involved, the situation becomes more complicated. In this case, an opponent's actions may not make sense except in the context of a team maneuver. Then the agent's *role* within the team must be modeled (Tambe, 1996b).

One reason that modeling other agents might be useful is that agents sometimes depend on each other for achieving their goals. Unlike in game theory where agents can cooperate or not depending on their utility estimation, there may be actions that *require* cooperation for successful execution. For example, two robots may be needed to successfully push a box, or, as in the pursuit domain, several agents may be needed to capture an opponent. Sichman and Demazeau (1995) analyze how the case of conflicting mutual models of different co-dependent agents can arise and be dealt with.

Resource management

Heterogeneous agents may have interdependent actions due to limited resources needed by several of the agents. Example domains include network traffic problems, including the network routing domain used in this book, in which several different agents must send information through the same network; and load balancing in which several computer processes or users have a limited amount of computing power to share among them.

One interesting network traffic problem called Braess' paradox has been studied from a multiagent perspective using GAs (Glance and Hogg, 1995). Braess' paradox is the phenomenon of adding more resources to a network but getting worse performance. When using a particular GA representation to represent different parts of a sample network that has usage-dependent resource costs, agents that are sharing the network and reasoning separately about which path of the network to use cannot achieve global optimal performance (Glance and Hogg, 1995). When the GA representation is improved, the system is able to find the globally optimal traffic flow (Arora and Sen, 1996).

Adaptive load balancing has been studied as a multiagent problem by allowing different agents to decide which processor to use at a given time. Using RL, heterogeneous agents can achieve reasonable load balance without any central control and without communication among agents (Schaerf et al., 1995). The agents keep track of how long a job takes when it is scheduled on a given resource, and they are given some incentive to explore untried processors or processors that did poorly in the past.

Social conventions

There has been some very interesting work done on how heterogeneous, non-communicating agents can reach "agreements," or make coinciding choices, if necessary. The locker-room agreement presented in Section 3.2 is an implementation of social conventions in a team of agents. As well as being used by the the communicating simulated robotic soccer agents, it is used by the non-communicating small-robot agents to achieve team coordination.

The focal point method is another example of social conventions (Fenster et al., 1995). The phenomenon of cultural (or programmed) preferences allows agents to "meet" without communicating. In this method, all else being equal, agents who need to meet should choose rare or extreme options.

Rather than coming from pre-analysis of the options as in the focal point method, conventions can emerge over time if agents are biased towards options that have been chosen, for example, most recently or most frequently in the past (Walker and Wooldridge, 1995).

ROLES

When agents have similar goals, they can be organized into a team. Each agent then plays a separate *role* within the team. With such a benevolent team of agents, one must provide some method for assigning different agents to different roles. The flexible teamwork structure presented in Section 3.3 provides one such method.

Prasad et al. (1996) study design agents that can either initiate or extend a design of a steam pump. In different situations, different agents are more effective at initiation and at extension. Thus a supervised learning technique is used to help agents learn what roles they should fill in different situations.

STEAM (Tambe, 1997) allows a team of agents to fill and switch roles dynamically. Particularly if a critical agent fails, another agent is able to replace it in its role so that the team can carry on with its mission.

If allowed to evolve independently, a group of agents might end up filling different roles in the domain or all end up with the same behavior. Balch (1998) investigates methods of encouraging behavioral diversity in a team of agents.

Homogeneous, Communicating MAS

The multiagent scenario with homogeneous, communicating agents is depicted in Figure 9.4. As in the homogeneous, non-communicating case (Figure 9.2), the agents are identical except that they are situated differently in the environment. However in this scenario, the agents can communicate directly as indicated by the arrows connecting the agents in Figure 9.4. From a practical point of view, the communication might be broadcast or posted on a "blackboard" for all to interpret, or it might be targeted point-to-point from an agent to another specific agent.

Communication raises several issues to be addressed in multiagent systems. However, in most cases, the issues are addressed in the literature with heterogeneous, communicating agents. In this subsection, I consider

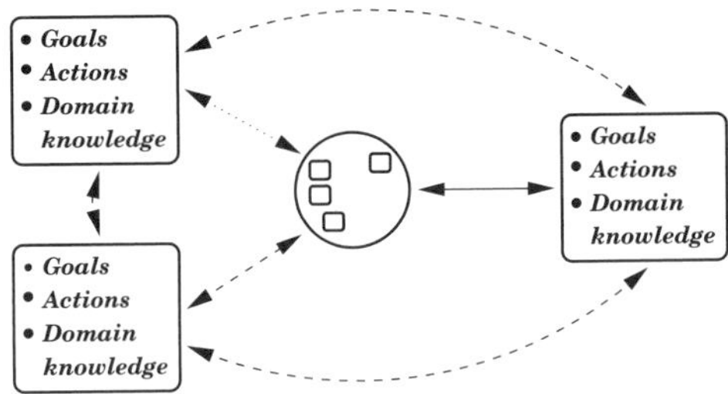

Figure 9.4
MAS with homogeneous, communicating agents. Only the sensor input and effector output of agents differ. Information can be transmitted directly among agents as indicated by the arrows between agents. Communication can either be broadcast or transmitted point-to-point.

distributed sensing, which is addressed with homogeneous, communicating agents as indicated in Table 9.4. Many more communication-related issues are addressed in the subsequent subsection devoted to *heterogeneous*, communicating multiagent systems.

Table 9.4
The issues and techniques for homogeneous, communicating multiagent systems as reflected in the literature.

Homogeneous, Communicating MAS
Issues
• Distributed sensing
Techniques
• Active sensing (Matsuyama, 1997)
• Query propagation for distributed traffic mapping (Moukas and Maes, 1997)

Distributed Sensing

The cooperative distributed vision project (Matsuyama, 1997) aims to construct and monitor a broad visual scene for dynamic three dimensional scene understanding by using multiple cameras, either stationary or on mobile robots. For example, consider the problem of tracking an individual car using cameras mounted at urban intersections. When the car leaves one camera's range and enters another's, there needs to be a way of identifying the two images as representing the same car, even though it probably looks different in the two cases (i.e. it is driving away from one camera and towards the other). The project combines active sensing—the ability to shift attention towards an area of higher uncertainty or interest—and communication among multiple sensing agents.

Another distributed sensing project is the trafficopter system (Moukas and Maes, 1997). In trafficopter, cars themselves collect and propagate traffic information to help each other decide on the best route to a given location. For example, a car driving in one direction might query an oncoming vehicle about traffic conditions up the road. By propagating such queries among vehicles, the original car can build a map of traffic conditions along different routes to its goal.

Our simulated robotic soccer agents use communication to achieve distributed sensing. In particular, the <selected-internal-state> in the communication paradigm presented in Section 3.4 can be used to transmit information that is visible to one agent and hidden to another. For example, in the soccer implementation, opponent and ball locations are communicated to agents that would otherwise not know their whereabouts.

Heterogeneous, Communicating MAS

The fully general multiagent scenario with heterogeneous, communicating agents is illustrated in Figure 9.5.

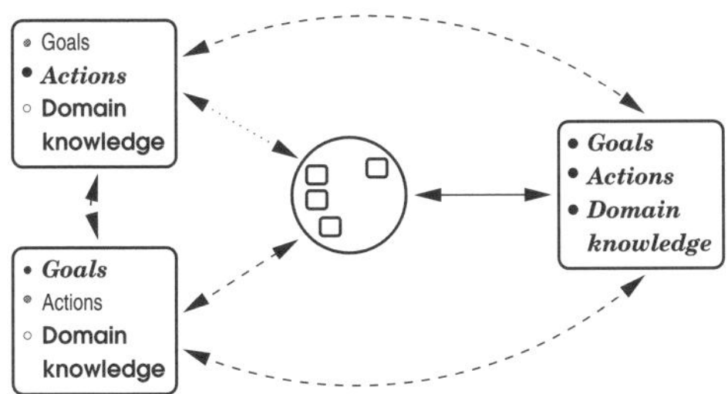

Figure 9.5
MAS with heterogeneous, communicating agents. Agents can be heterogeneous to any degree. Information can be transmitted directly among agents. Communication can either be broadcast or transmitted point-to-point.

Since heterogeneous communicating agents can choose not to communicate, and in some cases can also choose to be homogeneous or at least to minimize their heterogeneity, most of the issues discussed in the previous two scenarios apply in this one as well. Two of the most studied issues are communication protocols and theories of commitment. Already discussed in the context of the heterogeneous, non-communicating MAS scenario, the issue of benevolence vs. competitiveness becomes more complicated in the current context. These issues and others along with some of the existing techniques to deal with them are described below and summarized in Table 9.5.

Understanding each other

In all communicating multiagent systems, and particularly in domains with agents built by different designers, there must be some set language and protocol for the agents to use when interacting. Independent aspects of protocols are information content, message format, and coordination conventions. Among others, existing protocols for these three levels are: KIF for content (Genesereth and Fikes, 1992), KQML for message format (Finin et al., 1994), and COOL for coordination (Barbuceanu and Fox, 1995). There has been a lot of research done on refining these and other communication protocols.

One of the first industrial multiagent systems, ARCHON (Jennings and Wittig, 1992) successfully integrated several legacy systems. Applied in five different industrial settings, ARCHON successfully allows independently developed, heterogeneous computer systems to communicate in order to create collaborative, process control systems.

Creatures (Grand and Cliff, 1998) is a multiagent computer game based on sophisticated biological models. Agents have the ability to grow and learn, including a simple verb-object language, based on interactions with a human user or other agents in the environment.

Within the team member agent architecture presented in Section 3.2, agents understand each other based on a communication protocol defined within the locker-room agreement.

Planning communicative acts

When an agent transmits information to another agent, it has an effect just like any other action would have. Thus within a planning framework, one can define preconditions and effects for communicative acts. When combined with a model of other agents, the effect of a communication act might be to alter an agent's belief about the state of another agent or agents. The theory of communication as action is called *speech acts* (Cohen and Levesque, 1995; Lux and Steiner, 1995).

Table 9.5
The issues and techniques for heterogeneous, communicating multiagent systems as reflected in the literature.

Heterogeneous, Communicating MAS

Issues

- Understanding each other
- Planning communicative acts
- Benevolence vs. competitiveness
- Negotiation
- Resource management (schedule coordination)
- Commitment/decommitment

Techniques

- Language protocols: KIF (Genesereth and Fikes, 1992), KQML (Finin et al., 1994), COOL. (Barbuceanu and Fox, 1995)
- Legacy systems integration. (Jennings and Wittig, 1992)
- Language learning. (Grand and Cliff, 1998)
- Speech acts. (Cohen and Levesque, 1995; Lux and Steiner, 1995)
- Learning social behaviors. (Mataric, 1994b)
- Reasoning about truthfulness. (Rosenschein and Zlotkin, 1994; Sandholm and Lesser, 1996)
- Multiagent Q-learning. (Tan, 1993; Weiß, 1995)
- Training other agents' Q-functions (track driving). (Clouse, 1996)
- Minimize the need for training. (Potter et al., 1995)
- Cooperative co-evolution. (Bull et al., 1995)
- Contract nets for electronic commerce. (Sandholm and Lesser, 1995b)
- Market-based systems. (Huberman and Clearwater, 1995)
- Bayesian learning in negotiation: model others. (Zeng and Sycara, 1996)
- Market-based methods for distributed constraints. (Parunak et al., 1998)
- Generalized partial global planning (GPGP). (Decker and Lesser, 1995; Lesser, 1998)
- Learning to choose among coordination methods. (Sugawara and Lesser, 1995)
- Query response in information networks. (Sycara et al., 1996)
- Division of independent tasks. (Parker, 1994)
- Internal, social, and collective (role) commitments. (Castelfranchi, 1995)
- Commitment states (potential, pre, and actual) as planning states. (Haddadi, 1995)
- Belief/desire/intention (BDI) model: OASIS. (Rao and Georgeff, 1995)
- BDI commitments only over intentions. (Rao and Georgeff, 1995)
- Coalitions. (Zlotkin and Rosenschein, 1994; Shehory and Kraus, 1995; Sandholm and Lesser, 1995a)

Mataric adds a learning dimension to the idea of speech acts. Starting with the foraging behavior mentioned above (Mataric, 1994a), the agents can then learn to choose from among a set of social behaviors that includes broadcasting and listening (Mataric, 1994b). Q-learning is extended so that reinforcement can be received for direct rewards obtained by the agent itself or for rewards obtained by other agents.

When using communication as a planning action, the possibility arises of communicating misinformation in order to satisfy a particular goal. For instance, an agent may want another agent to believe that something is true. Rather than actually making it true, the agent might just *say* that it is true. For example, Sandholm and Lesser (1996) analyze a framework in which agents are allowed to "decommit" from agreements with other agents by paying a penalty to these other agents. They consider the case in which an agent might not be truthful in its decommitment, hoping that the other agent will decommit first. In such situations, agents must also consider what communications to believe (Rosenschein and Zlotkin, 1994).

The communication paradigm for single-channel, low-bandwidth unreliable communication environments presented in Section 3.4 safeguards against false communications with the <encoded-time-stamp> field. In the simulated robotic soccer implementation (Section 3.5), it is assumed that messages from teammates are truthful: only opponent messages could be deceptive.

Benevolence vs. competitiveness

Some studies involving competitive agents were described in the heterogeneous, non-communicating scenario in a previous subsection. In the current scenario, there are many more examples of competitive agents.

In the pursuit domain, multiagent Q-learning has been investigated (Tan, 1993). Agents help each other by exchanging reinforcement episodes and/or control policies. Similarly, competing Q-learners can bid against each other to earn the right to control a single system (Weiß, 1995). The highest bidder pays a certain amount to be allowed to act, then receives any reward that results from the action.

Another Q-learning approach, this time with benevolent agents, has been to explore the interesting idea of having one agent teach another agent through communication (Clouse, 1996). Starting with a *trainer* that has moderate expertise in a task, a learner can be rewarded for mimicking the trainer. Furthermore, the trainer can recommend to the learner what action to take in a given situation so as to direct the learner towards a reward state. Eventually, the learner is able to perform the task without any guidance.

While training is a useful concept, some research is driven by the goal of reducing the role of the human trainer. As opposed to the process of *shap-*

ing, in which the system designer develops simple behaviors and slowly builds them into more complex ones, populations appropriately seeded for competitive co-evolution can reduce the amount of designer effort. Potter and Grefenstette (1995) illustrate this effect in their domain described above in which two robots compete for a stationary pellet of food. Subpopulations of rules used by GAs are seeded to be more effective in different situations. Thus specialized subpopulations of rules corresponding to shaped behaviors tend to emerge.

GAs have also been used to evolve separate communicating agents to control different legs of a quadrapedal robot using cooperative co-evolution (Bull et al., 1995).

TPOT-RL as presented in Chapter 7 is another example of cooperative co-evolution. Independent agents learn policies that coordinate to create an effective team behavior.

Negotiation

Drawing inspiration from competition in human societies, several researchers have designed negotiating multiagent systems based on the law of supply and demand. In the *contract nets* framework (Smith, 1980), agents all have their own goals, are self-interested, and have limited reasoning resources. They bid to accept tasks from other agents and then can either perform the tasks (if they have the proper resources) or subcontract them to other agents. Agents must pay to contract their tasks out and thus shop around for the lowest bidder. Many multiagent issues arise when using contract nets (Sandholm and Lesser, 1995b).

In a similar spirit is an implemented multiagent system that controls air temperature in different rooms of a building (Huberman and Clearwater, 1995). A person can set one's thermostat to any temperature. Then depending on the actual air temperature, the agent for that room tries to "buy" either hot or cold air from another room that has an excess. At the same time, the agent can sell the excess air at the current temperature to other rooms. Modeling the loss of heat in the transfer from one room to another, the agents try to buy and sell at the best possible prices. The market regulates itself to provide equitable usage of a shared resource.

Zeng and Sycara (1996) study a competitive negotiation scenario in which agents use Bayesian Learning techniques to update models of each other based on bids and counter bids in a negotiation process.

The MarCon system (Parunak et al., 1998) uses market-based methods for distributed constraint problems. Designers at different points along a supply chain negotiate the characteristics of the overall design by buying and selling characteristics and propagating the resulting constraints.

Resource management

MarCon is an example of multiagent resource management: the design characteristics desired by one agent may consume the resources of another.

Similarly, generalized partial global planning (GPGP) allows several heterogeneous agents to post constraints, or commitments to do a task by some time, to each other's local schedulers and thus coordinate without the aid of any centralized agent (Decker and Lesser, 1995). A proposed general multiagent architecture based on GPGP contains five components: "local agent scheduling, multiagent coordination, organizational design, detection, and diagnosis (Lesser, 1998)."

In a heterogeneous, communicating multiagent system applied to diagnosis of a local area network, agents learn to choose among different coordination strategies based on the current situation (Sugawara and Lesser, 1993, 1995). Less sophisticated coordination methods require fewer network and time resources, but may lead to tasks failing to be executed or to redundant actions by multiple agents.

RETSINA (Sycara et al., 1996) uses three classes of heterogeneous, communicating agents to deliver information in response to specific user queries in information networks. RETSINA is able to satisfy the information requests of multiple users by searching multiple information sources, while considering network constraints and resource limitations of information agents. RETSINA has been used to implement several distributed network applications including a financial portfolio manager, a personal information manager and meeting scheduler, and a satellite visibility forecaster.

ALLIANCE and its learning variant L-ALLIANCE (Parker, 1994) use communication among heterogeneous robots to help divide independent tasks among the robots. With an emphasis on fault tolerance, agents only broadcast the task that they are currently working on. If the communication fails, multiple robots might temporarily try to do the same task, but they will eventually realize the conflict by observation and one will move on to a different task. In L-ALLIANCE, robots learn to evaluate each other's abilities with respect to specific tasks in order to more efficiently divide their tasks among the team.

Commitment/Decommitment

When agents communicate, they may decide to cooperate on a given task or for a given amount of time. In so doing, they make *commitments* to each other. Committing to another agent involves agreeing to pursue a given goal, possibly in a given manner, regardless of how much it serves one's own interests. Commitments can make systems run much more smoothly by providing a way for agents to "trust" each other, yet it is not obvious how to get self-interested agents to commit to others in a reasonable way. The theory of commitment and decommitment (when the commitment terminates) has consequently drawn considerable attention.

Castelfranchi (1995) defines three types of commitment: internal commitment—an agent binds itself to do something; social commitment—an agent commits to another agent; and collective commitment—an agent agrees to fill a certain role. Setting an alarm clock is an example of internal commitment to wake up at a certain time.

Commitment states have been used as planning states: potential cooperation, pre-commitment, and commitment (Haddadi, 1995). Agents can then use means-ends analysis to plan for goals in terms of commitment opportunities. This work is conducted within a model called belief/desire/intention, or BDI.

BDI is a popular technique for modeling other agents. Other agents' domain knowledge (beliefs) and goals (desires) are modeled as well as their "intentions," or goals they are currently trying to achieve and the methods by which they are trying to achieve them. The BDI model is used to build a system for air-traffic control, OASIS (Rao and Georgeff, 1995), which has been implemented for testing (in parallel with human operators who retain full control) at the airport in Sydney, Australia. Each aircraft is represented by a controlling agent which deals with a global sequencing agent. OASIS mixes reactive and deliberative actions in the agents: they can break out of planned sequences when coming across situations that demand immediate reaction. Since agents cannot control their beliefs or desires, they can only make commitments to each other regarding their intentions.

Finally, groups of agents may decide to commit to each other. Rather than the more usual two-agent or all-agent commitment scenarios, there are certain situations in which agents may want to form coalitions (Zlotkin and Rosenschein, 1994). Since this work is conducted in a game theory framework, agents consider the utility of joining a coalition in which they are bound to try to advance the utility of other members in exchange for reciprocal consideration. Shehory and Kraus (1995) present a distributed algorithm for task allocation when coalitions are either needed to perform tasks or more efficient that single agents. Sandholm and Lesser (1995a) use a vehicle routing domain to illustrate a method by which agents can form valuable coalitions when it is intractable to discover the optimal coalitions.

Within the context of this book, when using set-plays as presented within the flexible teamwork structure (Section 3.3), agents are committed to each other for the duration of the execution of the multiagent plan. If any agent fails to fill its set-play role, the plan is less likely to succeed.

Summary

This section has given an overview of prior research within the field of MAS, with emphasis on multiagent learning. Based on this detailed review of the literature, this book makes several contributions to the state of the art.

Several people have studied collaboration among agents (commitment, co-evolution, etc.), and several people have studied adversarial multiagent situations (game theory, Markov games, etc.). Yet there has been little effort towards studying situations in which agents reason about collaborating with other benevolent agents while at the same time trying to outwit one or more opponents. Our agents within the simulated robotic soccer domain are the first to operate in a real-time, noisy, collaborative and adversarial environment.

TPOT-RL (Section 7.2) is a multiagent RL algorithm for domains in which agents do not know the effects of their actions in terms of state transitions. While there are several multiagent RL approaches mentioned in this section (Tan, 1993; Littman, 1994; Mataric, 1994a; Clouse, 1996; Schaerf et al., 1995; Weiß, 1995), none is situated in an opaque-transition environment.

There have been some prior efforts towards having different agents change roles dynamically (Prasad et al., 1996; Tambe, 1997). But there is no previous system in which a team of agents operating in a real-time environment can dynamically change both its set of roles (formation) and role assignments within the formation. As illustrated in Figure 3.3 and implemented in the simulated robotic soccer implementation (Section 3.5) the flexible teamwork structure defined within the team member agent architecture (Section 3.3) contributes a method for agents to smoothly switch both formations and roles within a formation.

Several communicating multiagent systems were presented in this section. However, none addresses communication in single-channel, low-bandwidth, unreliable communication environments. The communication paradigm presented in Section 3.4 contributes a method for teams to communicate in such environments by taking advantage of the locker-room agreement within the team member agent architecture.

Finally, layered learning is a new approach to learning in complex systems, including those with multiple agents. While several multiagent learning systems are described in this section, none layers multiple machine learning techniques within a single application. As presented in Chapters 4–7, layered learning allowed us to connect learned individual skills, multiagent behaviors, and team behaviors to create a coherent team of agents in a complex, multiagent domain.

9.2 Robotic Soccer

Robotic soccer is a particularly good domain for studying multiagent systems. The main goal of any test bed is to facilitate the trial and evaluation of ideas that have promise in the real world (Decker, 1996a). A wide variety of real MAS issues can be studied in robotic soccer. In fact, all of the seventeen MAS issues listed in Table 9.1 can be feasibly studied in the soccer simulator.

Homogeneous, non-communicating MAS can be studied in robotic soccer by fixing the behavior of the opposing team and populating the team being studied with identical, mute players. To keep within the homogeneous agent scenario, the opponents must not be modeled as agents.

- In this context, the players can be *reactive or deliberative* to any degree. The extremely reactive agent might simply look for the ball and move straight at it, shooting whenever possible. At this extreme, the players may or may not have any knowledge that they are part of a team.
- On the other hand, players might *model each other*, thus enabling deliberative reasoning about whether to approach the ball or whether to move to a different part of the field in order to defend or to receive a pass.
- With players modeling each other, they may also reason about how to *affect each other's behaviors* in this inherently dynamic environment.
- It is possible to study the relative merits of *local and global perspectives* on the world. Robots can be given global views with the help of an overhead camera, and the soccer server comes equipped with an omniscient mode that permits global views. Simulated robotic soccer is usually approached as a problem requiring local sensing.

Heterogeneous, non-communicating MAS can also be studied in the robotic soccer domain.

- Since each player has several teammates with the same global goal and several opponents with the opposite goal, each player is both *benevolent and competitive* at the same time. This possibility for combination of collaborative and adversarial reasoning is a major feature of the domain.

- If the teams are learning during the course of a single game or over several games, all the issues of *evolving agents*, including the "arms race" and the credit-assignment problem, arise.

- In the soccer server, stamina is a resource assigned to each individual agent. At the team level, stamina is important for *resource management*: if too many agents are tired, the team as a whole will be ineffective. Therefore, it is to the team's advantage to distribute the running among the different agents.

- When trying to collaborate, players' actions are usually interdependent: to execute a successful pass, both the passer and the receiver must execute the appropriate actions. Thus *modeling each other* for the purpose of coordination is helpful. In addition, if opponents' actions can be predicted, then proactive measures might be taken to render them ineffective.

- *Social conventions*, such as programmed notions of when a given agent will pass or which agents should play defense, can also help coordination. The locker-room agreement is an example of social conventions within a team.

- Since communication is still not allowed, the players must have a reliable method for filling the different team *roles* needed on a soccer team (e.g. defender, forward, goaltender). The flexible teamwork structure presented in Section 3.5 is one such method.

Homogeneous, communicating MAS can be studied by again fixing the behavior of the opposing team and allowing teammates to communicate.

- *Distributed sensing* can be studied in this context due to the large amount of hidden state inherent in the soccer server (see Section 2.2). At any given moment, a particular agent can see only a small portion of the world. Only by communicating with teammates can it get a more complete picture of the world. In our communication paradigm presented in Section 3.4, the <selected-internal-state> field is designed for this purpose.

Heterogeneous, communicating MAS is perhaps the most appropriate scenario to study within the context of robotic soccer. Since the agents indeed are heterogeneous and can communicate, the full potential of the domain is realized in this scenario.

- With players sending messages to each other, they must have a language in order to *understand each other*. Our agents define such a language within the locker-room agreement.
- Especially in the single-channel, low-bandwidth communication environment modeled by the soccer server, agents must *plan their communicative acts*. If the opponents can understand the same language, a planned utterance can affect the knowledge of both teammates and opponents. The utility of communication must be carefully considered and the possibility of lying in order to fool the opponent arises. In addition, the low-bandwidth creates the condition that sending a message may prevent other messages from getting through.
- Like in the heterogeneous, non-communicating scenario, since agents have both teammates and adversaries, they must reason about being both *benevolent and competitive*.
- *Negotiation* protocols may be useful in the robotic soccer domain if different agents, based on their different sensory perspectives, have different opinions about what course of action would be best for the team.
- In a real-time environment, timing is very important for any team play, including a simple pass. Thus, *resource management* in terms of timing, or action coordination, is crucial.
- Protocols are also needed for *commitment* to team plays: the passer and receiver in a pass play must both agree to execute the pass. For more complex team plays, such as our set-plays, several players may need to commit to participate. But then the issue arises of how single-mindedly they must adhere to the committed play: when may they react to more pressing situations and ignore the commitment?

As demonstrated above, all of the MAS issues summarized in Table 9.1 can be studied in robotic soccer. I now review the research that has been conducted in this domain. First, I describe research conducted in the "early years", before organized robotic soccer workshops, that served as the foundations for the recent popularity of the domain. Second, I review some of the research presented at dedicated robotic soccer workshops held in conjunction with the international competitions described in Chapter 8, as well other contemporary robotic soccer-related research.

Foundations

Producing natural language commentary from real-time input, the SOCCER system (Andre et al., 1988) was the first AI research related to soccer. SOCCER analyzed *human* soccer games. By looking for triggers and terminations of events such as a player running or the ball being passed, SOCCER aims to announce important events without redundancy.

Robotic soccer was introduced as an interesting and promising domain for AI research at the Vision Interface conference in June, 1992 (Mackworth, 1993). Dynamite, the first working robotic soccer system (Barman et al., 1993; Sahota et al., 1995) was also described at that time. A ground-breaking system for robotic soccer, and the one that served as the inspiration and basis for my work, the Dynamite test bed was designed to be capable of supporting several robots per team, but most work has been done in a 1 vs. 1 scenario. It uses an overhead camera and color-based detection to provide global sensory information to the robots. Dynamite was used to introduce a decision making strategy called reactive deliberation which was used to choose from among seven hard-wired behaviors (Sahota, 1994). Subsequently, an RL approach based on high-level sensory predicates was used to choose from among the same hard-wired behaviors (Ford et al., 1994).

Asada et al. (1994a) developed the first robots equipped with on-board sensing capabilities. As mentioned in Section 5.5, these robots use learning from easy missions, an RL training technique, to learn to hit a stationary ball into the goal. One contribution of this work is the construction of state and action spaces that reduce the complexity of the learning task (Asada et al., 1996). As opposed to the action-dependent features used by TPOT-RL which create an abstract feature space prior to learning, states are clustered during learning based on the best action to take from each state. Another contribution is the combination of low-level behaviors, such as shooting and avoiding an opponent, that are learned using RL (Asada et al., 1994b; Uchibe et al., 1996). Rather than building the learned behaviors at different behavior levels as in layered learning, two previously learned control strategies are used to produce a new one, which then replaces the original two.

Minimax-Q learning for Markov games was first applied in an abstract simulated soccer game (Littman, 1994). This version of the domain is much simpler than the soccer server, having 800 states, 5 actions, and no hidden information. One player on each team moves in a grid world and the ball is always possessed by one of the players. Using minimax-Q, players learn optimal probabilistic policies for maneuvering past each other with the ball.

In research prior to that reported in this book, we conducted machine learning experiments in a simulator based closely on the Dynasim simulator (Sahota, 1996) which simulates the Dynamite robots mentioned above. First, we used memory-based learning to allow a player to learn when to shoot and when to pass the ball (Stone and Veloso, 1996a). We then used neural networks to teach a player to shoot a moving ball into particular parts of the goal (Stone and Veloso, 1996b). Based on training in a small region of the field, our agent was able to learn to successfully time its approach to a moving ball such that it could score from all areas of the field. These experiments served as the basis for our initial learning experiments in the soccer server (Stone and Veloso, 1996c).

In another early learning experiment in the soccer server, a player learned when to shoot and when to pass (Matsubara et al., 1996). As described in Section 5.5, the agent bases its decision on the positions of the ball, the goaltender, and one teammate.

The Competition Years

The research reported in the previous subsection confirmed the potential of robotic soccer as an AI research domain and justified the value of having large-scale competitions from a research perspective. Starting with the first competitions held in 1996 (Pre-RoboCup-96 and MiroSot-96) and continuing since then, there has been a great deal of robotic soccer-related research. It has been presented both at dedicated robotic soccer workshops held in conjunction with the competitions and in other scientific forums. In this subsection I review some of this recent robotic soccer research.

ROBOT HARDWARE

Much of the research inspired by competitions has been devoted to building robot hardware that is suitable for this challenging environment, e.g. (Achim et al., 1996; Hong et al., 1996; Hsia and Soderstrand, 1996; Kim et al., 1996; Shim et al., 1996). The emphasis in hardware approaches varies greatly. Some research focuses on fast and robust visual perception of the environment (Sargent et al., 1997; Cheng and Zelinsky, 1998; Han and Veloso, 1998). And some research focuses on automatic calibration of vision parameters (Shen et al.,

1998; Veloso and Uther, 1999) in response to the need for vision systems that work under various lighting conditions (conditions at competitions are never the same as in the lab). Instead of vision, one alternative approach is to use a laser range-finder for localization in the environment (Gutmann et al., 1998).

Other research focuses on robot path planning in crowded, dynamic, environments (Han et al., 1996; Kim and Chung, 1996). Path planning is particularly challenging with non-holonomic robots because they can only move straight in the direction that they are facing or in curved paths starting from their current location and direction. Our approach to non-holonomic robotic path planning is described in Appendix B, specifically in Section B.2. Omnidirectional robots can simplify path planning considerably: they do not have to consider the direction they are facing as a constraint (Price et al., 1998; Yokota et al., 1998).

In addition to robots developed specifically for the competitions, there have been robots created to exhibit special soccer-related skills. Shoobot (Mizuno et al., 1996, 1998) is a nomad-based robot that can dribble and shoot a soccer ball as it moves smoothly through an open space. The Sony legged robots (Fujita and Kageyama, 1997) walk on four legs. They have been used as the basis of an exclusively legged-robot soccer competition (Veloso et al., 1998c). And the Honda humanoid robots (Hirai, 1997) have been demonstrated kicking a real soccer ball and performing a penalty shot with a shooting and a goaltending robot. This demonstration indicates the feasibility of RoboCup's long-term goal of having a humanoid robot soccer competition on a real soccer field (Kitano et al., 1998).

Soccer Server Accessories

This book uses the soccer server described in Section 2.2 as a test bed for research in MAS and ML. In order to test the teamwork structure and communication paradigm presented in Chapter 3, our agents first needed to be equipped with the low-level individual skills described in Sections 3.5 and B.1 (Appendix B). Other approaches to building individual skills in the soccer server are present in the literature, e.g. (Burkhard et al., 1998; Pagello et al., 1998).

In addition to soccer-playing agent development, the soccer server has been used as a substrate for 3-dimensional visualization, real-time natural language commentary, and education research.

Figure 2.1 shows the 2-dimensional visualization tool that is included in the soccer server software. SPACE (Shinjoh, 1998) converts the 2-dimensional image into a 3-dimensional image, changing camera angle and rendering images in real time.

Another research challenge being addressed within the soccer server is producing natural language commentary of games as they proceed. Researchers aim to provide both low-level descriptions of the action, for example announcing which team is in possession of the ball, and high-level analysis of the play, for example commenting on the team strategies being used by the different teams. Commentator systems for the soccer server include ROCCO (Andre et al., 1998b), MIKE (Matsubara et al., 1999), and Byrne (Binsted, 1999).

Robotic soccer has also been used as the basis for education research. A survey of RoboCup-97 participants indicates that the majority of participants were students motivated principally by the research opportunities provided by the domain (Verner, 1999). There has also been an undergraduate AI programming course based on teaching students to create robotic soccer-playing agents in the soccer server (Coradeschi and Malec, 1999).

Multiagent Control and Robotic Soccer Strategy

The robotic soccer domain has inspired many different approaches to building and organizing teams of agents, including the team member agent architecture and layered learning as presented in this book.

Some research is based on applying existing programming methodologies to the robotic soccer domain. Team GAMMA (Noda, 1998) is built using Gaea (Nakashima et al., 1995), a logic programming language that is essentially a multi-threaded, multi-environment version of prolog. Gaea implements a dynamic subsumption architecture, allowing agents to override behaviors in different ways based on the current environment, or behavior context. Team ROGI (de la Rosa et al., 1997) is built using another programming methodology, namely agent-oriented programming (Shoham, 1990).

Other research, like our own, introduces new multiagent control methodologies and applies them to robotic soccer. For example, the MICROB robotic soccer team is an implementation of the Cassiopeia programming method (Drogoul and Collinot, 1998). Cassiopeia focuses on the organizational issues of multiagent tasks, analyzing the interdependencies of low-level skills and facilitating the formation of groups based on these interdependencies. Temporary organizations are formed based on the contract net framework (Smith, 1980). For example, the player with the ball might contract with another player to place itself in a particular location to receive a pass.

This approach differs from our own in that our agents position themselves autonomously, for instance using SPAR, and the agent with the ball decides autonomously where to pass: no negotiation is involved, enabling the players to act as quickly as possible.

Scerri (1998) presents another multi-layered approach to robotic soccer. However, unlike our own hierarchical approach, it does not involve the learning of any behaviors. In this approach, the different abstraction layers deal with different granularities of sensory input. For example, a low-level move-to-ball behavior is given the ball's precise location, while a high-level defend behavior—which might call go-to-ball—knows only that the ball is in the defensive half of the field. The Samba control architecture (Riekki and Roening, 1998) uses two behavior layers: the reactive layer which defines action maps from sensory input to actuator output; and the task layer which selects from among the action maps.

ISIS (Tambe et al., 1998) is a role-based approach to robotic soccer based on STEAM (Tambe, 1997). STEAM defines team behaviors that can be invoked dynamically. There has also been another formation-based approach to positioning agents on the soccer field (Matsumoto and Nagai, 1998). However, unlike in our dynamic formations with flexible positions, the player positions are static and the team formation cannot change dynamically. Several other researchers recognize the importance of decomposing the soccer task into different roles, e.g. (Coradeschi and Karlsson, 1998; Ch'ng and Padgham, 1998).

One approach with dynamically changing roles is developed in a soccer simulator other than the soccer server (Balch, 1998). Balch uses a behavioral diversity measure to encourage role learning in an RL framework, finding that providing a uniform reinforcement to the entire team is more effective than providing local reinforcements to individual players.

Often, definitions of robotic soccer positions involve fixed locations at which an agent should locate itself by default, e.g. (Gutmann et al., 1998; Matsumoto and Nagai, 1998). In contrast, as described in Section 3.5, our flexible positions allow players to adjust their locations within their roles. The ranges of flexibility are defined a priori as a part of the locker-room agreement. Observational reinforcement learning (Andou, 1998) allows agents to *learn* their positions dynamically based on the distribution of past ball locations in a game. A similar approach is also described in (Inoue and Wilkin, 1997).

In another learning approach, teammate and opponent capabilities are learned through repeated trials of specific actions (Nadella and Sen, 1997). This research is conducted in a soccer simulator in which the ball is always in possession of a player, eliminating the necessity for fine ball control. Each player has an assigned efficiency in the range [0, 1] for the execution of actions such as passing, tackling, and dribbling corresponding to the probability that the action will succeed. Agents do not know the abilities of themselves, their teammates, or the opponents. Instead, they learn to estimate them based on repeated trials. The agents can then base action decisions on the learned parameters.

All of the learning approaches described above, as well as the approach described in this book, are used to learn portions of an agent's behavior. Other aspects are created manually. In contrast, a few entirely learned soccer behaviors have been created.

Hexcer (Uther and Veloso, 1997) is an extension of the grid world soccer game described above (Littman, 1994). Rather than square grid locations, the world is defined as a lattice of hexagons. Thus the action space is increased and the geometric constraints are altered. The added complexity necessitates the development of generalized U-trees to allow agents to learn successful policies (Uther and Veloso, 1997). In hexcer, it is possible for agents to learn straight from sensors to actuators because, like Littman's simulation, hexcer has a much smaller state space than the soccer server and the agents have no hidden state.

As mentioned in Section 4.5, the RoboCup-97 and RoboCup-98 competitions each included one team created using genetic programming (Koza, 1992). In both cases, the goal was to learn entirely from agent sensors to actuators in the soccer server. The first attempt (Luke et al., 1998) was eventually scaled down, although a successful team was created based on some manually created low-level skills. The following year, Darwin United (Andre and Teller, 1999) entered an entirely learned team.

Summary

Within this large and growing body of research in the robotic soccer domain, this book fills several gaps:

- While there are several role-based approaches, and at least one examination of possible team formations ((Matsumoto and Nagai, 1998)), no other robotic soccer system enables its agents to dynamically switch both roles and formations.
- No other implemented system includes pre-defined, multiagent plans (set-plays) for frequently occurring situations.

- Our communication paradigm for single-channel, low-bandwidth, unreliable communication environments, such as that of the soccer server, is the only such paradigm presented.
- While there have been many learning approaches to robotic soccer, including several within the soccer server, no other system layers multiple learning modules as we do using layered learning.

Nonetheless, even with all of the above contributions by us and by others, there is still a lot of room for new AI research within the robotic soccer domain. The next and concluding chapter outlines some of these potential future directions as well as summarizing the contributions of this book.

10 Conclusions and Future Work

Motivated by the challenges inherent in the soccer server, a simulated robotic soccer domain, this book contributes several techniques for building successful agents in real-time, noisy, collaborative and adversarial environments. This chapter reviews the book's scientific contributions to the fields of Multiagent Systems and Machine Learning (Section 10.1) and then discusses promising directions for future research in this challenging class of domain (Section 10.2).

10.1 Contributions

The four main contributions of this book are summarized as follows.

• The **team member agent architecture** presented in Chapter 3 is suitable for PTS domains: domains with team synchronization opportunities interleaved with periods of real-time, dynamic action and limited communication. The team member agent architecture incorporates a locker-room agreement, which includes the definition of a flexible teamwork structure including mechanisms for task decomposition and dynamic role assignment. Roles, team formations, and multiagent set-plays are defined.
For PTS domains with limited communication (as opposed to no communication) possible during the dynamic periods, the locker-room agreement also defines inter-agent communication protocols. This book presents a communication paradigm for PTS domains with single-channel, low-bandwidth, unreliable communication environments. This communication paradigm facilitates team coordination while being robust to lost messages and active interference from opponents.
The team member agent architecture is implemented both in simulated robotic soccer and in real robotic soccer. Empirical results demonstrate the effectiveness of the teamwork structure and communication paradigm implementations.

• **Layered learning** (Chapter 4) is a hierarchical ML paradigm applicable in complex domains in which learning a mapping directly from sensors to actuators is intractable. Given a hierarchical task decomposition, layered learning allows for learning at each level of the hierarchy, with learning at each level directly affecting learning at the next higher level.
Layered learning is applied in simulated robotic soccer as a set of three in-

terconnecting learned behaviors. At the lowest layer, ball interception, an individual skill, is learned (Chapter 5). This learned individual skill is used as part of the training behavior for learning pass evaluation, a multiagent behavior (Chapter 6). The learned multiagent behavior is then used to create the input space for learning pass selection, a team behavior (Chapter 7). All of the learned behaviors are validated empirically in controlled testing scenarios.

• **TPOT-RL** (Chapter 7) is a new multiagent reinforcement learning method. TPOT-RL is designed for complex domains in which agents cannot necessarily observe the state transitions caused by their or other agents' actions. It exploits local, action-dependent features to aggressively generalize its input representation for learning and partitions the task among the agents, allowing them to simultaneously learn collaborative policies by observing the long-term effects of their actions. TPOT-RL is applicable in domains with large state spaces and limited training opportunities.
TPOT-RL is developed and tested in the simulated robotic soccer domain. It is also successfully applied in another multiagent domain, namely network routing.

• The **CMUnited simulated robotic soccer system** (Chapters 3–8 and Appendices B–D) is a fully implemented and operational team of simulated robotic soccer agents which has performed successfully at international tournaments. This book contributes algorithmic details of the CMUnited implementation, as well as its source code.

10.2 Future Directions

Future Directions within Robotic Soccer

The challenges inherent in the simulated robotic soccer domain have motivated the research reported in this book. While CMUnited has performed successfully in competitions as a result of this research, there are still many challenges within robotic soccer to be addressed. These challenges could be addressed either within robotic soccer or within a similar real-time, collaborative, and adversarial domain.

Short-term, on-line learning and prediction. The on-line learning implemented in this book—TPOT-RL—takes many games against a fixed opponent to learn an effective behavior. It is still an open question whether useful on-line learning can be accomplished in this domain within the course of a single

10-minute game. For example, can the actions of a particular opponent agent be learned quickly enough that predictions can be exploited before the end of the game?

Opponent modeling. All of the robotic soccer behaviors created in this book have either ignored opponents' behaviors or considered them a part of the environment. Explicit modeling of opponents' behaviors and short-term goals may facilitate the adaptation of behaviors to specific adversarial situations[1].

On-line multiagent planning. The set-plays created as part of our flexible teamwork structure are pre-compiled multiagent plans. They are created ahead of time for use in situations that occur repeatedly within the domain. The creation of multiagent plans on-line for use during an unanticipated situation remains an open research problem.

Since the robotic soccer simulator changes periodically, adding new challenges to replace those that have been successfully met, I anticipate additional research challenges from this domain in the future. For example, if the soccer server moves from a 2-dimensional to a 3-dimensional simulation, or if the visual information format is changed to simulate video camera input, the low-level skills will become more challenging to create, thus introducing additional learning opportunities. In addition, if heterogeneous agents or a coach agent are introduced into the environment, the resulting collaborative and adversarial aspects of the domain will present new research challenges.

This book contributes several successful techniques for building agents in the robotic soccer domain. However, it is not yet a "solved" domain.

Future Directions within the Contributed Algorithms

In this subsection I discuss future research directions regarding the main contributions of this book: the team member agent architecture, layered learning, and TPOT-RL. Each contribution has been implemented in simulated robotic soccer and at most one other domain. In all three cases, an important future direction is the application of these algorithms to additional domains. Broad applications can verify the algorithms' generality as well as helping to identify their most important features for achieving successful results.

---

1 The CMUnited-99 simulator team, created after the research reported in this book was conducted, makes use of some explicit teammate and opponent modeling.

TEAM MEMBER AGENT ARCHITECTURE

Automatic set-play definition. The flexible teamwork structure provides a specification for how to execute pre-compiled, multiagent plans, or *set-plays*. However, these set-plays must currently be input to the system. A general mechanism for automatically defining set-plays would be a useful direction for future research.

One possible approach to automatically defining set-plays is to use a probabilistic planning algorithm such as Weaver (Blythe, 1998). Since PTS domains are dynamic, a probabilistic planner is needed to deal with unpredictable environmental changes. In noisy domains, the probabilistic methods are also needed to handle the uncertain effects of agents' actuators.

In order to use such a planning algorithm, one must define an *initial state*, a *goal state*, and a set of *operators*. The initial state is the situation in which the set-play is called, the goal state is the team's joint goal G (or an intermediate state on a path of states towards G), and the operators are the agents' actuators in the domain. Since set-plays are defined as part of the locker-room agreement, the planning algorithm could create a set-play for the entire team at once. The team could then break the plan into its individual roles in order to encode it within the locker-room agreement.

When to switch roles. The flexible teamwork structure defined within the team member agent architecture defines a mechanism by which agents can smoothly switch roles within a formation. However, we have not discovered any useful heuristics governing *when* agents should switch roles. Defining such heuristics would be an interesting extension to our teamwork structure.

For example, if agent a_1 is filling role r_1 and agent a_2 is filling role r_2, one clear reason to switch roles would be if a_1 has more of the resources necessary for filling r_2 than does a_2 and likewise a_2 for r_1. In this and other situations in which homogeneous agents might switch roles, the cost to the team in terms of possible discontinuities of roles being filled and in terms of inconsistent agent impressions of the mapping $A \mapsto R$ must be considered.

In addition to being implemented in simulated robotic soccer, the team member agent architecture, including the flexible teamwork structure, has been applied in real robotic soccer. Since our robots do not use inter-agent communication, the communication paradigm for PTS domains with single-channel, low-bandwidth, unreliable communication environments does not apply on our current robots. For soccer-playing robots with inter-agent communication capabilities, however, the communication paradigm can be applied.

An important direction of future work is to apply the team member agent architecture, the teamwork structure, and the communication paradigm to domains other than robotic soccer. The most obvious extension is to other team-sports domains, such as American football. As opposed to soccer, football has much more frequent synchronization opportunities: between every play, teammates can discuss their next play. Even so, formations can change during the course of a single play. And like in soccer, each formation consists of a set of roles that are each defined with some flexibility left to the player that fills it. The communication environment during the dynamic periods is also quite similar to that of soccer: it is single-channel, low-bandwidth, and unreliable. In football, set-plays would be a much more prevalent part of the locker-room agreement.

As mentioned in Section 3.8, there are several examples of non-sports-related PTS domains, including multi-spacecraft missions (Stone, 1997), search and rescue domains, hospital/factory maintenance (Decker, 1996b), battlefield combat (Tambe, 1997), and network routing. Another PTS domain with single-channel, low-bandwidth, unreliable communication is multi-robot systems with audio communication (Fujita and Kageyama, 1997). Applying the team member agent architecture to some of these domains is an important direction for future work.

LAYERED LEARNING

More learned layers. The layered learning implementation in this book consists of three learned layers ranging from an individual behavior to a team behavior. The end of Section 4.3 details the possible extension of this implementation to include another team behavior and an adversarial behavior. Successfully implementing these or other additional learned layers would be an interesting avenue for future research.

Automatic task decomposition. Layered learning works with a given task decomposition. However, it could be combined with a method for learning task decompositions. As presented in Section 4.1,

> let A be an algorithm for learning task decompositions within a domain. Suppose that A does not have an objective metric for comparing different decompositions. Applying layered learning on the task decomposition and quantifying the resulting performance can be used as a measure of the utility of A's output.

The creation of an algorithm A for learning task decompositions is a challenging open research direction.

Error propagation. In this book, each of the learned layers is validated in a controlled testing scenario, demonstrating the effectiveness of the learned behavior. However, no study is made of the propagation of errors from one layer to the next. It is possible that errors at initial layers could hurt performance at all subsequent layers. However, since learned layers are trained individually, it is also possible that the learning at subsequent layers could compensate for earlier errors and thus render them inconsequential. A detailed study of error propagation and compensation within layered learning implementations is a promising area for future research.

Layered learning is applied in simulated robotic soccer in this book. A possible next step is to apply layered learning in real robotic soccer as well. In this case, the same task decomposition as is used in simulated robotic soccer might apply.

In general, layered learning applies in domains that are too complex for tractably learning a mapping directly from an agent's sensory inputs to its actuator outputs. Many real-world domains fit this characteristic. For example, layered learning could be applied in a multiagent search and rescue domain. Like in robotic soccer, agents could learn individual, multiagent, team, and adversarial behaviors.

TPOT-RL

Choosing a representation. One of the key responsible factors for TPOT-RL's success in both simulated robotic soccer and network routing is the choice of input representation for learning. In particular, the action-dependent feature function $e(s, a)$ determines the representation of the learned function. In the case of robotic soccer, the input representation is constructed from the previously learned layer in layered learning.

In both implementations of TPOT-RL in this book, a single input representation is successfully used. However, other representations are possible. For example, in robotic soccer, rather than using the learned pass-evaluation function as e, the agents could perhaps learn based on the distance of the closest opponent to the pass target.

Quantifying the effect of learned TPOT-RL behaviors as a function of the input representation used would be an interesting result.

Choosing a reward function. Similarly, the implementations of TPOT-RL in this book vary the agents' reward function only minimally. As with all reinforcement learning methods, the reward function has an important effect on what is learned. It would be interesting to quantify the effects of the reward function on the learned behaviors when using TPOT-RL.

As presented in Section 7.5, TPOT-RL applies in domains with the following characteristics:

- There are multiple agents organized in a team.
- There are opaque state transitions.
- There are too many states and/or not enough training examples for traditional RL techniques to work.
- The target concept is non-stationary.
- There is long-range reward available.
- There are action-dependent features available.

In addition to simulated robotic soccer and network packet-routing, such domains include information networks, distributed logistics, and rescue missions. As with all of the book's contributions, it is a valuable direction of future research to apply TPOT-RL to these other multiagent domains.

10.3 Concluding Remarks

In short, this book contributes techniques for building agents in a particularly complex class of real-world domains: real-time, noisy, collaborative and adversarial multiagent environments. I believe that AI agents will be applied to this type of domain more and more frequently in the near future. I hope that the book's contributions will prove useful in addressing the problems that arise in these domains, and, ultimately, will improve our understanding of what it takes to build complete, AI agents.

A List of Acronyms

Following is the list of acronyms used in this book.

AAAI: American Association of Artificial Intelligence

AI: Artificial Intelligence

BDI: Belief/Desires/Intentions

DAG: Directed Acyclic Graph

DAI: Distributed Artificial Intelligence

DT: Decision Tree

GA: Genetic Algorithm

GPGP: Generalized Partial Global Planning

ICMAS: International Conference on Multi-Agent Systems

IJCAI: International Joint Conference on Artificial Intelligence

IROS: International Conference on Intelligent Robotic Systems

KIF: Knowledge Interchange Format

KQML: Knowledge Query and Manipulation Language

MAS: Multi-Agent Systems

MiroSot: Micro-Robot Soccer Tournament

ML: Machine Learning

NN: Neural Network

OPL: Only Play Left

OPR: Only Play Right

PLOS: Predictive, Locally Optimal Skills

PRW: Prefer Right Wing

PTS: Periodic Team Synchronization

RCF: Receiver Choice Function

RL: Reinforcement Learning

RMM: Recursive Modeling Method

SPAR: Strategic Positioning using Attraction and Repulsion

TPOT-RL: Team-Partitioned, Opaque-Transition Reinforcement Learning

B Robotic Soccer Agent Skills

This appendix complements the description of the CMUnited implementations described in Chapter 3. The implementation details of the simulated and robotic agent skills are presented. In the context of the team member agent architecture, the skills are low-level external behaviors culminating in action primitives.

B.1 CMUnited-98 Simulator Agent Skills

The skills available to CMUnited-98 players include kicking, dribbling, ball interception, goaltending, defending, and clearing. The common thread among these skills is that they are all *predictive, locally optimal skills* (PLOS). They take into account predicted world states as well as predicted effects of future actions in order to determine the optimal primitive action from a local perspective, both in time and in space.

Even though the skills are predictive, the agent *commits* to only one action during each cycle. When the time comes to act again, the situation is completely reevaluated. If the world is close to the anticipated configuration, then the agent will stay in the same behavior mode and carry on with the same skill, acting similarly to the way it predicted on previous cycles. However, if the world is significantly different, the agent will arrive at a new sequence of actions rather than being committed to a previous plan. Again, it will only execute the first step in the new sequence.

Many of the skills presented here were developed in collaboration with Riley (Stone et al., 1999).

Kicking

Recall from Section 2.2 that an agent can only kick the ball when it is within the `kickable_area` = `player_size` + `ball_size` + `kickable_margin` = 1.885 with the current server parameters.

As a first level of abstraction when dealing with the ball, all reasoning is done as a desired trajectory for the ball for the next cycle. Before a kick is actually sent to the server, the difference between the ball's current velocity and the ball's desired velocity is used to determine the kick to actually perform. If the exact trajectory can not be obtained, the ball is kicked such that the direction is correct, even if the speed is not.

In order to effectively control the ball, a player must be able to kick the ball in any direction. In order to do so, the player must be able to move the ball from one side of its body to the other without the ball colliding with the player. This behavior is called the *turnball* behavior. It was developed based on code released by the PaSo'97 team(Pagello et al., 1998). The desired trajectory of a turnball kick is calculated by getting the ray from the ball's current position that is tangent to a circle around the player (see Figure B.1(a)). Note that there are two possible such rays which correspond to the two directions that the ball can be turned around the player. Care is taken to ensure that the ball stays well within the kickable area from kick to kick so that the player keeps control of the ball.

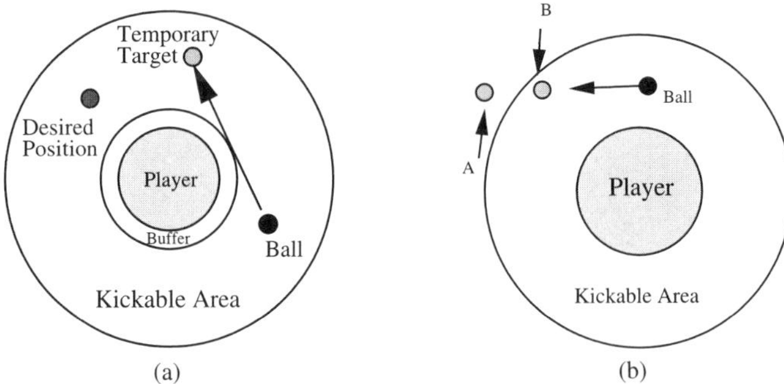

Figure B.1
(a) The turnball skill. (b) Basic kicking with velocity prediction.

The next important skill is the ability to kick the ball in a given direction, either for passing or shooting. The first step is to figure out the target speed of the ball. If the agent is shooting, the target speed is the maximum ball speed, but for a pass, it might be better to kick the ball slower so that the receiving agent can intercept the ball more easily. In this case, the agent must take into account the ball's deceleration over time when determining how hard to kick the ball.

In order to get the ball to the desired speed, several kicks in succession are usually required. By putting the ball to the side of the player (relative to the desired direction of the kick) the agent can kick the ball several times in succession. If a higher ball speed is desired, the agent can use the turnball kicks to back the ball up so that enough kicks can be performed to accelerate the ball.

This skill is predictive in that it looks at future velocities of the ball given different possible kicks. In some cases, doing a weaker kick one cycle may keep the ball in the kickable area so that another kick can be executed the following cycle. In Figure B.1(b), the agent must choose between two possible kicks. Kicking the ball to position A will result in the ball not being kickable next cycle; if the ball is already moving quickly enough, this action may be correct. However, a kick to position B followed by a kick during the next cycle may result in a higher overall speed. Short term velocity prediction is the key to these decisions.

Dribbling

Dribbling is the skill which allows the player to move down the field while keeping the ball close to the player the entire time. The basic idea is fairly simple: alternate kicks and dashes so that after one of each, the ball is still close to the player.

Every cycle, the agent looks to see that if it dashes this cycle, the ball will be in its kickable area (and not be a collision) at the next cycle. If so, then the agent dashes, otherwise it kicks. A kick is always performed assuming that on the next cycle, the agent will dash. As an argument, the low-level dribbling code takes the angle relative to the direction of travel at which the player should aim the ball (see Figure B.2). This is called the "dribble angle" and its valid values are $[-90, 90]$. Deciding what the dribble angle should be is discussed in the next subsection.

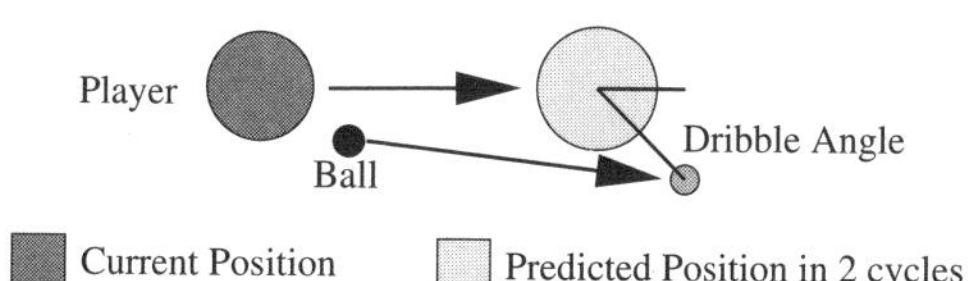

Figure B.2
The basic dribbling skill.

First the predicted position of the agent (in 2 cycles) is calculated:

$$p_{new} = p_{current} + v + (v * pdecay + a)$$

where p_{new} is the predicted player position, $p_{current}$ is the current position of the player, v is the current velocity of the player, $pdecay$ is the server parameter `player_decay`, and a is the acceleration that a dash gives. As presented in Section 2.2, the a value is usually just the dash power times the `dash_power_rate` in the direction the player is facing, but stamina may need to be taken into account.

Added to p_{new} is a vector in the direction of the dribble angle and length such that the ball is in the kickable area. This is the target position p_{target} of the ball. Then the agent gets the desired ball trajectory by the following formula:

$$traj = \frac{p_{target} - p_{ball}}{1 + bdecay}$$

where $traj$ is the target trajectory of the ball, p_{ball} is the current ball position, and $bdecay$ is the server parameter `ball_decay`. This process is illustrated in Figure B.2.

If for some reason this kick cannot be done (it would be a collision for example), then a turnball kick is done to get the ball in the right position. Then the next cycle, a normal dribble kick should work.

As can be seen from these calculations, the basic dribbling is highly predictive of the positions and velocities of the ball and player. It is also local in that it only looks 2 cycles ahead and recomputes the best action every cycle.

Smart Dribbling

The basic dribbling takes one parameter that was mentioned above: the dribble angle. Smart dribbling is a skill layered on the basic dribbling skill that decides the best dribble angle based on opponent positions. Intuitively, the agent should keep the ball away from the opponents, so that if an opponent is on the left, the ball is kept on the right, and vice versa.

The agent considers all nearby opponents that it knows about. Each opponent is given a “vote” about what the dribble angle should be; each opponent votes for the valid angle $[-90, 90]$ that is farthest from itself. For example, an opponent at 45 degrees, would vote for -90, while an opponent at -120 degrees would vote for 60. Each opponent’s vote is weighted by the distance and angle relative to the direction of motion. Closer opponents and opponents more in front of the agent are given more weight (see Figure B.3).

Ball Interception

There are two types of ball interception, referred to as active and passive interception. The passive interception is used only by the goaltender in some particular cases, while the rest of the team uses only the active interception. Each cycle, the interception target is recomputed so that the most up to date

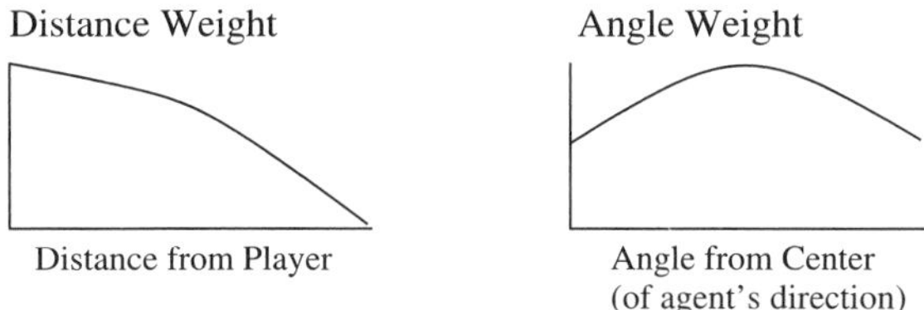

Figure B.3
The weights for smart dribbling.

information about the world is used.

The active interception is similar to the one used by the Humboldt '97 team(Burkhard et al., 1998). The active interception predicts the ball's position on successive cycles, and then tries to predict whether the player will be able to make it to that spot before the ball does, taking into account stamina and the direction that the player is facing. The agent aims for the earliest such spot.

This process can be used for teammates as well as for the agent itself. Thus, the agent can determine which player should go for the ball, and whether it can get there before the opponents do.

The passive interception is much more geometric. The agent determines the closest point along the ball's current trajectory that is within the field. By prediction based on the ball's velocity, the agent decides whether it can make it to that point before the ball. If so, then the agent runs towards that point.

These analytic ball-interception skills were developed in a later version of the simulator (version 4) than the learned ball-interception skill described in Chapter 5 (version 2). These routines were not appropriate in version 2 of the simulator because players were not given information about the ball's instantaneous velocity in their visual information. In addition, sensory information arrived much less frequently (every 500 msec as opposed to the current 150 msec). Therefore, in version 2 of the soccer server, it was much harder to accurately predict the ball's future path.

Goaltending

The assumption behind the movement of the goaltender is that the worst thing that could happen to the goaltender is to lose sight of the ball. The sooner the goaltender sees a shot coming, the greater chance it has of preventing a goal. Therefore, the goaltender generally uses the widest view mode (`view_width` = *wide*) and uses backwards dashing when appropriate to keep the ball in view while positioning itself in situations that are not time-critical.

Every cycle that the ball is in the defensive zone, the goaltender looks to see if the ball is in the midst of a shot. It does this by extending the ray of the ball's position and velocity and intersecting that with the baseline of the field. If the intersection point is in the goaltender box and the ball has sufficient velocity to get there, the ball is considered to be a shot (though special care is used if an opponent can kick the ball this cycle). Using the passive interception if possible (see the previous subsection), the goaltender tries to get in the path of the ball and then run at the ball to grab it. In this way, if the goaltender misses a catch or kick, the ball may still collide with the goaltender and thus be stopped.

When there is no shot coming, the goaltender positions itself in anticipation of a future shot. Based on the angle of the ball relative to the goal, the goaltender picks a spot in the goal to guard; call this the "guard point." The further the ball is to the side of the field, the further the goaltender guards to that side. Then, a rectangle is computed that shrinks as the ball gets closer (though it never shrinks smaller than the goaltender box). The line from the guard point to the ball's current position is intersected with the rectangle, and that is the desired position of the goaltender.

Defending

CMUnited-98 agents are equipped with two different defending modes: opponent tracking and opponent marking. In both cases, a particular opponent player is selected as the target against which to defend. This opponent can either be selected individually or as a defensive unit via communication (the latter is the case in CMUnited-98).

In either case, the agent defends against this player by observing its position over time and position itself strategically so as to minimize its usefulness to the other team. When *tracking*, the agent stays between the opponent and the goal at a generous distance, thus blocking potential shots. When *marking*, the agent stays close to the opponent on the ball-opponent-goal angle bisector, making it difficult for the opponent to receive passes and shoot towards the goal. Defensive marking and tracking positions are illustrated in Figure B.4.

When marking and tracking, it is important for the agent to have accurate knowledge about the positions of both the ball and the opponent (although the ball position is not strictly relevant for tracking, it is used for the decision of whether or not to be tracking). Thus, when in the correct defensive position, the agent always turns to look at the object (opponent or ball) in which it is

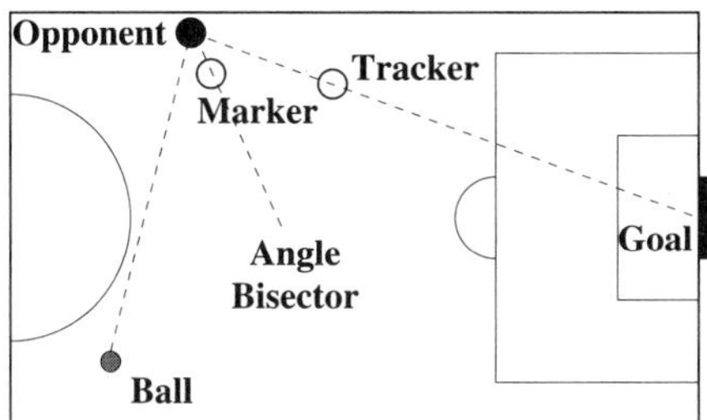

Figure B.4
Positioning for defensive tracking and marking.

least confident of the correct position. The complete algorithm, which results in the behavior of doggedly following a particular opponent and glancing back and forth between the opponent and ball, is as follows:

- If the ball position is unknown, look for the ball.
- Else, if the opponent position is unknown, look for the opponent.
- Else, if not in the correct defensive position, move to that position.
- Else, look towards the object, ball or opponent, which has been seen less recently (lower confidence value).

This defensive behavior is locally optimal in that it defends according to the opponent's current position, following it around rather than predicting its future location. However, the defensive positioning is chosen in anticipation of the opponent's future possible actions, i.e. receiving a pass or shooting.

Clearing

When in a defensive position, it is often advantageous to just send the ball upfield, clearing it from the defensive zone. If the agent decides that it cannot pass or dribble while in a defensive situation, it clears the ball. The important decision in clearing the ball is where to clear it to. The best clears are upfield, but not to the middle of the field (you don't want to center the ball for the opponents), and also away from the opponents.

The actual calculation is as follows. Every angle is evaluated with respect to its usefulness, and the expected degree of success. The usefulness is a sine curve with a maximum of 1 at 30 degrees, .5 at 90 degrees, and 0 at -90, where a negative angle is towards the middle of the field. The actual equation is (Θ is in degrees):

$$\text{usefulness}(\Theta) = \frac{sin(\frac{3}{2}\Theta + 45) + 1}{2} \tag{B.1}$$

The expected degree of success is evaluated by looking at an isosceles triangle with one vertex where the ball is, and congruent sides extending in the direction of the target being evaluated. For each opponent in the triangle, its distance from the center line of the triangle is divided by the distance from the player on that line. For opponent C in Figure B.5, these values are w and d respectively. The expected success is the product of all these quotients. In Figure B.5, opponent A would not affect the calculation, being outside the triangle, while opponent B would lower the expected success to 0, since it is on the potential clear line ($w = 0$).

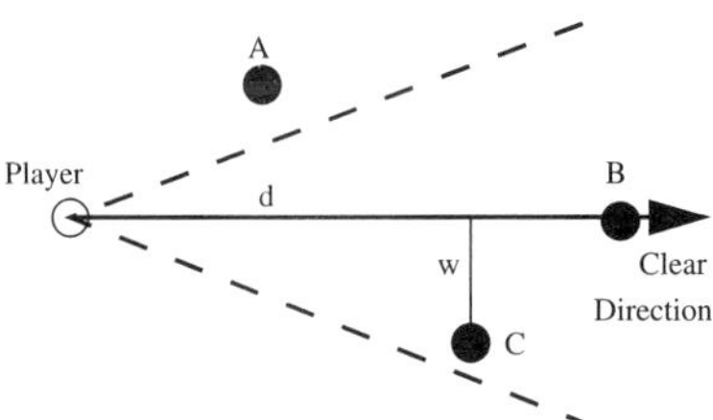

Figure B.5
Measuring the expected success of a clear.

By multiplying the usefulness and expected success together for each possible clear angle, and taking the maximum, the agent gets a crude approximation to maximizing the expected utility of a clear.

Closely related to clearing, there is another behavior called offensive "sending." Rather than trying to clear the ball to the sides, the agent sends the ball to the middle of the offensive zone in the hope that a teammate will catch up to the ball before the defenders. This is useful if the agent is too tired or unable to dribble for some reason. It is especially useful to beat an offsides trap because it generally requires the defenders to run back to get the ball.

The only difference between offensive sending and defensive clearing is the usefulness function. For sending, the usefulness function is linear, with slope determined by the agent's y position on the field. The closer the agent is to the sideline, the steeper the slope, and the more that it favors sending to the middle of the field.

B.2 CMUnited-97 Small-Robot Skills

The skills available to the CMUnited-97 robots include path-planning, two forms of ball handling, obstacle avoidance, goaltending, and pass evaluation (Veloso and Stone, 1998).

Non-holonomic Path Generation

The non-holonomic path planning problem has been addressed by many researchers, e.g., (Latombe, 1991; Fujimura, 1991). However, most of the algorithms deal with static worlds and generate pre-planned global paths. In the robot soccer domain, this pre-planning is not possible as the domain is inherently dynamic and response times need to be very fast. Furthermore, the world dynamics include possible interference from other robots (e.g., pushing), making precisely mapped out paths ineffective and unnecessary.

Implemented by Han and described in detail in (Han and Veloso, 1998), the navigational movement for the CMUnited-97 robots is done via reactive control. The control rules were inspired by the Braitenburg vehicle (Braitenburg, 1984).

Ball Handling

If a robot is to accurately direct the ball towards a target position, it must be able to approach the ball from a specified direction. Using the ball prediction from the vision system, the robot aims at a point on the far side of the target position. The robots are equipped with two methods of doing so:

- **Ball collection:** Moving behind a ball and knocking it towards the target.
- **Ball interception:** Waiting for the ball to cross its path and then intercepting the moving ball towards the target.

When using the ball collection behavior, the robot considers a line (line a in Figure B.6(a)) from the target position to the ball's current or predicted position, depending on whether or not the ball is moving. The robot then plans a path to a point on line a and behind the ball such that it does not hit the ball on the way and such that it ends up facing the target position. Finally, the robot accelerates to the target. Figure B.6(a) illustrates this behavior.

When using the ball interception behavior (Figure B.6(b)), on the other hand, the robot considers a line from *itself* to the target position (line a) and determines where the ball's path (line b) will intersect this line. The robot then

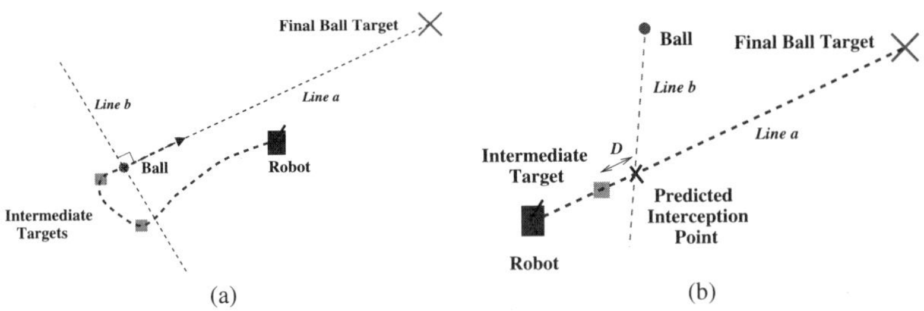

Figure B.6
Single-agent behaviors to enable team collaboration (a) Ball collection (aiming for a pass or to the goal); (b) Ball interception (receiving a pass).

positions itself along this line so that it will be able to accelerate to the point of intersection at the same time that the ball arrives.

In practice, the robot chooses from between its two ball handling routines based on whether the ball will eventually cross its path at a point such that the robot could intercept it towards the goal. Thus, the robot gives precedence to the ball interception routine, only using ball collection when necessary. When using ball collection, it actually aims at the ball's predicted location a fixed time in the future so as to eventually position itself in a place from which it can intercept the ball towards the target.

Obstacle Avoidance

In the robotic soccer field, there are often obstacles between the robot and its goal location. Our robots try to avoid collisions by planning a path around the obstacles. Due to the highly dynamic nature of this domain, our obstacle avoidance algorithm uses closed-loop control by which the robots continually replan their goal positions around obstacles. In the event that an obstacle blocks the direct path to the goal location, the robot aims to one side of the obstacle until it is in a position such that it can move directly to its original goal. Rather than planning the entire path to the goal location at once, the robot just looks ahead to the first obstacle in its way under the assumption that other robots are continually moving around. Using the reactive control described above, the robot continually reevaluates its target position. For an illustration, see Figure B.7.

The robot starts by trying to go straight towards its final target along line a. When it comes across an obstacle within a certain distance of itself and of line

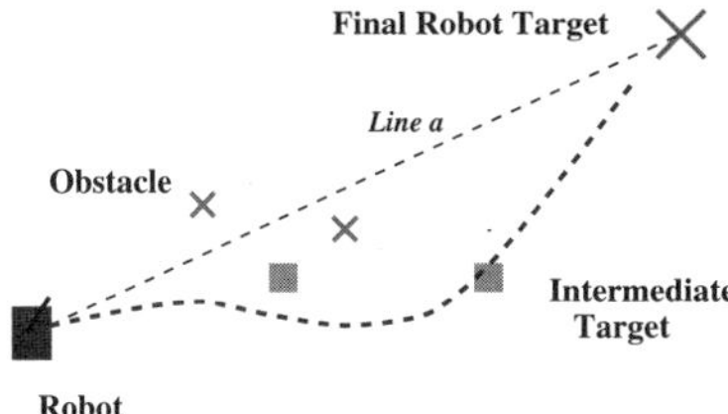

Figure B.7
Obstacle avoidance through dynamic generation of intermediate targets.

a, it aims at an intermediate target to the side, and slightly beyond the obstacle. The robot goes around the obstacle the short way, unless it is at the edge of the field. Using reactive control, the robot continually recomputes line a until the obstacle is no longer in its path. As it comes across further obstacles, it aims at additional intermediate targets until it obtains an unobstructed path to the final target.

Even with obstacle avoidance in place, the robots can occasionally get stuck against other robots or against the wall. Particularly if opponent robots do not use obstacle avoidance, collisions are inevitable. When unable to move, our robots identify the source of the problem as the closest obstacle and "unstick" themselves by moving away. In order to prevent looping, they move a considerable distance from the closest obstacle before considering themselves unstuck. Once free, normal control resumes.

Goaltending

The goaltender robot has both special hardware and special software. Thus, it does not switch positions or active modes like the others. The goaltender's physical frame is distinct from that of the other robots in that it is as long as allowed under the RoboCup-97 rules (18cm) so as to block as much of the goal as possible. The goaltender's role is to prevent the ball from entering the goal. It stays parallel to and close to the goal, aiming always to be directly even with the ball's lateral coordinate on the field.

Ideally, simply staying even with the ball would guarantee that the ball would never get past the goaltender. However, since the robots cannot accelerate as fast as the ball can, it would be possible to defeat such a behavior. Therefore, the goaltender continually monitors the ball's trajectory. In some cases it moves to the ball's predicted destination point ahead of time. The decision of when to move to the predicted ball position is both crucial and difficult, as illustrated in Figure B.8. Our goaltender robot currently takes into account the predicted velocity and direction of the ball to select its moves. If the ball is moving slowly, it tries to stay even with the ball as shown by the solid goaltender robot; if the ball is moving quickly, it goes directly to its predicted position as shown by the dashed goaltender robot.

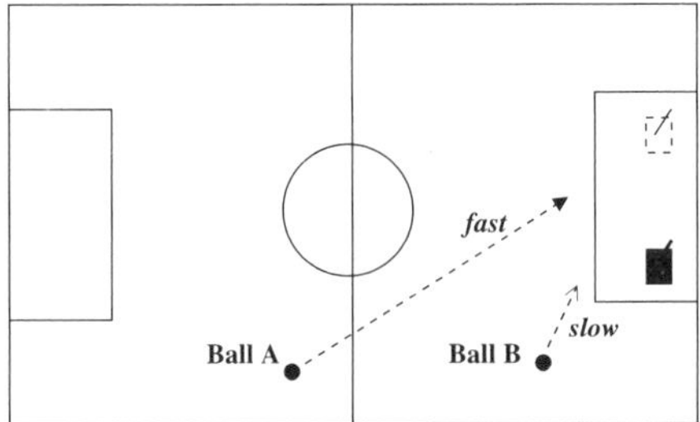

Figure B.8
Goaltending.

Run-time Evaluation of Collaborative Opportunities

Unlike the simulated agents which use a learned pass evaluation function (see Chapter 6), the robots do not have any learned modules. Instead, they use a special-purpose pass-evaluation procedure.

When in active mode, the robots use an evaluation function that takes into account teammate and opponent positions to determine whether to pass the ball or whether to shoot. In particular, as part of the formation definition, each position has a set of positions to which it considers passing (see Chapter 3). For example, a defender might consider passing to any forward or midfielder, while a forward would consider passing to other forwards, but not backwards to a midfielder or defender.

For each such position that is occupied by a teammate, the robot evaluates the pass to that position as well as evaluating its own shot. To evaluate each possible pass, the robot computes the *obstruction-free-index* of the two line segments that the ball must traverse if the receiver is to shoot the ball (lines b and c in Figure B.9). In the case of a shot, only one line segment must be considered (line a). The *value* of each possible pass or shot is the product of the relevant obstruction-free-indices. Robots can be biased towards passing or shooting by further multiplying the values by a factor determined by the relative proximities of the active robot and the potential receivers to the goal. The robot chooses the pass or shot with the maximum value. The obstruction-free-index of line segment l is computed by the following algorithm (variable names correspond to those in Figure B.9):

1. *obstruction-free-index* = 1.
2. For each opponent O:
   - Compute the distance x from O to l and the distance y along l to l's origin, i.e. the end at which the ball will be kicked by the robot (See Figure B.9).
   - Define constants *min-dist* and *max-denominator*. Opponents farther than *min-dist* from l are not considered. When discounting *obstruction-free-index* in the next step, the y distance is never considered to be larger than *max-denominator*. For example, in Figure B.9, the opponent near the goal would be evaluated with y = *max-denominator*, rather than its actual distance from the ball. The reasoning is that beyond distance *max-denominator*, the opponent has enough time to block the ball: the extra distance is no longer useful.
   - if $x <$ *min-dist* and $x < y$, *obstruction-free-index* = *obstruction-free-index* $\times$ $x/MIN(\textit{max-demoninator}, y)$.
3. return *obstruction-free-index*.

Thus the obstruction-free-index reflects how easily an opponent could intercept the pass or the subsequent shot. The closer the opponent is to the line and the farther it is from the ball, the better chance it has of intercepting the ball.

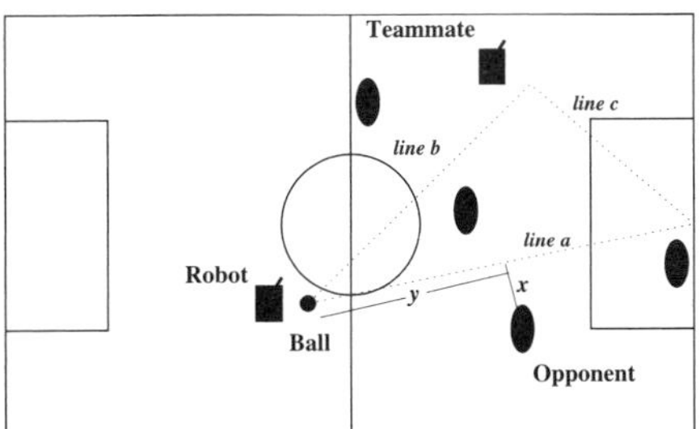

Figure B.9
Run-time pass evaluation based on the positions of opponents.

C CMUnited-98 Simulator Team Behavior Modes

This appendix describes the detailed conditions and effects of the behavior modes used by the CMUnited-98 simulator agents. As laid out in Chapter 3, specifically in Section 3.5, the agents have several behavior modes. In the context of the team member agent architecture, the choice of behavior mode is the top-level external behavior. The full set of modes is:

- Goaltend
- Localize
- Before kick off
- Face ball
- Set-play
- Recover
- Get onside
- Handle ball
- Active offense
- Auxiliary offense
- Passive offense
- Active defense
- Auxiliary defense
- Passive defense

Here I present the detailed conditions and effects of these behavior modes.

C.1 Conditions

During each simulator cycle, an agent's first step towards choosing an action is to reevaluate its behavior mode. They use the following rule-based system. Some of the conditions depend on an evaluation of which team currently has *possession* of the ball. The agent evaluates which of all the players on the field could intercept the ball's path most quickly. If it is an opponent, then the opponent team has possession. Otherwise, the agent's own team has possession.

The agent uses the first of the following rules that applies.

- If playing the goaltender position: use goaltend mode.
- If own location is unknown: use localize mode.
- If the server's play mode is "before kickoff:" use before kickoff mode.
- If the ball's location is unknown: use face ball mode.
- If there is a set-play defined for the situation and playing a position involved in the play: use set-play mode.
- If there is a set-play defined for the situation and *not* playing a position involved in the play: use passive offense mode.
- If the ball is kickable (within `kickable_area`): use handle ball mode.
- If stamina is lower than the server's threshold for decrementing the `recovery` parameter (`recover_dec_thr` × `stamina_max`) : use recover mode.
- If the ball is not moving and no teammate is closer to the ball: use active offense mode.
- If no teammate could intercept the ball's current trajectory more quickly (taking into account what is known about own and teammates' current staminas): use active offense mode.
- If able to intercept the ball's current trajectory, the opponents have possession of the ball, and no more than one teammate is closer to the ball: use active defense mode.
- If expecting to receive a pass (a teammate has recently announced an intention to execute such a pass): use face ball mode.
- If in an offside position: use get onside mode.
- If playing a defender position:
  - –If own team is in possession of the ball and the ball is further back on the field than own position: use auxiliary offense mode.
  - –If recently assigned to mark an opponent: use auxiliary defense mode.
  - –Otherwise: use passive defense mode.
- If playing a midfielder position:
  - –If the opponents have possession: use passive offense mode.
  - –Otherwise: use auxiliary offense mode.
- Otherwise (if playing a forward position):
  - –If the ball is close to the home of the position being played (within 30 meters on the field's lengthwise axis): use auxiliary offense mode.
  - –Otherwise: use passive offense mode

C.2 Effects

The effects of being in the different behavior modes are as follows:

Goaltend: Execute the goaltender skill detailed in Appendix B.

Localize: Turn until visual information is sufficient to determine own location on the field.

Before kick off: Move to a location appropriate for kickoffs (on own side of the field and close to own position's home location). Then face the ball.

Face ball: If the ball's location is unknown, turn until it is visible. Otherwise, turn directly towards the ball.

Set-play: Fill the appropriate role in the appropriate set-play for the current situation. There are defensive and offensive set-plays defined for all dead-ball situations (kickoffs, corner kicks, free kicks, etc.). The number of players involved in each set play varies from 1 (1 player gets in front of the ball when it's the opponent's kick in) to 5 (see the corner kick example in Section 3.5). Agents use the current team formation to map formation positions to set-play positions based on geographical proximity. As set-play positions have behaviors associated with them, the agent involved in a set-play executes its assigned behavior either until the play is over or until a time-limit expires. Then it returns to choosing from among the other behavior modes as usual.

Recover: Stay still until stamina recovers above the server's threshold for decrementing the `recovery` parameter: (`recover_dec_thr` × `stamina_max`).

Get onside: Move to a position that is not offside, i.e. in front of the opponent's last defender.

Handle ball: One of the most important decisions in the robotic soccer domain arises when the agent has control of the ball. In this state, it has the options of dribbling the ball in any direction, passing to any teammate, shooting the ball, clearing the ball, or simply controlling the ball.

In CMUnited-98, the agent uses a complex heuristic decision mechanism, incorporating a machine learning module, to choose its action. The best teammate to receive a potential pass (called *potential receiver* below) is determined by a decision tree trained off-line (see Chapter 6). Following is a rough sketch of the decision-making process without all of the parametric details. The referenced low-level skills are described in Section B.1.

To begin with, since kicks (i.e. shots, passes, and clears) can take several cycles to complete (Section B.1), the agent remembers the goal of a previously started kick and continues executing it. When no kick is in progress (do the first that applies):

- If close to the opponent's goal and no defenders are blocking the path to the goal (defined as a cone with vertex at the ball): shoot or dribble based on the goaltender's position, the position of the closest opponent, and the distance to the goal.
- At the other extreme, if close to the agent's own goal and there is an opponent nearby: clear the ball (see Section B.1).
- If approaching the line of the last opponent defender: dribble the ball forward if possible; otherwise send the ball past the defender (see Section B.1).
- If the potential receiver is closer to the goal and has a clear shot: pass to the potential receiver.
- If no opponents are in the direct path to the goal: dribble to the goal (see Section B.1).
- If fairly close to the opponent's goal and there is at most one opponent in front of the goal: shoot.
- If no opponents are in the way of one of the corner flags: dribble towards the corner flag.
- If there is a potential receiver: pass.
- If it's possible to hold onto the ball without moving (at most one opponent is nearby): hold the ball.
- Otherwise: Kick the ball away (clear).

Active offense: Intercept the ball as described in Section B.1.

Auxiliary offense: Use the SPAR variant of flexible positioning to try to get open to receive a pass (see Section 3.5).

Passive offense: Use ball-dependent flexible positioning (see Section 3.5).

Active defense: Go towards the ball even though another teammate might also be going towards it. As the second player to the ball, this player tries to block the opponent from dribbling away from the first teammate to the ball.

Auxiliary defense: Mark or track an opponent as described in Section B.1. The defensive unit captain assigns defenders their opponents to mark so that each opponent is covered.

Passive defense: Use ball-dependent flexible positioning (see Section 3.5).

D CMUnited Simulator Team Source Code

The source code of the CMUnited simulator teams is an on-line appendix. It is located at the following URL:

http://www.cs.cmu.edu/~pstone/book

The page at this URL includes links to the CMUnited-97 simulator team source code and portions of the CMUnited-98 simulator team source code. Executables are also available.

References

Achim, S., Stone, P., and Veloso, M. (1996). Building a dedicated robotic soccer system. In *Proceedings of the IROS-96 Workshop on RoboCup*, pages 41–48, Osaka, Japan.

Agre, P. and Chapman, D. (1987). Pengi: An implementation of a theory of activity. In *Proceedings of the National Conference on Artificial Intelligence*, pages 268–272.

Andou, T. (1998). Refinement of soccer agents' positions using reinforcement learning. In Kitano, H., editor, *RoboCup-97: Robot Soccer World Cup I*, pages 373–388. Springer Verlag, Berlin.

Andre, D., Corten, E., Dorer, K., Gugenberger, P., Joldos, M., Kummeneje, J., Navratil, P. A., Noda, I., Riley, P., Stone, P., Takahashi, R., and Yeap, T. (1998a). Soccer server manual, version 4.0. Technical Report RoboCup-1998-001, RoboCup. At URL http://ci.etl.go.jp/~noda/soccer/server/Documents.html.

Andre, D. and Teller, A. (1999). Evolving team darwin united. In Asada, M. and Kitano, H., editors, *RoboCup-98: Robot Soccer World Cup II*. Springer Verlag, Berlin.

Andre, E., Herzog, G., and Rist, T. (1988). On the simultaneous interpretation of real world image sequences and their natural language description: The system soccer. In *Proc. of the 8th ECAI*, pages 449–454, Munich.

Andre, E., Herzog, G., and Rist, T. (1998b). Generating multimedia presentations for RoboCup soccer games. In Kitano, H., editor, *RoboCup-97: Robot Soccer World Cup I*, pages 200–215. Springer Verlag, Berlin.

Arai, S., Miyazaki, K., and Kobayashi, S. (1997). Generating cooperative behavior by multi-agent reinforcement learning. In *Sixth European Workshop on Learning Robots*, Brighton, UK.

Arkin, R. (1992). Cooperation without communication: Multi-agent schema based robot navigation. *Journal of Robotic Systems*, 9(3):351–364.

Arkin, R. C. (1987). *Towards Cosmopolitan Robots: Intelligent Navigation in Extended Man-Made Environments*. PhD thesis, University of Massachusetts.

Arkin, R. C. (1998). The 1997 AAAI mobile robot competition and exhibition. *AI Magazine*, 19(3):13–17.

Arora, N. and Sen, S. (1996). Resolving social dilemmas using genetic algorithms. In *Adaptation, Coevolution and Learning in Multiagent Systems: Papers from the 1996 AAAI Spring Symposium*, pages 1–5, Menlo Park,CA. AAAI Press. AAAI Technical Report SS-96-01.

Asada, M. and Kitano, H., editors (1999). *RoboCup-98: Robot Soccer World Cup II*. Lecture Notes in Artificial Intelligence 1604. Springer Verlag, Berlin.

Asada, M., Kuniyoshi, Y., Drogoul, A., Asama, H., Mataric, M., Duhaut, D., Stone, P., and Kitano, H. (1998). The RoboCup physical agent challenge: Phase-I. *Applied Artificial Intelligence*, 12:251–263.

Asada, M., Noda, S., and Hosoda, K. (1996). Action-based sensor space categorization for robot learning. In *Proc. of IEEE/RSJ International Conference on Intelligent Robots and Systems 1996 (IROS '96)*, pages 1502–1509.

Asada, M., Noda, S., Tawaratsumida, S., and Hosoda, K. (1994a). Purposive behavior acquisition on a real robot by vision-based reinforcement learning. In *Proc. of MLC-COLT (Machine Learning Confernce and Computer Learning Theory) Workshop on Robot Learning*, pages 1–9.

Asada, M., Uchibe, E., Noda, S., Tawaratsumida, S., and Hosoda, K. (1994b). Coordination of multiple behaviors acquired by vision-based reinforcement learning. In *Proc. of IEEE/RSJ/GI International Conference on Intelligent Robots and Systems 1994*, pages 917–924.

Balch, T. (1998). *Behavioral Diversity in Learning Robot Teams*. PhD thesis, College of Computing, Georgia Institute of Technology.

Balch, T. and Arkin, R. C. (1995). Motor schema-based formation control for multiagent robot teams. In *Proceedings of the First International Conference on Multi-Agent Systems (ICMAS-95)*, pages 10–16, Menlo Park, California. AAAI Press.

Barbuceanu, M. and Fox, M. S. (1995). COOL: A language for describing coordination in multi agent systems. In *Proceedings of the First International Conference on Multi-Agent Systems (ICMAS-95)*, pages 17–24, Menlo Park, California. AAAI Press.

Barman, R. A., Kingdon, S. J., Little, J. J., Mackworth, A. K., Pai, D. K., Sahota, M., Wilkinson, H., and Zhang, Y. (1993). DYNAMO: Real-time experiments with multiple mobile robots. In *Intelligent Vehicles Symposium*, pages 261–266, Tokyo.

Benda, M., Jagannathan, V., and Dodhiawala, R. (1986). On optimal cooperation of knowledge sources - an empirical investigation. Technical Report BCS–G2010–28, Boeing Advanced Technology Center, Boeing Computing Services, Seattle, Washington.

Binsted, K. (1999). Character design for soccer commentary. In Asada, M. and Kitano, H., editors, *RoboCup-98: Robot Soccer World Cup II*. Springer Verlag, Berlin.

Blythe, J. (1998). *Planning Under Uncertainty in Dynamic Domains*. PhD thesis, Computer Science Department, Carnegie Mellon University, Pittsburgh, PA.

Bond, A. H. and Gasser, L. (1988). An analysis of problems and research in DAI. In Bond, A. H. and Gasser, L., editors, *Readings in Distributed Artificial Intelligence*, pages 3–35. Morgan Kaufmann Publishers, San Mateo, CA.

Bowling, M., Stone, P., and Veloso, M. (1996). Predictive memory for an inaccessible environment. In *Proceedings of the IROS-96 Workshop on RoboCup*, pages 28–34, Osaka, Japan.

Boyan, J. A. and Littman, M. L. (1994). Packet routing in dynamically changing networks: A reinforcement learning approach. In Cowan, J. D., Tesauro, G., and Alspector, J., editors, *Advances In Neural Information Processing Systems 6*. Morgan Kaufmann Publishers.

Boyan, J. A. and Moore, A. W. (1995). Generalization in reinforcement learning: Safely approximating the value function. In Tesauro, G., Touretzky, D., and Leen, T., editors, *Advances in Neural Information Processing Systems*, volume 7. The MIT Press.

Braitenburg, V. (1984). *Vehicles – experiments in synthetic psychology*. MIT Press.

Brooks, R. A. (1986). A robust layered control system for a mobile robot. *IEEE Journal of Robotics and Automation*, RA-2:14–23.

Bull, L., Fogarty, T., and Snaith, M. (1995). Evolution in multi-agent systems: Evolving communicating classifier systems for gait in a quadrupedal robot. In Forrest, S., editor, *Proceedings of the Sixth International Conference on Genetic Algorithms*, pages 382–388, San Mateo,CA. Morgan Kaufman.

Burkhard, H.-D., Hannebauer, M., and Wendler, J. (1998). AT Humboldt — development, practice and theory. In Kitano, H., editor, *RoboCup-97: Robot Soccer World Cup I*, pages 357–372. Springer Verlag, Berlin.

Caro, G. D. and Dorigo, M. (1998). AntNet: Distributed stigmergetic control for communications networks. *Journal of Artificial Intelligence Research*, 9:317–365.

Castelfranchi, C. (1995). Commitments: From individual intentions to groups and organizations. In *Proceedings of the First International Conference on Multi-Agent Systems (ICMAS-95)*, pages 41–48, Menlo Park, California. AAAI Press.

Cheng, G. and Zelinsky, A. (1998). Real-time vision processing for a soccer playing mobile robot. In Kitano, H., editor, *RoboCup-97: Robot Soccer World Cup I*, pages 144–155. Springer Verlag, Berlin.

Ch'ng, S. and Padgham, L. (1998). From roles to teamwork: a framework and architecture. *Applied Artificial Intelligence*, 12:211–232.

Clouse, J. A. (1996). Learning from an automated training agent. In Weiß, G. and Sen, S., editors, *Adaptation and Learning in Multiagent Systems*. Springer Verlag, Berlin.

Cohen, P. R. and Levesque, H. J. (1995). Communicative actions for artificial agents. In *Proceedings of the First International Conference on Multi-Agent Systems (ICMAS-95)*, pages 65–72, Menlo Park, California. AAAI Press.

Cohen, P. R., Levesque, H. J., and Smith, I. (1999). On team formation. In Hintikka, J. and

Tuomela, R., editors, *Contemporary Action Theory*. Synthese. to appear.

Conte, R., Castelfranchi, C., and Dignum, F. (1999). Autonomous norm-acceptance. In Müller, J. P., Singh, M. P., and Rao, A. S., editors, *Intelligent Agents V — Proceedings of the Fifth International Workshop on Agent Theories, Architectures, and Languages (ATAL-98)*, volume 1555 of *Lecture Notes in Artificial Intelligence*, pages 99–112. Springer-Verlag, Heidelberg.

Coradeschi, S. and Karlsson, L. (1998). A role-based decision-mechanism for teams of reactive and coordinating agents. In Kitano, H., editor, *RoboCup-97: Robot Soccer World Cup I*, pages 112–122. Springer Verlag, Berlin.

Coradeschi, S. and Malec, J. (1999). How to make a challenging AI course enjoyable using the RoboCup soccer simulation system. In Asada, M. and Kitano, H., editors, *RoboCup-98: Robot Soccer World Cup II*. Springer Verlag, Berlin.

Crites, R. H. and Barto, A. G. (1996). Improving elevator performance using reinforcement learning. In Touretzky, D. S., Mozer, M. C., and Hasselmo, M. E., editors, *Advances in Neural Processing Systems 8*, Cambridge, MA. MIT Press.

Dayan, P. and Hinton, G. E. (1993). Feudal reinforcement learning. In Hanson, S. J., Cowan, J. D., and Giles, C. L., editors, *Advances in Neural Information Processing Systems 5*. Morgan Kaufmann, San Mateo, CA.

de la Rosa, J. L., Oller, A., Vehi, J., and Puyol, J. (1997). Soccer team based on agent-oriented programming. *Robotics and Autonomous Systems*.

Decker, K. S. (1987). Distributed problem solving: A survey. *IEEE Transactions on Systems, Man, and Cybernetics*, 17(5):729–740.

Decker, K. S. (1996a). Distributed artificial intelligence testbeds. In O'Hare, G. M. P. and Jennings, N. R., editors, *Foundations of Distributed Artificial Intelligence*, pages 119–138. Wiley Interscience.

Decker, K. S. (1996b). Task environment centered simulation. In Prietula, M., Carley, K., and Gasser, L., editors, *Simulating Organizations: Computational Models of Institutions and Groups*. AAAI Press/MIT Press.

Decker, K. S. and Lesser, V. R. (1995). Designing a family of coordination algorithms. In *Proceedings of the First International Conference on Multi-Agent Systems (ICMAS-95)*, pages 73–80, Menlo Park, California. AAAI Press.

Dietterich, T. G. (1998). The MAXQ method for hierarchical reinforcement learning. In *Proceedings of the Fifteenth International Conference on Machine Learning*. Morgan Kaufmann.

Digney, B. L. (1996). Emergent hierarchical control structures: Learning reactive/hierarchical relationships in reinforcement environments. In *Proceedings of the 4th International Conference of Simulation of Adaptive Behavior*, pages 363–372. MIT Press.

Drogoul, A. and Collinot, A. (1998). Applying an agent-oriented methodology to the design of artificial organizations: A case study in robotic soccer. *Autonomous Agents and Multi-Agent Systems*, 1(1):113–129.

Durfee, E. H. (1992). What your computer really needs to know, you learned in kindergarten. In *Proceedings of the Tenth National Conference on Artificial Intelligence*, Philadelphia, PA. Morgan Kaufman.

Durfee, E. H. (1995). Blissful ignorance: Knowing just enough to coordinate well. In *Proceedings of the First International Conference on Multi-Agent Systems (ICMAS-95)*, pages 406–413, Menlo Park, California. AAAI Press.

Durfee, E. H., Lesser, V. R., and Corkill, D. D. (1989). Trends in cooperative distributed problem solving. *IEEE Transactions on Knowledge and Data Engineering*, 1(1):63–83.

Fenster, M., Kraus, S., and Rosenschein, J. S. (1995). Coordination without communication: Experimental validation of focal point techniques. In *Proceedings of the First International Conference on Multi-Agent Systems (ICMAS-95)*, pages 102–108, Menlo Park, California. AAAI Press.

Finin, T., McKay, D., Fritzson, R., and McEntire, R. (1994). KQML: An information and knowledge exchange protocol. In Fuchi, K. and Yokoi, T., editors, *Knowledge Building and Knowledge Sharing*. Ohmsha and IOS Press.

Ford, R., Boutilier, C., and Kanazawa, K. (1994). Exploiting natural structure in reinforcement learning: Experience in robot soccer-playing. Unpublished Manuscript.

Fujimura, K. (1991). *Motion Planning in Dynamic Environments*. Springer-Verlag.

Fujita, M. and Kageyama, K. (1997). An open architecture for robot entertainment. In *Proceedings of the First International Conference on Autonomous Agents*, pages 435–442, Marina del Rey, CA.

Garland, A. and Alterman, R. (1996). Multiagent learning through collective memory. In *Adaptation, Coevolution and Learning in Multiagent Systems: Papers from the 1996 AAAI Spring Symposium*, pages 33–38, Menlo Park,CA. AAAI Press. AAAI Technical Report SS-96-01.

Gat, E. (1998). Three-layer architectures. In KortenKamp, D., Bonasso, R. P., and Murphy, R., editors, *Artificial Intelligence and Mobile Robots*, pages 195–210. AAAI Press, Menlo Park, CA.

Genesereth, M. R. and Fikes, R. E. (1992). Knowledge interchange format, version 3.0 reference manual. Technical Report Logic-92-1, Computer Science Department, Stanford University.

Glance, N. S. and Hogg, T. (1995). Dilemmas in computational societies. In *Proceedings of the First International Conference on Multi-Agent Systems (ICMAS-95)*, pages 117–124, Menlo Park, California. AAAI Press.

Goldman, C. and Rosenschein, J. (1994). Emergent coordination through the use of cooperative state-changing rules. In *Proceedings of the Twelfth National Conference on Artificial Intelligence*, pages 408–413, Philadelphia, PA. Morgan Kaufman.

Grand, S. and Cliff, D. (1998). Creatures: Entertainment software agents with artificial life. *Autonomous Agents and Multi-Agent Systems*, 1(1):39–58.

Grefenstette, J. and Daley, R. (1996). Methods for competitive and cooperative co-evolution. In *Adaptation, Coevolution and Learning in Multiagent Systems: Papers from the 1996 AAAI Spring Symposium*, pages 45–50, Menlo Park,CA. AAAI Press. AAAI Technical Report SS-96-01.

Grosz, B. J. (1996). Collaborative systems. *AI Magazine*, 17(2):67–85.

Gutmann, J.-S., Hattzack, W., Herrmann, I., Nebel, B., Rittinger, F., Topor, A., Weigel, T., and Welsch, B. (1998). The CS Freiburg team. In Asada, M., editor, *Proceedings of the second RoboCup Workshop*, pages 451–458, Paris, France.

Haddadi, A. (1995). Towards a pragmatic theory of interactions. In *Proceedings of the First International Conference on Multi-Agent Systems (ICMAS-95)*, pages 133–139, Menlo Park, California. AAAI Press.

Han, K. and Veloso, M. (1997). Physical model based multi-objects tracking and prediction in robosoccer. In *Working Note of the AAAI 1997 Fall Symposium*. AAAI, MIT Press.

Han, K. and Veloso, M. (1998). Reactive visual control of multiple non-holonomic robotic agents. In *Proceedings of the International Conference on Robotics and Automation*, Leuven,Belgium.

Han, W.-G., Baek, S.-M., Kuc, T.-Y., and Kwan, S. K. (1996). Path planning of visual-served multiple mobile robots using the genetic algorithms. In *Proceedings of the Micro-Robot World Cup Soccer Tournament*, pages 57–63, Taejon, Korea. IEEE Robotics and Automation Society.

Haynes, T. and Sen, S. (1996). Evolving behavioral strategies in predators and prey. In Weiß, G. and Sen, S., editors, *Adaptation and Learning in Multiagent Systems*, pages 113–126. Springer Verlag, Berlin.

Haynes, T., Wainwright, R., Sen, S., and Schoenefeld, D. (1995). Strongly typed genetic programming in evolving cooperation strategies. In Forrest, S., editor, *Proceedings of the Sixth International Conference on Genetic Algorithms*, pages 271–278, San Mateo, CA. Morgan Kaufman.

Hirai, K. (1997). Development of the Honda humanoid robot. Presentation at the CMU robotics institute seminar. At URL http://www.honda.co.jp/home/hpr/e_news/robot/.

Holland, O. (1996). Multiagent systems: Lessons from social insects and collective robotics. In *Adaptation, Coevolution and Learning in Multiagent Systems: Papers from the 1996 AAAI Spring Symposium*, pages 57–62, Menlo Park,CA. AAAI Press. AAAI Technical Report SS-96-01.

Hong, S.-G., Eom, T.-D., Jeong, I.-K., Choi, C., Shin, J.-H., and Lee, J.-J. (1996). Development of soccer-playing robots: Control, cooperation, and strategy. In *Proceedings of the Micro-Robot World Cup Soccer Tournament*, pages 134–141, Taejon, Korea. IEEE Robotics and Automation Society.

Horikawa, K., Aida, M., and Sugawara, T. (1996). Traffic control scheme under the communication delay of high-speed networks. In *Proceedings of the Second International Conference on Multi-Agent Systems (ICMAS-96)*, pages 111–117, Menlo Park, California. AAAI Press.

Hsia, T. C. and Soderstrand, M. (1996). Development of a micro robot system for playing soccer games. In *Proceedings of the Micro-Robot World Cup Soccer Tournament*, pages 149–152, Taejon, Korea. IEEE Robotics and Automation Society.

Huber, M. J. and Durfee, E. H. (1995). Deciding when to commit to action during observation-based coordination. In *Proceedings of the First International Conference on Multi-Agent Systems (ICMAS-95)*, pages 163–170, Menlo Park, California. AAAI Press.

Huberman, B. and Clearwater, S. H. (1995). A multi-agent system for controlling building environments. In *Proceedings of the First International Conference on Multi-Agent Systems (ICMAS-95)*, pages 171–176, Menlo Park, California. AAAI Press.

Inoue, N. and Wilkin, S. (1997). Learning system for the formation and the pass-play. Presented at the poster session of the IROS-96 workshop on RoboCup.

Jennings, N. R., Sycara, K., and Wooldridge, M. (1998). A roadmap of agent research and development. *Autonomous Agents and Multi-Agent Systems*, 1(1):7–38.

Jennings, N. R. and Wittig, T. (1992). Archon: Theory and practice. In Avouris, N. M. and Gasser, L., editors, *Distributed Artificial Intelligence: Theory and Praxis*, pages 179–195. Kluwer Academic Press.

Kaelbling, L. P., Cassandra, A. R., and Littman, M. L. (1994). Acting optimally in partially observable stochastic domains. In *Proceedings of the Twelfth National Conference on Artificial Intelligence*.

Kaelbling, L. P., Littman, M. L., and Moore, A. W. (1996). Reinforcement learning: A survey. *Journal of Artificial Intelligence Research*, 4:237–285.

Kim, D.-Y. and Chung, M. J. (1996). Path planning for multi-mobile robots in the dynamic environment. In *Proceedings of the Micro-Robot World Cup Soccer Tournament*, pages 127–132, Taejon, Korea. IEEE Robotics and Automation Society.

Kim, J.-H., editor (1996). *Proceedings of the Micro-Robot World Cup Soccer Tournament*, Taejon, Korea.

Kim, K.-H., Ko, K.-W., Kim, J.-G., Lee, S.-H., and Cho, H. S. (1996). Multiple micro robots playing robot soccer game. In *Proceedings of the Micro-Robot World Cup Soccer Tournament*, pages 38–43, Taejon, Korea. IEEE Robotics and Automation Society.

Kitano, H., editor (1996). *Proceedings of the IROS-96 Workshop on RoboCup*, Osaka, Japan.

Kitano, H., editor (1998). *RoboCup-97: Robot Soccer World Cup I*. Springer Verlag, Berlin.

Kitano, H. and Asada, M. (1998). RoboCup humanoid challenge: That's one small step for a robot, one giant leap for mankind. In *Proceedings of the International Conference on Intelligent Robotics and Systems*, Victoria, Canada.

Kitano, H., Asada, M., Noda, I., and Matsubara, H. (1998). RoboCup: Robot world cup. *Crossroads*, 4.3.

Kitano, H., Takokoro, S., Noda, I., Matsubara, H., Takahashi, T., Shinjou, A., and Shimada, S. (1999). RoboCup rescue: Search and rescue in large-scale disasters as a domain for autonomous agents research. In *Proceedings of the IEEE International Conference on Man, System, and Cybernetics*.

Kitano, H., Tambe, M., Stone, P., Veloso, M., Coradeschi, S., Osawa, E., Matsubara, H., Noda, I., and Asada, M. (1997). The RoboCup synthetic agent challenge 97. In *Proceedings of the Fifteenth International Joint Conference on Artificial Intelligence*, pages 24–29, San Francisco, CA. Morgan Kaufmann.

Koza, J. R. (1992). *Genetic Programming*. MIT Press.

LaBlanc, M. L. and Henshaw, R. (1994). *The World Encyclopedia of Soccer*. Visible Ink Press.

Latombe, J.-C. (1991). *Robot Motion Planning*. Kluwer Academic Publishers, Boston.

Lesser, V. (1998). Reflections on the nature of multi-agent coordination and its implications for an agent architecture. *Autonomous Agents and Multi-Agent Systems*, 1(1):89–112.

Lesser, V. R. (1995). Multiagent systems: An emerging subdiscipline of AI. *ACM Computing Surveys*, 27(3):340–342.

Levy, R. and Rosenschein, J. S. (1992). A game theoretic approach to the pursuit problem. In *Working Papers of the 11th International Workshop on Distributed Artificial Intelligence*, pages 195–213.

Lin, L.-J. (1993). *Reinforcement Learning for Robots Using Neural Networks*. PhD thesis, School of Computer Science, Carnegie Mellon University, Pittsburgh, PA.

Littman, M. and Boyan, J. (1993). A distribute reinforcement learning scheme for network routing. Technical Report CMU-CS-93-165, Computer Science Department, Carnegie Mellon University, Pittsburgh, PA.

Littman, M. L. (1994). Markov games as a framework for multi-agent reinforcement learning. In *Proceedings of the Eleventh International Conference on Machine Learning*, pages 157–163, San Mateo, CA. Morgan Kaufman.

Luke, S., Hohn, C., Farris, J., Jackson, G., and Hendler, J. (1998). Co-evolving soccer softbot team coordination with genetic programming. In Kitano, H., editor, *RoboCup-97: Robot Soccer World Cup I*, pages 398–411, Berlin. Springer Verlag.

Lux, A. and Steiner, D. (1995). Understanding cooperation: an agent's perspective. In *Proceedings of the First International Conference on Multi-Agent Systems (ICMAS-95)*, pages 261–268, Menlo Park, California. AAAI Press.

Mackworth, A. K. (1993). On seeing robots. In Basu, A. and Li, X., editors, *Computer Vision: Systems, Theory, and Applications*, pages 1–13. World Scientific Press, Singapore.

Maes, P. and Brooks, R. A. (1990). Learning to coordinate behaviors. In *Proceedings of the Eighth National Conference on Artificial Intelligence*, pages 796–802. Morgan Kaufmann.

Mahadevan, S. and Connell, J. (1991). Scaling reinforcement learning to robotics by exploiting the subsumption architecture. In *Proceedings of the Eighth International Workshop on Machine Learning*, pages 328–332.

Maio, D. and Rizzi, S. (1995). Unsupervised multi-agent exploration of structured environments. In *Proceedings of the First International Conference on Multi-Agent Systems (ICMAS-95)*, pages 269–275, Menlo Park, California. AAAI Press.

Mataric, M. J. (1994a). Interaction and intelligent behavior. MIT EECS PhD Thesis AITR–1495, MIT AI Lab.

Mataric, M. J. (1994b). Learning to behave socially. In *Third International Conference on Simulation of Adaptive Behavior*.

Mataric, M. J. (1995). Designing and understanding adaptive group behavior. *Adaptive Behavior*, 4(1).

Matsubara, H., Frank, I., Tanaka-Ishii, K., Noda, I., Nakashima, H., and Hasida, K. (1999). Automatic soccer commentary and RoboCup. In Asada, M. and Kitano, H., editors, *RoboCup-98: Robot Soccer World Cup II*. Springer Verlag, Berlin.

Matsubara, H., Noda, I., and Hiraki, K. (1996). Learning of cooperative actions in multi-agent systems: a case study of pass play in soccer. In *Adaptation, Coevolution and Learning in Multiagent Systems: Papers from the 1996 AAAI Spring Symposium*, pages 63–67, Menlo Park,CA. AAAI Press. AAAI Technical Report SS-96-01.

Matsumoto, A. and Nagai, H. (1998). Decision making by the characteristics and the interaction in multi-agent robotics soccer. In Kitano, H., editor, *RoboCup-97: Robot Soccer World Cup I*, pages 132–143. Springer Verlag, Berlin.

Matsuyama, T. (1997). Cooperative distributed vision. In *Proceedings of the First International workshop on Cooperative Distributed Vision*, Kyoto, Japan.

McCallum, A. K. (1996). Learning to use selective attention and short-term memory in sequential tasks. In *From Animals to Animats: Proceedings of the Fourth International Conference of the Simulation of Adaptive Behavior*. MIT Press.

Mizuno, H., Kourogi, M., Kawamoto, Y., and Muraoka, Y. (1998). A method applied for soccer's behaviors using proper feedback and feedforward control. In Kitano, H., editor, *RoboCup-97: Robot Soccer World Cup I*, pages 156–167. Springer Verlag, Berlin.

Mizuno, H., Kourogi, M., and Muraoka, Y. (1996). Building shoobot possible to dribble and shoot. In *Proceedings of the IROS-96 Workshop on RoboCup*.

Moore, A. W. and Atkeson, C. G. (1993). Prioritized sweeping: Reinforcement learning with less data and less time. *Machine Learning*, 13:103–130.

Mor, Y. and Rosenschein, J. (1995). Time and the prisoner's dilemma. In *Proceedings of the First International Conference on Multi-Agent Systems (ICMAS-95)*, pages 276–282, Menlo Park, California. AAAI Press.

Moukas, A. and Maes, P. (1997). Trafficopter: A distributed collection system for traffic information. At URL http://trafficopter.www.media.mit.edu/projects/trafficopter/.

Mueller, J. P. (1996). *The Design of Intelligent Agents: A Layered Approach*. Springer-Verlag, Berlin.

Müller, J. P. (1999). The right agent (architecture) to do the right thing. In Müller, J. P., Singh, M. P., and Rao, A. S., editors, *Intelligent Agents V — Proceedings of the Fifth International Workshop on Agent Theories, Architectures, and Languages (ATAL-98)*, volume 1555 of *Lecture Notes in Artificial Intelligence*, pages 211–225. Springer-Verlag, Heidelberg.

Nadella, R. and Sen, S. (1997). Correlating internal parameters and external performance: learning soccer agents. In Weiß, G., editor, *Distributed Artificial Intelligence Meets Machine Learning*, pages 137–150. Springer-Verlag.

Nakashima, H., Noda, I., and Ohsawa, I. (1995). Organic programming for multi-agents. In Lesser, V., editor, *Proceedings of the First International Conference on Multi-Agent Systems*, page 459, San Francisco, CA. MIT Press.

Newell, A. (1990). *Unified Theories of Cognition*. Harvard University Press, Cambridge, MA.

Newell, A. and Simon, H. A. (1972). *Human Problem Solving*. Prentice-Hall, Inc., Englewood Cliffs, NJ.

Noda, I. (1998). Team GAMMA: Agent programming on gaea. In Kitano, H., editor, *RoboCup-97: Robot Soccer World Cup I*, pages 500–507. Springer Verlag, Berlin.

Noda, I., Matsubara, H., Hiraki, K., and Frank, I. (1998). Soccer server: A tool for research on multiagent systems. *Applied Artificial Intelligence*, 12:233–250.

Ono, N. and Fukumoto, K. (1997). A modular approach to multi-agent reinforcement learning. In Weiß, G., editor, *Distributed Artificial Intelligence Meets Machine Learning*, pages 25–39. Springer-Verlag.

Pagello, E., Montesello, F., D'Angelo, A., and Ferrari, C. (1998). A reactive architecture for RoboCup competition. In Kitano, H., editor, *RoboCup-97: Robot Soccer World Cup I*, pages 434–442. Springer Verlag, Berlin.

Parker, L. E. (1994). *Heterogeneous Multi-Robot Cooperation*. PhD thesis, Massachusetts

Institute of Technology.

Parunak, H. V. D. (1996). Applications of distributed artificial intelligence in industry. In O'Hare, G. M. P. and Jennings, N. R., editors, *Foundations of Distributed Artificial Intelligence*, pages 139–164. Wiley Interscience.

Parunak, H. V. D., Ward, A., and Sauter, J. (1998). A systematic market approach to distributed constraint problems. In *Proceedings of the Third International Conference on Multi-Agent Systems*, pages 455–456.

Pell, B., Bernard, D. E., Chien, S. A., Gat, E., Muscettola, N., Nayak, P. P., Wagner, M. D., and Williams, B. C. (1998). An autonomous spacecraft agent prototype. *Autonomous Robots*, 5(1).

Permpoontanalarp, Y. (1995). Generalised proof-theory for multi-agent autoepistemic reasoning. In *Proceedings of the First International Conference on Multi-Agent Systems (ICMAS-95)*, pages 304–311, Menlo Park, California. AAAI Press.

Potter, M. A., Jong, K. A. D., and Grefenstette, J. J. (1995). A coevolutionary approach to learning sequential decision rules. In Forrest, S., editor, *Proceedings of the Sixth International Conference on Genetic Algorithms*, pages 366–372, San Mateo,CA. Morgan Kaufman.

Prasad, M. V. N., Lesser, V. R., and Lander, S. E. (1996). Learning organizational roles in a heterogeneous multi-agent system. In *Adaptation, Coevolution and Learning in Multiagent Systems: Papers from the 1996 AAAI Spring Symposium*, pages 72–77, Menlo Park,CA. AAAI Press. AAAI Technical Report SS-96-01.

Price, A., Jennings, A., and Kneen, J. (1998). RoboCup97: An omnidirectional perspective. In Kitano, H., editor, *RoboCup-97: Robot Soccer World Cup I*, pages 320–332. Springer Verlag, Berlin.

Quinlan, J. R. (1993). *C4.5: Programs for Machine Learning*. Morgan Kaufmann, San Mateo, CA.

Rao, A. S. and Georgeff, M. P. (1995). BDI agents: From theory to practice. In *Proceedings of the First International Conference on Multi-Agent Systems (ICMAS-95)*, pages 312–319, Menlo Park, California. AAAI Press.

Ridley, M. (1997). *The Origins of Virtue : Human Instincts and the Evolution of Cooperation*. Viking Press.

Riekki, J. and Roening, J. (1998). Playing soccer by modifying and combining primitive reactions. In Kitano, H., editor, *RoboCup-97: Robot Soccer World Cup I*, pages 74–87. Springer Verlag, Berlin.

RoboCup (1997). RoboCup web page. At URL http://www.robocup.org.

Rosenschein, J. S. and Zlotkin, G. (1994). *Rules of Encounter*. MIT Press.

Rosin, C. D. and Belew, R. K. (1995). Methods for competitive co-evolution: Finding opponents worth beating. In Forrest, S., editor, *Proceedings of the Sixth International Conference on Genetic Algorithms*, pages 373–380, San Mateo,CA. Morgan Kaufman.

Roychowdhury, S., Arora, N., and Sen, S. (1996). Effects of local information on group behavior. In *Adaptation, Coevolution and Learning in Multiagent Systems: Papers from the 1996 AAAI Spring Symposium*, pages 78–83, Menlo Park,CA. AAAI Press. AAAI Technical Report SS-96-01.

Sahota, M. K. (1994). Reactive deliberation: An architecture for real-time intelligent control in dynamic environments. In *Proceedings of the Twelfth National Conference on Artificial Intelligence*, pages 1303–1308.

Sahota, M. K. (1996). Dynasim user guide. At URL http://www.cs.ubc.ca/nest/lci/soccer.

Sahota, M. K., Mackworth, A. K., Barman, R. A., and Kingdon, S. J. (1995). Real-time control of soccer-playing robots using off-board vision: the Dynamite testbed. In *IEEE International Conference on Systems, Man, and Cybernetics*, pages 3690–3663.

Salustowicz, R. P., Wiering, M. A., and Schmidhuber, J. (1998). Learning team strategies: Soccer case studies. *Machine Learning*.

Samuel, A. L. (1959). Some studies in machine learning using the game of checkers. *IBM Journal of Research and Development*, 3:211–229. Reprinted in E. A. Feigenbaum and J. Feldman, editors, *Computers and Thought*, McGraw-Hill, New York 1963.

Sandholm, T. and Lesser, V. (1995a). Coalition formation among bounded rational agents. In *Proceedings of the Fourteenth International Joint Conference on Artificial Intelligence*, pages 662–669, Los Angeles, CA. Morgan Kaufman.

Sandholm, T. and Lesser, V. (1995b). Issues in automated negotiation and electronic commerce: Extending the contract net framework. In *Proceedings of the First International Conference on Multi-Agent Systems (ICMAS-95)*, pages 328–335, Menlo Park, California. AAAI Press.

Sandholm, T. and Lesser, V. (1996). Advantages of a leveled commitment contracting protocol. In *Proceedings of the Thirteenth National Conference on Artificial Intelligence*, pages 126–133, Menlo Park,California. AAAI Press.

Sandholm, T. W. and Crites, R. H. (1996). On multiagent Q-learning in a semi-competitive domain. In Weiß, G. and Sen, S., editors, *Adaptation and Learning in Multiagent Systems*. Springer Verlag, Berlin.

Sargent, R., Bailey, B., Witty, C., and Wright, A. (1997). Dynamic object capture using fast vision tracking. *AI Magazine*, 18(1):65–72.

Scerri, P. (1998). A multi-layered behavior based system for controlling RoboCup agents. In Kitano, H., editor, *RoboCup-97: Robot Soccer World Cup I*, pages 467–474. Springer Verlag, Berlin.

Schaerf, A., Shoham, Y., and Tennenholtz, M. (1995). Adaptive load balancing: A study in multi-agent learning. *Journal of Artificial Intelligence Research*, 2:475–500.

Schmidhuber, J. (1996). A general method for multi-agent reinforcement learning in unrestricted environments. In *Adaptation, Coevolution and Learning in Multiagent Systems: Papers from the 1996 AAAI Spring Symposium*, pages 84–87, Menlo Park,CA. AAAI Press. AAAI Technical Report SS-96-01.

Sen, S., editor (1996). *Adaptation, Coevolution and Learning in Multiagent Systems: Papers from the 1996 AAAI Spring Symposium*, Menlo Park,CA. AAAI, AAAI Press. AAAI Technical Report SS-96-01.

Shapire, R. E. (1990). The strength of weak learnability. *Machine Learning*, 5:197–227.

Shehory, O. and Kraus, S. (1995). Task allocation via coalition formation among autonomous agents. In *Proceedings of the Fourteenth International Joint Conference on Artificial Intelligence*, pages 655–661, Los Angeles, CA. Morgan Kaufman.

Shen, W.-M., Adibi, J., Adobbati, R., Cho, B., Erdem, A., Moradi, H., Salemi, B., and Tejada, S. (1998). Building integrated mobile robots for soccer competition. In *Proceedings of the International Conference on Robotics and Automation*.

Shim, H.-S., Jung, M.-J., Kim, H.-S., Choi, I.-H., Han, W.-S., and Kim, J.-H. (1996). Designing distributed control architecture for cooperative multiagent systems. In *Proceedings of the Micro-Robot World Cup Soccer Tournament*, pages 19–25, Taejon, Korea. IEEE Robotics and Automation Society.

Shinjoh, A. (1998). RoboCup-3D: The construction of intelligent navigation system. In Kitano, H., editor, *RoboCup-97: Robot Soccer World Cup I*, pages 188–199. Springer Verlag, Berlin.

Shoham, Y. (1990). Agent-oriented programming. Technical Report CS-1335-90, Computer Science Dept., Stanford University.

Sichman, J. S. and Demazeau, Y. (1995). Exploiting social reasoning to deal with agency level inconistency. In *Proceedings of the First International Conference on Multi-Agent Systems (ICMAS-95)*, pages 352–359, Menlo Park, California. AAAI Press.

Simmons, R., Veloso, M., and Smith, S., editors (1998). *Proceedings of The Fourth International Conference on Artificial Intelligence Planning Systems*, Pittsburgh,PA. AAAI Press.

Singh, S. P., Jaakkola, T., and Jordan, M. I. (1994). Learning without state-estimation in partially observable Markovian decision processes. In *Proc. 11th International Conference on Machine Learning*, pages 284–292. Morgan Kaufmann.

Singh, S. P. and Sutton, R. S. (1996). Reinforcement learning with replaceing eligibility traces. *Machine Learning*, 22:123–158.

Smith, R. G. (1980). The contract net protocol: High-level communication and control in a distributed problem solver. *IEEE Transactions on Computers*, C-29(12):1104–1113.

Stone, P. (1997). Multiagent learning for autonomous spacecraft constellations. In *Proceedings of the NASA Workshop on Planning and Scheduling for Space*.

Stone, P. (1998). *Layered Learning in Multi-Agent Systems*. PhD thesis, Computer Science Department, Carnegie Mellon University, Pittsburgh, PA. Available as technical report CMU-CS-98-187.

Stone, P. and Veloso, M. (1996a). Beating a defender in robotic soccer: Memory-based learning of a continuous function. In Touretzky, D. S., Mozer, M. C., and Hasselmo, M. E., editors, *Advances in Neural Information Processing Systems 8*, pages 896–902, Cambridge, MA. MIT Press.

Stone, P. and Veloso, M. (1996b). Towards collaborative and adversarial learning: A case study in robotic soccer. In *Adaptation, Coevolution and Learning in Multiagent Systems: Papers from the 1996 AAAI Spring Symposium*, pages 88–92, Menlo Park,CA. AAAI Press. AAAI Technical Report SS-96-01.

Stone, P. and Veloso, M. (1996c). Using machine learning in the soccer server. In *Proceedings of the IROS-96 Workshop on RoboCup*, pages 19–27, Osaka, Japan.

Stone, P. and Veloso, M. (1997). Multiagent systems: A survey from a machine learning perspective. Technical Report CMU-CS-97-193, Computer Science Department, Carnegie Mellon University, Pittsburgh, PA.

Stone, P. and Veloso, M. (1998a). The CMUnited-97 simulator team. In Kitano, H., editor, *RoboCup-97: Robot Soccer World Cup I*. Springer Verlag, Berlin.

Stone, P. and Veloso, M. (1998b). Communication in domains with unreliable, single-channel, low-bandwidth communication. In Drogoul, A., Tambe, M., and Fukuda, T., editors, *Collective Robotics*, pages 85–97. Springer Verlag, Berlin.

Stone, P. and Veloso, M. (1998c). A layered approach to learning client behaviors in the RoboCup soccer server. *Applied Artificial Intelligence*, 12:165–188.

Stone, P. and Veloso, M. (1998d). Towards collaborative and adversarial learning: A case study in robotic soccer. *International Journal of Human-Computer Studies*, 48(1):83–104.

Stone, P. and Veloso, M. (1998e). Using decision tree confidence factors for multiagent control. In *Proceedings of the Second International Conference on Autonomous Agents*.

Stone, P. and Veloso, M. (1999a). Layered learning. In *Proceedings of the IJCAI-99 Workshop on Learning About, From, and With Other Agents*, Stockholm,Sweden.

Stone, P. and Veloso, M. (1999b). Task decomposition and dynamic role assignment for real-time strategic teamwork. In Müller, J. P., Singh, M. P., and Rao, A. S., editors, *Intelligent Agents V — Proceedings of the Fifth International Workshop on Agent Theories, Architectures, and Languages (ATAL-98)*, volume 1555 of *Lecture Notes in Artificial Intelligence*, pages 293–308. Springer-Verlag, Heidelberg.

Stone, P. and Veloso, M. (1999c). Task decomposition, dynamic role assignment, and low-bandwidth communication for real-time strategic teamwork. *Artificial Intelligence*, 110(2):241–273.

Stone, P. and Veloso, M. (1999d). Team-partitioned, opaque-transition reinforcement learning. In Asada, M. and Kitano, H., editors, *RoboCup-98: Robot Soccer World Cup II*. Springer Verlag, Berlin. Also in *Proceedings of the Third International Conference on Autonomous Agents*,1999.

Stone, P., Veloso, M., and Riley, P. (1999). The CMUnited-98 champion simulator team. In Asada, M. and Kitano, H., editors, *RoboCup-98: Robot Soccer World Cup II*. Springer Verlag,

Berlin.

Subramanian, D., Druschel, P., and Chen, J. (1997). Ants and reinforcement learning: A case study in routing in dynamic networks. In *Proceedings of the Fifteenth International Joint Conference on Artificial Intelligence*, San Francisco, CA. Morgan Kaufmann.

Sugawara, T. and Lesser, V. (1993). On-line learning of coordination plans. COINS technical report 93-27, University of Massachussetts Computer Science Department.

Sugawara, T. and Lesser, V. (1995). Learning coordination plans in distributed OS environments. In Lesser, V., editor, *Proceedings of the First International Conference on Multi-Agent Systems*, page 462, San Francisco, CA. MIT Press.

Sutton, R. S. (1988). Learning to predict by the methods of temporal differences. *Machine Learning*, 3:9–44.

Sycara, K. (1998). Multiagent systems. *AI Magazine*, 19(2):79–92.

Sycara, K., Decker, K., Pannu, A., Williamson, M., and Zeng., D. (1996). Distributed intelligent agents. *IEEE Expert.*

Tambe, M. (1995). Recursive agent and agent-group tracking in a real-time , dynamic environment. In *Proceedings of the First International Conference on Multi-Agent Systems (ICMAS-95)*, pages 368–375, Menlo Park, California. AAAI Press.

Tambe, M. (1996a). Teamwork in real-world, dynamic environments. In *Proceedings of the Second International Conference on Multi-Agent Systems (ICMAS-96)*, Menlo Park, California. AAAI Press.

Tambe, M. (1996b). Tracking dynamic team activity. In *Proceedings of the Thirteenth National Conference on Artificial Intelligence*, Menlo Park, California. AAAI Press.

Tambe, M. (1997). Towards flexible teamwork. *Journal of Artificial Intelligence Research*, 7:81–124.

Tambe, M., Adibi, J., Al-Onaizan, Y., andGal A. Kaminka, A. E., Marsela, S. C., Muslea, I., and Tallis, M. (1998). Using an explicit model of teamwork in RoboCup-97. In Kitano, H., editor, *RoboCup-97: Robot Soccer World Cup I*, pages 123–131. Springer Verlag, Berlin.

Tan, M. (1993). Multi-agent reinforcement learning: Independent vs. cooperative agents. In *Proceedings of the Tenth International Conference on Machine Learning*, pages 330–337.

Tesauro, G. (1994). TD-Gammon, a self-teaching backgammon program, achieves master-level play. *Neural Computation*, 6(2):215–219.

Uchibe, E., Asada, M., and Hosoda, K. (1996). Behavior coordination for a mobile robot using modular reinforcement learning. In *Proc. of IEEE/RSJ International Conference on Intelligent Robots and Systems 1996 (IROS '96)*, pages 1329–1336.

Uther, W. T. B. and Veloso, M. M. (1997). Generalizing adversarial reinforcement learning. In *Proceedings of the AAAI Fall Symposium on Model Directed Autonomous Systems.*

Veloso, M., Bowling, M., Achim, S., Han, K., and Stone, P. (1999a). The CMUnited-98 champion small robot team. In Asada, M. and Kitano, H., editors, *RoboCup-98: Robot Soccer World Cup II*. Springer Verlag, Berlin.

Veloso, M., Pagello, E., and Kitano, H., editors (2000). *RoboCup-99: Robot Soccer World Cup III*. Springer Verlag, Berlin. To appear.

Veloso, M. and Stone, P. (1998). Individual and collaborative behaviors in a team of homogeneous robotic soccer agents. In *Proceedings of the Third International Conference on Multi-Agent Systems*, pages 309–316.

Veloso, M., Stone, P., and Bowling, M. (1999b). Anticipation as a key for collaboration in a team of agents: A case study in robotic soccer. In *Proceedings of SPIE*, volume 3839.

Veloso, M., Stone, P., and Han, K. (1998a). CMUnited-97: RoboCup-97 small-robot world champion team. *AI Magazine*, 19(3):61–69.

Veloso, M., Stone, P., and Han, K. (1999c). The CMUnited-97 robotic soccer team: Perception and multi-agent control. *Robotics and Automated Systems*. To appear. Also in *Proceedings of the Second International Conference on Autonomous Agents*, May 1998.

Veloso, M., Stone, P., Han, K., and Achim, S. (1998b). The CMUnited-97 small-robot team. In Kitano, H., editor, *RoboCup-97: Robot Soccer World Cup I*, pages 242–256. Springer Verlag, Berlin.

Veloso, M. and Uther, W. (1999). The CMTrio-98 Sony legged robot team. In Asada, M. and Kitano, H., editors, *RoboCup-98: Robot Soccer World Cup II*. Springer Verlag, Berlin.

Veloso, M., Uther, W., Fujita, M., Asada, M., and Kitano, H. (1998c). Playing soccer with legged robots. In *Proceedings of IROS-98, Intelligent Robots and Systems Conference*, Victoria, Canada.

Verner, I. (1999). RoboCup: A challenging environment for engineering education. In Asada, M. and Kitano, H., editors, *RoboCup-98: Robot Soccer World Cup II*. Springer Verlag, Berlin.

Walker, A. and Wooldridge, M. (1995). Understanding the emergence of conventions in multi-agent systems. In *Proceedings of the First International Conference on Multi-Agent Systems (ICMAS-95)*, pages 384–389, Menlo Park, California. AAAI Press.

Wang, X. (1996). Planning while learning operators. In *Proceedings of the Third International Conference on AI Planning Systems*.

Watkins, C. J. C. H. (1989). *Learning from Delayed Rewards*. PhD thesis, King's College, Cambridge, UK.

Weiß, G. (1995). Distributed reinforcement learning. *Robotics and Autonomous Systems*, 15:135–142.

Weiß, G., editor (1997). *Distributed Artificial Intelligence Meets Machine Learning*, volume 1221. Springer Verlag, Berlin.

Weiß, G. and Sen, S., editors (1996). *Adaptation and Learning in Multiagent Systems*. Springer Verlag, Berlin.

Wolpert, D. H. (1992). Stacked generalization. *Neural Networks*, 5:241–259.

Woodworth, R. S. (1938). *Experimental Psychology*. H. Hold and co., New York.

Yokota, K., Ozaki, K., Matsumoto, A., Kawabata, K., Kaetsu, H., and Asama, H. (1998). Omni-directional autonomous robots cooperating for team play. In Kitano, H., editor, *RoboCup-97: Robot Soccer World Cup I*, pages 333–347. Springer Verlag, Berlin.

Zeng, D. and Sycara, K. (1996). Bayesian learning in negotiation. In *Adaptation, Coevolution and Learning in Multiagent Systems: Papers from the 1996 AAAI Spring Symposium*, pages 99–104, Menlo Park,CA. AAAI Press. AAAI Technical Report SS-96-01.

Zhao, J. and Schmidhuber, J. (1996). Incremental self-improvement for life-time multi-agent reinforcement learning. In *Proceedings of the 4th International Conference of Simulation of Adaptive Behavior*, pages 363–372. MIT Press.

Zlotkin, G. and Rosenschein, J. S. (1994). Coalition, cryptography, and stability: Mechanisms for coalition formation in task oriented domains. In *Proceedings of the Twelfth National Conference on Artificial Intelligence*, pages 432–437, Menlo Park, California. AAAI Press.